LEARNING TO PROGRAM

IN

STRUCTURED COBOL

by

Edward Yourdon
Chris Gane
Trish Sarson

YOURDON inc.
1133 Avenue of the Americas
New York, New York 10036

## INTRODUCTION

This book is intended for people with no previous knowledge of computers, who want to learn to program in COBOL, the most widely used computer language. The book incorporates the methods and styles of "structured" programming, which have been shown to be more productive than traditional programming techniques.

The book can either be used for self-study, or as the text for an industrial or college course. If you are an instructor, please read the following Notes for Instructors which discuss possible uses as a textbook.

If you plan to use the book to study COBOL on your own, you will find the frequent questions and exercises very helpful, especially if you work them _before_ checking the answers provided.

We have tried to make your learning easy, thorough, and fun. If you can actually run some of the exercise programs on a computer, you will enhance your learning, and find it fascinating to build up a realistic commercial data processing system.


## NOTES FOR INSTRUCTORS

One of the objectives of this book is to serve with Part II, as a text for a six-week full-time course or a three-semester college course for people with little or no prior exposure to data processing.

Apart from teaching COBOL entirely in the context of structured programming, the course design incorporates several well-established educational techniques which have not, so far as we know, been applied in this area before. They are:

- the concept of COBOL as a "foreign language"

- the concept of the spiral curriculum

- the concept of the "theory/practice sandwich."

## COBOL as a foreign language

It is known that the teaching of a foreign language via a grammar is not as effective as teaching via a set of syntactic structures. That is, it is better to learn a language by learning basic conversational exchanges such as "Have you got an X? Yes, I have an X" rather than to learn "I have, you have, he has, she has,..." If we view COBOL in this light, we see that the standards manual and manufacturer's reference manuals are *grammars* of COBOL; they set forth the rules of the language in a formal way, exploring all the options of each statement, however obscure and rarely used. Many texts and courses explain the reference manual, but essentially follow the same pattern. In this text, and in courses based on it, we have used the four structures -- process, decision, loop, and CASE -- as the building blocks and taught the language with a structural rather than a grammatical orientation.

Regarding COBOL as a foreign language also suggests that we keep to a minimum the history and geography of the "country" concerned. While we do not question that a well-rounded professional should know the history of data processing from Hollerith to HISAM, we take the view that history is irrelevant to the beginner, and confusing insofar as it is of no help in performing his central task of solving problems with code. Likewise, while a professional COBOL programmer should know enough about the architecture of the hardware to appreciate the implications of alternative coding techniques, the beginner needs only a very simple model of main storage and common peripherals. We have taken pains to concentrate initially on the production of readable, changeable code, rather than any considerations of run-time efficiency; for example, binary representation is not discussed until Chapter 8 in Part II.

## The spiral curriculum

Usually the topics in a subject can be arranged in a linear order, one after another. This is very difficult in teaching programming, because of the amount of interdependence between topics; the instructor is in the chicken-and-egg situation of not being able to teach topic A properly before the students know about topic B, and not being able to teach B before they know about A. The solution is to design a *spiral* curriculum in which all topics are treated several times at progressively increasing levels of detail. As you will see, the book has in fact five levels to the spiral:

Chapter 1:        a brief explanation of the whole program
development process, and a walk-through of
a simple COBOL program

Chapters 2,3,4,5,6:    establishing the basic structures and
                       language subset, with a thorough dis-
                       cussion of COBOL logic

Chapters 7,8,9:        the use of auxiliary storage, a larger
                       subset of the language, and internal data
                       representation

Chapters 10,11,12:     the remainder of the language facilities:
                       tables, advanced I/O, program-to-program
                       communication, and teleprocessing

Chapters 13,14,15:     considerations of program quality,
                       structured design, testing and debugging
                       strategies, efficiency and optimization.


## The theory/practice sandwich

It is often a temptation for someone who is expert in a subject to
teach theory at a more profound level than is desirable.  This is partly
because the more deeply one understands the theory behind a subject, the
simpler it appears.  So the instructor may feel that the subject can be
made simple to the learner by teaching the underlying theory at the same
depth as the instructor understands it.  This is a fallacy; the learner
needs to start with familiar, concrete things and simple skills, and
then learn abstract concepts.  After a while, he can treat these abstract
concepts as concrete things and then learn deeper level concepts and so
on.  Introducing the subject of computer programming by teaching binary
arithmetic is a case in point; it is true that, at a deep level, the
computer is merely performing operations on binary strings, but that is
no help to the beginner.  The temptation to teach too much theory too
early can be resisted by asking "What is the simplest act of mastery
the learner can do next?  What is the minimum theory he must know in
order to do that act of mastery?"  So we get the idea of the "theory/
practice sandwich"; a curriculum which, within each spiral, has the
structure

              minimum theory
              simple act of mastery
              next item of minimum theory
              next act of mastery

              and so on.

The sequence of acts of mastery the book is built around is:

> read a simple program
> make a small modification to a program
> write a card-to-print program
> enhance the program to do some arithmetic
> enhance the program to do complex logic
> enhance the program to write a tape file
> maintain the tape file
> use the tape file to create an indexed disk file
> use the indexed disk file in a simple
>     accounting system
>
> and so on.

The use of the COPY library is dealt with as early as Chapter 5, and the program exercises build on each other in such a way as to involve the maximum of learning with the minimum of coding and key-punching.

Suggested lesson plans and lecture notes for the first 30 sessions of a course (three hours per session) are set out in Appendix C.

# CHAPTER 1:  MAKING THE COMPUTER DO WHAT YOU WANT

## 1.1    CLERKS, COMPUTERS, COMPILERS, AND COBOL

You've probably heard a lot about computers before picking up this book.  Some of it may be alarming, about how computers are invading our lives and taking over; some of it may be very optimistic, about how computers will do all the boring work, leaving people a life of ease and leisure.  Neither of these statements is true, of course, and by the end of the book we hope you'll be in a position to make up your own mind about the meaning of computers (from a position of strength), because you will be giving the orders.

Because that is what being a programmer is all about: giving the orders to the computers.  Think of the computer as a clerk without any common sense and yourself as the clerk's boss.  Whatever you tell the clerk to do, he will do exactly that, incredibly fast, and drawing on a vast memory of what you and others have told him in the past. But if you tell the computer to send out a check for $100,000 when you meant only $100, the computer will blindly obey and pay out the $100,000.

So the key thing about your job as a programmer is to understand in practical terms what work people need done by the computer, and then to translate those needs very, very exactly into code the computer can read and obey.  Computers work by streams of coded electronic pulses, which we shall discuss in detail later in the book.  These pulses are of course meaningless to humans, so a variety of computer language translators have been developed, which take in commands in an English-like language and transform them into coded electronic instructions which work the computer.  The most common of these languages is COBOL, which is a contraction of COmmon Business Oriented Language.  The vast majority of computers have a translator (called a compiler) which takes in COBOL commands and produces the coded instructions (called Machine Language) which drive that computer.

To see how this programming process works in practice, let's go through a simple computer job and see what is involved.  Don't worry if you don't understand all the details of how the job is done; we'll discuss the details in later chapters.  The most important thing for you is to see how the parts of the process fit together; then the details will make sense when you come to learn them.

Suppose the firm you work for has decided to start selling by mail order. They have advertised in the national magazines and newspapers and gotten back a veritable blizzard of cut-out coupons -- 30,000 in all -- asking for catalogs. Have you ever seen 30,000 coupons? Going through them by hand is a chore. We have the job of sending out catalogs to all these people, and for that we need labels. Also we want to capture these names and addresses on the computer so we can send out further mailings. The first problem we find on looking through the coupons is that while most people have filled in their name, address, and phone number correctly, some have just given their name and phone number. So the first job we are asked to do is to write a program which will produce a list of all the people who have sent in coupons, and mark prominently the ones whose addresses are missing, so that someone can go through the list, call them, and complete the entry.

The list opposite represents the first 20 coupons of the 30,000. You will see that the names and addresses are typed in three columns, and that in some cases the address lines are missing. Just to get an idea of the amount of paper involved, if these addresses were typed like this, 30 on a page, how many sheets would be needed for all 30,000? How thick a stack of paper would this be? If it takes a typist one minute to type a label, how long would it take to type the labels each time you wanted to mail something to all 30,000 people?

What we want to do is print all 30,000 names and addresses on computer stationery, which you've probably seen. Computer print-out paper is continuous, with folds between pages, and holds 60 lines per page. It often has holes down both sides to allow the toothed wheels in the computer printer to move the paper.

Where the coupon had no address, as in the case of Dr. Quackenbush, Ms. diGiacomo, and Mr. Buchwald, we want to have the computer print a very obvious message ("flagging" is the computer jargon). Figure 1.1 shows what the print-out will look like.

Victor S Grasper
990 Gauntlet Ave
Burlingame CA 94010
(415) 243-7022

Dr P. Quackenbush

(602) 852-4822

Frances Paisano
2521 Edge Street
Fort Lee NJ 07024
(201) 614-7525

Ian S Inkerman
59 Pecan Valley Rd
Montvale NJ 07645
(201) 103-6061

Barbara diGiacomo

(918) 726-4401

C. Enchaine
212 Sleepy Hollow Dr
Greenwich CT 06830
(203) 886-7431

Saralee James
Parthenon Court
Athens MO 64065
(816) 542-0535

Scarlett O'Hara
Suite 414 Nat Bank
New Orleans LA 70012
(504) 815-1147

Lucy Lakeshore
7328 Main Street
Chicago IL 60619
(312) 838-9903

Susan Krupman
131 W 32nd Street
New York NY 10001
(212) 465-0330

I. Morris Good
1313 Porpoise
Dallas TX 75219
(214) 225-7013

Mel Harrison
4 Newton Plaza
Syracuse NY 13210
(315) 747-2121

Digital Datagrab
Apt 4R, 400 John St
Chicago IL 60611
(312) 494-1014

B. Hugh Thompson
1111 Sutter
San Francisco,
  CA 94103
(415) 263-4857

C.P. Foster Inc
8th & Chestnut
Philadelphia PA 77055
(215) 229-5575

Starlet Q. Freebody
12277 Sunset Blvd
Los Angeles CA 90024
(213) 574-2179

B Buchwald

(202) 936-1212

Francis T. Nord
1905 N. County Road
Minneapolis MN 55436
(612) 501-0631

John Woodside
12074 Milam
Houston TX 77023
(713) 292-8996

Z. Robertski
12 Jefferson Road
Newton MA 02160
(617) 569-8505

etc.

| | | | | | |
|---|---|---|---|---|---|
| VICTOR S GRASPER | 990 GAUNTLET AVENUE | BURLINGAME | CA94010 | 415 243-7022 | |
| DR P. BLACKENBUSH | | | | 602 852-4822 | **** ADDRESS MISSING **** |
| FRANCES PAISANO | 2521 EDGE STREET | FORT LEE | NJ07024 | 201 614-7525 | |
| IAN S INKERMAN | 59 PECAN VALLEY RD | MONTVALE | NJ07645 | 201 103-6061 | |
| BARBARA DI.IACOMO | | | | 918 726-4401 | **** ADDRESS MISSING **** |
| C. ENCHAINE | 212 SLEEPY HOLLOW DRGREENWICH | | CT06830 | 203 886-7431 | |
| SARALEE JAMES | PARTHENON COURT | ATHENS | MO64065 | 816 542-0535 | |
| SCARLETT O'HARA | STE 414 NAT BANK | NEW ORLEANS | LA70012 | 504 815-1147 | |
| LUCY LAKESHORE | 7328 MAIN STREET | CHICAGO | IL60619 | 312 838-9903 | |
| SUSAN KRUPMAN | 131 W 32ND STREET | NEW YORK | NY10001 | 212 465-0330 | |
| I. MORRIS GOOD | 1313 PORPOISE | DALLAS | TX75219 | 214 225-7013 | |
| MEL HARRISON | 4 NEWTOWN PLAZA | SYRACUSE | NY13210 | 315 747-2121 | |
| DIGITAL DATAGRAB | APT 4R, 400 JOHN ST | CHICAGO | IL60611 | 312 494-1014 | |
| B. HUGH THOMPSON | 1111 SUTTER | SAN FRANCISCO | CA94103 | 413 263-4857 | |
| C. P. FOSTER INC | 8TH & CHESTNUT | PHILADELPHIA | PA77055 | 215 229-5575 | |
| STARLET W. FREEBODY | 12277 SUNSET BLVD | LOS ANGELES | CA90024 | 213 574-2179 | |
| B BUCHWALD | | | | 202 936-1212 | **** ADDRESS MISSING **** |
| FRANCIS T. NCRD | 1905 N. COUNTY ROAD | MINNEAPOLIS | MN55436 | 612 501-0631 | |
| JOHN WCUDSICE | 12074 MILAM | HOUSTON | TX77023 | 713 292-8996 | |
| Z. ROBERTSKI | 12 JEFFERSON ROAD | NEWTOWN | MA02160 | 617 569-8505 | |

Figure 1.1    A computer print-out of names, addresses, and phone numbers, with missing addresses flagged

As you can see from the print-out opposite, we have made the computer list the names, addresses, and phone numbers one to a line, and flag the missing addresses with a warning message.

## 1.2   *CODING THE DATA TO GET IT INTO A COMPUTER*

Obviously, before the computer can print, it has got to read in the data somehow.  There are several ways of getting data from the form humans read and use, such as handwriting, into a form which the machine can convert to coded pulses (called "machine-readable form").  The most common way is to punch holes in cards using a machine called a key-punch, with a typewriter-like keyboard.  A picture of a card with Victor Grasper's data is shown below; study it carefully and see if you can figure out the combinations of hole-positions which correspond to each letter and number on the top row.

```
VICTOR S GRASPER     990 GAUNTLET AVE     BURLINGAME    CA 94010 415243-7022
```

Each group of columns is called a field.  The whole card is said to contain a record, and a set of such cards makes up a file.  Of course, there can be any number of records in the file, and up to 80 fields in each record.  If you had punched a card for every coupon, you would have 30,000 cards; since a tray of 2,000 cards is about 2 feet long, you would have a file of cards 30 feet long!

As well as a card file of this type, the computer treats the print-out as being a file, with each line on the print-out being a record.

The specimen card below shows that each of the 80 columns can carry either a digit (0 through 9), or a letter (A through Z), or a special character (+, -, *, etc.), or be blank and represent a space.

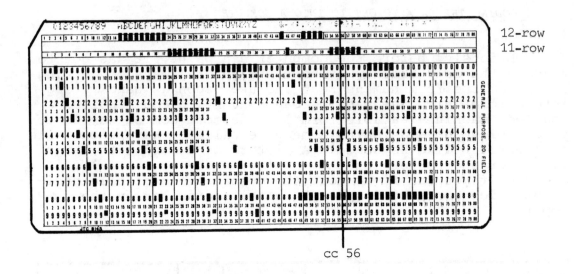

12-row
11-row

cc 56

Every column in a row is printed with the row number, except for the top two rows, which for historical reasons are called the 11-row and the 12-row as shown.

A digit is coded as a single punch in the appropriate row; a letter is coded as two punches; e.g., A is a 12-punch plus a 1-punch.  Special characters have varying numbers of punches, e.g., the asterisk (*) is 11-4-8.  This is shown above in card column 56 (abbreviated "cc 56").

Punched cards with the characters printed along the top are said to be <u>interpreted</u>.  You may sometimes need to read <u>uninterpreted cards</u>; don't bother to memorize the codes, just use this specimen for reference.

If you have access to a key-punch, get someone to show you how to use it at this point, and punch yourself a set of 20 cards with the 20 names, addresses, and phone numbers listed previously.  Be sure to use the same columns for the same type of data, uniform with Victor Grasper's card; that is, always start the name in cc 1, the address in cc 21, the city in cc 41, the state in cc 54, the zip code in cc 56, and the phone number in cc 61.

In order to get the data on them into a computer, the cards must be stacked and fed into a card reader, which senses where the holes have been punched in each card, either with fine metal brushes, or with light rays.  The hole-positions are converted into coded electronic pulses which are fed along a cable into the Central Processing Unit (CPU), which is the brain of the computer.  The picture below shows an IBM System/370 Model 135 with a 2540 Card Reader/Punch and a 1403 Printer, which takes the pulses along another cable from the CPU and produces the print-out.

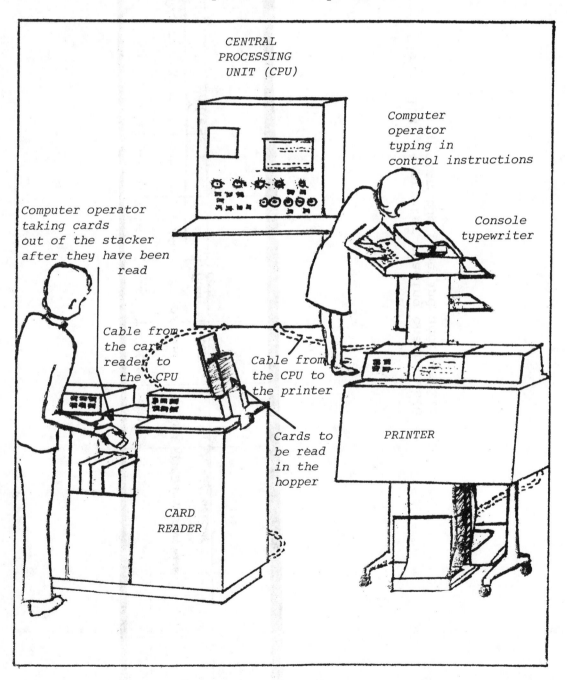

CENTRAL
PROCESSING
UNIT (CPU)

Computer
operator
typing in
control instructions

Console
typewriter

Computer operator
taking cards
out of the stacker
after they have been
read

Cable from
the card
reader to
the CPU

Cable from
the CPU to
the printer

Cards to
be read
in the
hopper

PRINTER

CARD
READER

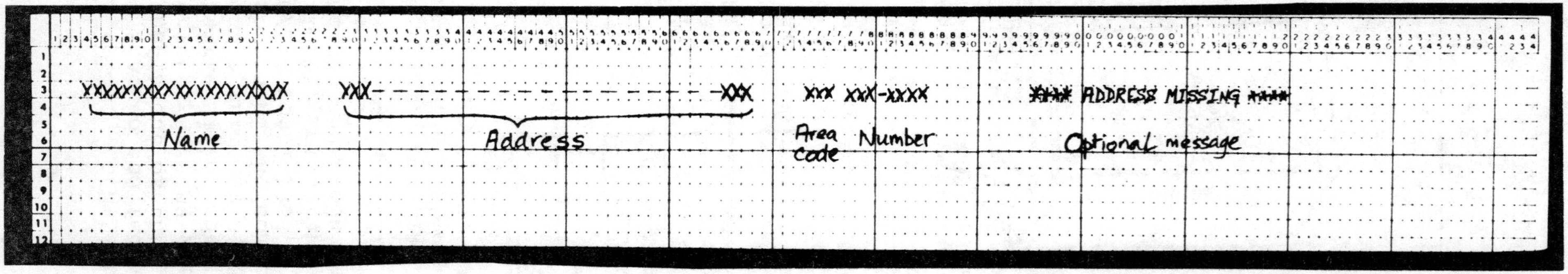

Figure 1.2 A printer spacing chart, used to plan the name and address listing

Look at the layout of the printer listing (Fig. 1.2).
This shows a printer spacing chart, which is the form the
programmer uses to plan the print-out.  Compare the position
of the fields on the printer listing with the fields on the
input card.  You will see that the lengths are still the
same, but they are spaced out across the whole 132 columns
of the printer.  (Some printers have 120 columns, some 144,
but 132 is most usual.)

Check back to the actual print-out shown in Fig. 1.1
and see how the printer spacing chart corresponds.

Now, what do you, the programmer, have to do to get
the computer to read these cards, and list them on the
printer in this format, detecting cards with no address and
writing out the message

**** ADDRESS MISSING ****

Well, you have to write the necessary instructions
(which make up the "program"), punch them on cards also,
and feed them into the computer ahead of time so that it
knows what to do with the name and address cards when you
feed them in.

The next page shows how you would write the instructions for this particular job.  Don't worry if you don't
follow everything that is written there; just read the
program and the annotations, and we'll get to details later.

SAMPLE-1

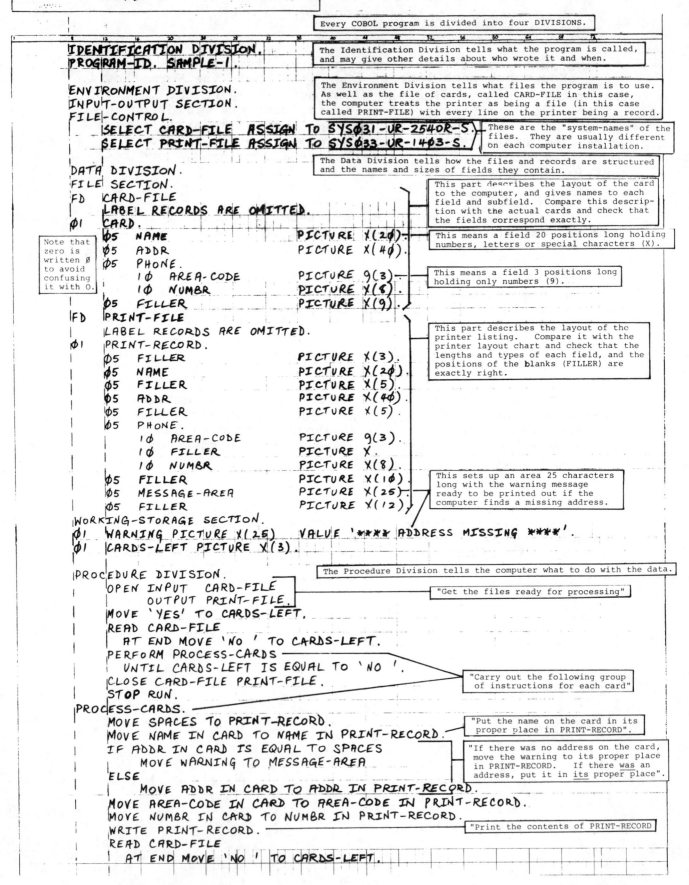

Every COBOL program is divided into four DIVISIONS.

```
IDENTIFICATION DIVISION.
PROGRAM-ID. SAMPLE-1.
```

The Identification Division tells what the program is called, and may give other details about who wrote it and when.

```
ENVIRONMENT DIVISION.
INPUT-OUTPUT SECTION.
FILE-CONTROL.
    SELECT CARD-FILE ASSIGN TO SYS031-UR-2540R-S.
    SELECT PRINT-FILE ASSIGN TO SYS033-UR-1403-S.
```

The Environment Division tells what files the program is to use. As well as the file of cards, called CARD-FILE in this case, the computer treats the printer as being a file (in this case called PRINT-FILE) with every line on the printer being a record.

These are the "system-names" of the files. They are usually different on each computer installation.

```
DATA DIVISION.
FILE SECTION.
FD  CARD-FILE
    LABEL RECORDS ARE OMITTED.
01  CARD.
    05  NAME                    PICTURE X(20).
    05  ADDR                    PICTURE X(40).
    05  PHONE.
        10  AREA-CODE           PICTURE 9(3).
        10  NUMBR               PICTURE X(8).
    05  FILLER                  PICTURE X(9).
FD  PRINT-FILE
    LABEL RECORDS ARE OMITTED.
01  PRINT-RECORD.
    05  FILLER                  PICTURE X(3).
    05  NAME                    PICTURE X(20).
    05  FILLER                  PICTURE X(5).
    05  ADDR                    PICTURE X(40).
    05  FILLER                  PICTURE X(5).
    05  PHONE.
        10  AREA-CODE           PICTURE 9(3).
        10  FILLER              PICTURE X.
        10  NUMBR               PICTURE X(8).
    05  FILLER                  PICTURE X(10).
    05  MESSAGE-AREA            PICTURE X(25).
    05  FILLER                  PICTURE X(12).
WORKING-STORAGE SECTION.
01  WARNING PICTURE X(25)    VALUE '**** ADDRESS MISSING ****'.
01  CARDS-LEFT PICTURE X(3).
```

The Data Division tells how the files and records are structured and the names and sizes of fields they contain.

This part describes the layout of the card to the computer, and gives names to each field and subfield. Compare this description with the actual cards and check that the fields correspond exactly.

Note that zero is written 0 to avoid confusing it with O.

This means a field 20 positions long holding numbers, letters or special characters (X).

This means a field 3 positions long holding only numbers (9).

This part describes the layout of the printer listing. Compare it with the printer layout chart and check that the lengths and types of each field, and the positions of the blanks (FILLER) are exactly right.

This sets up an area 25 characters long with the warning message ready to be printed out if the computer finds a missing address.

```
PROCEDURE DIVISION.
    OPEN INPUT  CARD-FILE
         OUTPUT PRINT-FILE.
    MOVE 'YES' TO CARDS-LEFT.
    READ CARD-FILE
      AT END MOVE 'NO ' TO CARDS-LEFT.
    PERFORM PROCESS-CARDS
      UNTIL CARDS-LEFT IS EQUAL TO 'NO '.
    CLOSE CARD-FILE PRINT-FILE.
    STOP RUN.
PROCESS-CARDS.
    MOVE SPACES TO PRINT-RECORD.
    MOVE NAME IN CARD TO NAME IN PRINT-RECORD.
    IF ADDR IN CARD IS EQUAL TO SPACES
        MOVE WARNING TO MESSAGE-AREA
    ELSE
        MOVE ADDR IN CARD TO ADDR IN PRINT-RECORD.
    MOVE AREA-CODE IN CARD TO AREA-CODE IN PRINT-RECORD.
    MOVE NUMBR IN CARD TO NUMBR IN PRINT-RECORD.
    WRITE PRINT-RECORD.
    READ CARD-FILE
      AT END MOVE 'NO ' TO CARDS-LEFT.
```

The Procedure Division tells the computer what to do with the data.

"Get the files ready for processing"

"Carry out the following group of instructions for each card"

"Put the name on the card in its proper place in PRINT-RECORD".

"If there was no address on the card, move the warning to its proper place in PRINT-RECORD. If there was an address, put it in its proper place".

"Print the contents of PRINT-RECORD"

Figure 1.3   SAMPLE-1

And that's all there is to it!


	You punch each line of the COBOL program on a card and feed the cards in while running your computer's COBOL compiler program (which is already stored there ready for use).


	The compiler will check that everything has been punched correctly, as far as it can, and print out a listing of the cards with messages about anything the compiler can find wrong ("diagnostics").  You may have to repunch some cards and rerun the compiler.  When you have a "clean compilation" -- no serious diagnostics -- the computer will store the electronic instructions representing SAMPLE-1 ready for use.


	Then you instruct the computer to prepare SAMPLE-1 for a "run" and feed in the data cards with name, address, and phone numbers, to get the print-out.


	Before reading further in this book, we strongly recommend that you punch up SAMPLE-1 exactly as shown, get someone to show you how to use your computer's COBOL compiler, and run your 20 data cards through.  Be sure you punch exactly what is written; every space and every period means something to the computer, as you will see later on.  It's quite a thrill to get your first compilation and print-out, and once you've seen the various stages in the cycle, everything else will make much more sense.


	The listing on the next page shows how the program should look when printed out from your cards.

```
00001              IDENTIFICATION DIVISION.
00002              PROGRAM-ID. SAMPLE-1.
00003              ENVIRONMENT DIVISION.
00004              INPUT-OUTPUT SECTION.
00005              FILE-CONTROL.
00006                  SELECT CARD-FILE  ASSIGN TO SYS031-UR-2540R-S.
00007                  SELECT PRINT-FILE ASSIGN TO SYS033-UR-1403-S.
00008              DATA DIVISION.
00009              FILE SECTION.
00010              FD  CARD-FILE
00011                  LABEL RECORDS ARE OMITTED.
00012              01  CARD.
00013                  05  NAME                     PICTURE    X(20).
00014                  05  ADDR                     PICTURE    X(40).
00015                  05  PHONE.
00016                      10  AREA-CODE            PICTURE    9(3).
00017                      10  NUMBR                PICTURE    X(8).
00018                  05  FILLER                   PICTURE    X(9).
00019              FD  PRINT-FILE
00020                  LABEL RECORDS ARE OMITTED.
00021              01  PRINT-RECORD.
00022                  05  FILLER                   PICTURE    X(3).
00023                  05  NAME                     PICTURE    X(20).
00024                  05  FILLER                   PICTURE    X(5).
00025                  05  ADDR                     PICTURE    X(40).
00026                  05  FILLER                   PICTURE    X(5).
00027                  05  PHONE.
00028                      10  AREA-CODE            PICTURE    9(3).
00029                      10  FILLER               PICTURE    X.
00030                      10  NUMBR                PICTURE    X(8).
00031                  05  FILLER                   PICTURE    X(10).
00032                  05  MESSAGE-AREA             PICTURE    X(25).
00033                  05  FILLER                   PICTURE    X(12).
00034              WORKING-STORAGE SECTION.
00035              01  WARNING PICTURE X(25)   VALUE '**** ADDRESS MISSING ****'.
00036              01  CARDS-LEFT PICTURE X(3).
00037              PROCEDURE DIVISION.
00038                  OPEN INPUT  CARD-FILE
00039                       OUTPUT PRINT-FILE.
00040                  MOVE 'YES' TO CARDS-LEFT.
00041                  READ CARD-FILE
00042                    AT END MOVE 'NO ' TO CARDS-LEFT.
00043                  PERFORM PROCESS-CARDS
00044                    UNTIL CARDS-LEFT IS EQUAL TO 'NO '.
00045                  CLOSE CARD-FILE PRINT-FILE.
00046                  STOP RUN.
00047              PROCESS-CARDS.
00048                  MOVE SPACES TO PRINT-RECORD.
00049                  MOVE NAME IN CARD TO NAME IN PRINT-RECORD.
00050                  IF ADDR IN CARD IS EQUAL TO SPACES
00051                      MOVE WARNING TO MESSAGE-AREA
00052                  ELSE
00053                      MOVE ADDR IN CARD TO ADDR IN PRINT-RECORD.
00054                  MOVE AREA-CODE IN CARD TO AREA-CODE IN PRINT-RECORD.
00055                  MOVE NUMBR IN CARD TO NUMBR IN PRINT-RECORD.
00056                  WRITE PRINT-RECORD.
00057                  READ CARD-FILE
```

Figure 1.4   SAMPLE-4 listing

CHAPTER 2:  PROCESSES, DECISIONS, AND LOOPS


Now that you've seen what is involved in writing and running a COBOL program, let's look more closely at some of the instructions we used.


## 2.1    MOVING DATA FROM FIELD TO FIELD


The MOVE statement is probably the statement you'll use most as a COBOL programmer.  If you look back at the MOVE statements in SAMPLE-1, you'll see they are all of the general form:

MOVE first-field TO second-field

where first-field and second-field vary depending on what you want to do.  If first-field is WARNING and second-field is MESSAGE-AREA, the general form becomes:

MOVE WARNING TO MESSAGE-AREA.


Picture the inside of the computer as consisting of thousands of storage positions, each normally capable of holding one character.  When you write the Data Division (a portion of your COBOL program which we will define in Chapter 3), you reserve some of these storage positions for your program.  WARNING is a field 25 positions long, with those positions filled like this:

WARNING:       **** ADDRESS MISSING ****

You set it up this way in the Working Storage section of the Data Division in SAMPLE-1.


MESSAGE-AREA is a field 25 positions long, defined as part of PRINT-RECORD, and full of blanks (spaces).  When the computer obeys your MOVE instruction, it copies data from WARNING to MESSAGE-AREA position by position working from the left, like this:

WARNING:         **** ADDRESS MISSING ****

Rest of PRINT-RECORD      1 2 3 4   etc.

                          MESSAGE-AREA

This whole MOVE operation may take as much as one ten-thousandth of a second!

- 13 -

The important thing to remember is that since the MOVE takes place from left to right, if MESSAGE-AREA is shorter than WARNING, the computer will stop copying characters when it comes to the end of MESSAGE-AREA.

Q.   What would be put in MESSAGE-AREA if it were only 10 positions long?

A.   **** ADDRE

Since the MOVE is a copy operation, the contents of the field you are copying (WARNING) are left unchanged. If there was anything in MESSAGE-AREA before the MOVE, however, it will be over-written and lost. If WARNING were shorter than MESSAGE-AREA, then when all of WARNING has been moved, the rest of MESSAGE-AREA will be filled up with blanks.

To illustrate the possibilities, cover up the right-hand column below and work out for each case what will be in FIELD-A and FIELD-B after the computer executes the instruction

MOVE FIELD-A TO FIELD-B.

Assume in each case that FIELD-A and FIELD-B have been defined appropriately in the Data Division.

| | BEFORE MOVE | | AFTER MOVE | |
|---|---|---|---|---|
| | FIELD-A | FIELD-B | FIELD-A | FIELD-B |
| Case 1: | N A M E | G O N E | N A M E | N A M E |
| | | | | (Fields are the same length so NAME over-writes GONE) |
| Case 2: | N A M E | G O N E T O | N A M E | N A M E ⌀ ⌀ |
| | | | | (FIELD-B is longer so it is filled up with blanks) |
| Case 3: | N A M E | G O | N A M E | N A |
| | | | | (Moving stops when FIELD-B is full) |

Q. What would happen to FIELD-A if, after the MOVE shown in Case 2 above, you commanded

MOVE FIELD-B TO FIELD-A.

A. FIELD-A would still contain NAME.


Q. If MOVEing a field destroys the receiving field, how could you swap the contents of two locations in main storage?

A. You would need to set up a third location, say one called FIELD-C, and store one field in there temporarily, like this:


FIELD-A         FIELD-B         FIELD-C

|N|A|M|E|       |G|O|N|E|       |ø|ø|ø|ø|


1. MOVE FIELD-B TO FIELD-C.

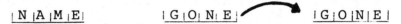

2. MOVE FIELD-A TO FIELD-B.

3. MOVE FIELD-C TO FIELD-A.

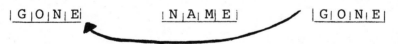

Thus you have swapped over FIELD-A and FIELD-B.


When you are programming, always imagine what the contents of the computer storage will be like at every step. If it helps you, draw little diagrams like the ones above. Remember to distinguish the name of a field (the "data-name") which stays the same throughout a given program, from the contents or value of that field at a particular point in time; the contents will change every time you do something in the program to modify the field.

Q. In the swapping example above, which are data-names and which are field contents?

A. FIELD-A, FIELD-B, FIELD-C are data-names; NAME, GONE are field contents or values.

Generally speaking, computer main storage stays the way you set it until you reset it with another MOVE or similar instruction. Very often, as well, the part of main storage that your program uses has been used earlier by someone else's program, and a lot of your fields may start out filled by someone else's garbage. So before you get to work, you must initialize the fields you are going to use (indeed, if you don't, your program has a high likelihood of misbehaving -- either printing garbage or not executing at all). One way of doing this is to MOVE SPACES to them. SPACES is a special reserved name supplied to you by COBOL, which provides you with all the spaces (blanks) you need for any field.

Statement 48 in SAMPLE-1 says:

MOVE SPACES TO PRINT-RECORD.

PRINT-RECORD is a field 132 positions long which is used to build each line of print-out. Fields from each card are moved into it but nothing is moved into the FILLER fields between columns. So we MOVE SPACES to clear out anybody else's garbage that may be there.

Take the card that holds statement 48 out of SAMPLE-1, recompile and rerun the program. See what you get on the print-out.

SPACES will give you as many spaces as you need to fill the field in question; you don't have to specify how many spaces you want.

*2.3*     *QUALIFIED DATA-NAMES*

In SAMPLE-1 we wrote:

MOVE NAME IN CARD TO NAME IN PRINT-RECORD.

In the Data Division, there are in fact two fields both called NAME. Obviously, if you wrote MOVE NAME TO NAME the computer would not know which you meant and you would get a rude message when you compiled the program telling you so.

Data-names such as field names must be written so as to be unique within a program. You can make them so either by giving each field a different, though meaningful, name, or by providing additional information, as above.

For example, you could have called the fields in the card NAME-IN, ADDR-IN, and PHONE-IN, and the fields in the print-line NAME-OUT, and so on.  You would then write MOVE NAME-IN to NAME-OUT and the computer would know exactly which fields you were talking about.

Or, as in SAMPLE-1, you can qualify a data-name by adding the name of the item of which it is a part, writing NAME IN CARD or NAME OF CARD.  The computer knows what you mean by reading the Data Division.

## 2.4    LITERALS

Suppose you want to set a field to a specific value -- say to put CALIF in a five-position field called STATE. COBOL allows you to do this directly by writing:

```
MOVE 'CALIF' TO STATE.
```

You put quotation marks around the specific value (called a literal) so the computer knows you don't mean some field called CALIF, defined in the Data Division.  The quotation marks must be single quotes (not the usual ", or double quotes).

Q.    How would you put the value 243-7022 in an
      eight-position field called NUMB?

A.    MOVE '243-7022' TO NUMB.

Where a pure number is concerned, you don't need to include it in quotes, because a pure number can't be a data-name.  So

```
MOVE 212 TO AREA-CODE.
```

would be OK.  Note that in the Data Division of SAMPLE-1, AREA-CODE was defined with a PICTURE 9(3), meaning a field three positions long, containing only pure numbers (digits 0 through 9, with maybe a + or - sign, and/or a decimal point).

Q.    How would you put the value 1492 in a field
      called YEAR, defined with a PICTURE 9(4)?

A.    MOVE 1492 TO YEAR.

Q.    Why can't you write

                MOVE 243-7022 TO NUMB.

A.    243-7022 is a non-numeric literal (not a pure
      number) because it contains a hyphen; it must
      be enclosed in quotes.


    If the field is to contain a decimal point, the PICTURE
must show where by including a V.   Thus

            RATE    PICTURE 99V99

is a field which could be 19.95 or 14.00 or 01.25 or any such
number.  No space is left for an actual decimal point in the
field; instead its position is understood from the PICTURE.

Q.    How would you define a numeric field called PI,
      whose value is approximated by 3.14159?

A.    PI    PICTURE 9V9{5} or 9V99999. *


## 2.5    'MOVE'ING NUMBERS


    When the computer receives an instruction to move one
numeric field to another numeric field, instead of working
from left to right, it aligns the decimal point in the
sending field with the decimal point in the receiving field.

    PIC is a standard abbreviation for PICTURE, which we
shall use in the future.  If FIELD-1 is defined PIC 999V99
and contains.

                | 3 | 2 | 1.4 | 6 |

and is MOVEd to FIELD-2, defined PIC 999V9, FIELD-2 will then
contain

                | 3 | 2 | 1.4 |

You must be extremely careful when MOVEing numeric fields or
you will lose digits.  Note that we wrote the decimal point
in its understood position between the digits, not in a space
all its own.

_____

* Note that we use this special type face for extracts from
  programs; { and } are the right and left parentheses.


                        - 18 -

If in doubt, draw diagrams to verify what will happen.
Two rules:

1. When the compiler detects empty positions in the
   receiving fields, it fills them up with zeroes.

2. When no decimal point is specified in the sending
   field, the compiler assumes it is in the right-most
   position.

Bearing these rules in mind and remembering that the
computer works outwards from the decimal point, what will
be the contents of FIELD-2 in the cases below after executing

MOVE FIELD-1 TO FIELD-2.

| | BEFORE MOVE | | AFTER MOVE |
|---|---|---|---|
| | FIELD-1 | FIELD-2 | FIELD-2 |
| Case 1: | PIC 99V99 <br> 1 2.7 1 | PIC 99V99 <br> 8 7.2 1 | 1 2.7 1 |
| Case 2: | PIC 9(3) <br> 3 1 4 | PIC 99V99 <br> 8 7.2 1 | 1 4.0 0 <br> (3 is lost; two decimal places filled with zeros) |
| Case 3: | PIC 9V999 <br> 3.1 4 3 | PIC 99V99 <br> 8 7.2 1 | 0 3.1 4 <br> (2 is lost; leading zero is supplied) |
| Case 4: | PIC 9(4)V9(4) <br> 1 2.3 4.5 6 7 8 | PIC 99V99 <br> 8 7.2 1 | 3 4.5 6 |

Just as you could set an alphanumeric field like
PRINT-RECORD to blanks by moving spaces, so you can set a
numeric field to zero by writing, for example:

MOVE ZEROS TO FIELD-1.

This is useful for initializing numeric fields.

In SAMPLE-1, the phone number punched in each card is defined as being composed of two fields: AREA-CODE PIC 9(3) and NUMBR PIC X(8). Defined this way, NUMBR is not a pure numeric field because it has a hyphen in it between the first three digits which represent the telephone exchange and the last four digits which represent the telephone number.

Q.   How could you redefine these 11 characters or card columns so that all three fields of the number are numeric and can be manipulated separately?

A.       AREA-CODE        PIC 9(3).
         EXCHANGE         PIC 9(3).
         HYPHEN           PIC X.    ◄──────── a hyphen is not
         TEL-NUMBR        PIC 9(4).            a pure number.

Q.   How would you set all the positions of a field called PHONE to zero?

A.   MOVE ZEROS TO PHONE.

Q.   How would you set up the number (212) 936-4096 in the fields defined above, field by field?

A.   MOVE 212 TO AREA-CODE.
     MOVE 936 TO EXCHANGE.
     MOVE '-' TO HYPHEN.   ◄──────── must have quote marks
     MOVE 4096 TO TEL-NUMBR.          because it is a
                                      non-numeric literal.

There are a number of other more complex possibilities in defining and moving fields, and we will look at them in detail in Part II, Chapter 9.

Apart from reading in cards and writing their contents on the printer, the most important thing that SAMPLE-1 does is to test each card to see whether it has an address or not, and to take a different action depending on whether the address is present or blank.  This is done with the IF statement (lines 50 through 53 in the program):

```
IF ADDR IN CARD IS EQUAL TO SPACES
    MOVE WARNING TO MESSAGE-AREA
ELSE
    MOVE ADDR IN CARD TO ADDR IN PRINT-RECORD.
```

(Note that there is only one period, and it comes at the end of the whole statement.)


The general form is:

```
IF condition is true
    Carry out specified operation
ELSE
    Carry out different operation.
```

The IF statement, properly programmed, enables the computer to make decisions and to appear to "think."  Of course, the computer is not really thinking; it's the programmer working out the IF statements who is doing the thinking which the machine will follow mechanically.


The conditions tested by the IF can be extremely complex as we shall see in Chapter 6.  For the moment, let us just concentrate on testing whether one field is equal to another, or equal to a literal.

Q.    Suppose you wanted to move FIELD-A to
      FIELD-B if AREA-CODE was 202; if AREA-CODE
      was anything else, you wanted to move
      FIELD-A to FIELD-C.  How would you
      code the test?

A.    IF AREA-CODE IS EQUAL TO 202
          MOVE FIELD-A TO FIELD-B
      ELSE
          MOVE FIELD-A TO FIELD-C.

Though COBOL does not require it, we recommend that you code the ELSE statement on a line alone, aligned with its corresponding IF, and indent the imperative statements.  This makes the structure of the text clear to the eye, which as you will see later is very important when the IFs get at all complex.  Most important of all is to be consistent, so you learn to identify standard constructs by this format.

Q.   Code a sentence which tests whether PHONE is
     punched in a card read by the program or not;
     if present, move PHONE to PRINT-LINE; if not,
     move WARNING-3 to MESSAGE-AREA.

A.   IF PHONE IN CARD IS EQUAL TO SPACES
          MOVE WARNING-3 TO MESSAGE-AREA
     ELSE
          MOVE PHONE IN CARD TO PHONE IN PRINT-LINE.

The ELSE clause can contain more than one imperative
statement.  For instance, you could write:

     IF PHONE IN CARD IS EQUAL TO SPACES
          MOVE WARNING-3 TO MESSAGE-AREA
     ELSE
          MOVE AREA-CODE IN CARD TO AREA-CODE IN PRINT-LINE
          MOVE NUMBR IN CARD TO NUMBR IN PRINT-LINE.

Once again, note that there is only one period, right at the
end of the sentence.  This sort of decision can be shown
graphically, which sometimes helps display the control structure.

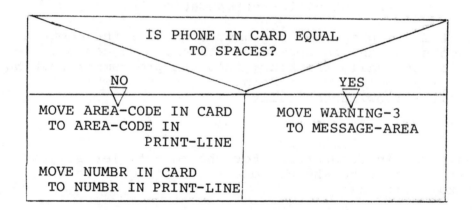

If the answer to the question in the central triangle is "Yes,"
then the right-hand rectangle is processed.  If the answer is
"No," the statements in the left-hand rectangle are obeyed.

If the "false" alternative requires no action, but the
"true" does, you can leave out the ELSE part.
For instance:

     IF AREA-CODE IS EQUAL TO 312
          MOVE 'CHICAGO NUMBER' TO MESSAGE-AREA.
     MOVE PHONE IN CARD TO PHONE IN PRINT-LINE.

Q.   What does this code do?

- 22 -

A. Tests if the area code is 312 and if so, moves a message to that effect ready to be printed. No matter what the area code, the whole number is moved in preparation for printing.

Graphically, this looks like:

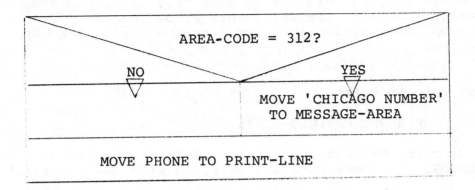

AREA-CODE = 312?

NO          YES

MOVE 'CHICAGO NUMBER'
TO MESSAGE-AREA

MOVE PHONE TO PRINT-LINE

For obvious reasons, a rectangle containing an IF-ELSE structure is known as a "decision box"; a rectangle containing a MOVE or series of MOVEs is a "process box." The boxes can be put together in any order and are read from top to bottom.

Q. Write the code (program instructions) which will express process-decision-process.

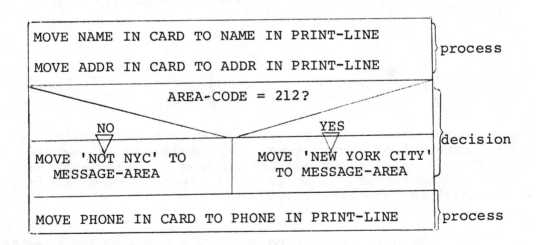

MOVE NAME IN CARD TO NAME IN PRINT-LINE
MOVE ADDR IN CARD TO ADDR IN PRINT-LINE        }process

AREA-CODE = 212?

NO          YES

MOVE 'NOT NYC' TO          MOVE 'NEW YORK CITY'
MESSAGE-AREA               TO MESSAGE-AREA        }decision

MOVE PHONE IN CARD TO PHONE IN PRINT-LINE        }process

A.    MOVE NAME IN CARD TO NAME IN PRINT-LINE.
      MOVE ADDR IN CARD TO ADDR IN PRINT-LINE.
      IF AREA-CODE IS EQUAL TO 212
          MOVE 'NEW YORK CITY' TO MESSAGE-AREA
      ELSE
          MOVE 'NOT NYC' TO MESSAGE-AREA.
      MOVE PHONE IN CARD TO PHONE IN PRINT-LINE.

Very often in a program we want to execute a group
of instructions, either once or many times.  In order
to do this we have to label these instructions as a group
called a procedure.  For example, in SAMPLE-1, PROCESS-CARDS
is written starting in column 8 to show that it is the name
of a procedure, and all the statements which follow
PROCESS-CARDS (beginning four columns to the right) make up
the procedure.

If we were to write:

PERFORM PROCESS-CARDS.

this means "carry out all the statements following the name
PROCESS-CARDS, then come back and carry on with the program."

So we can diagram the flow of control (the sequence in
which instructions are executed) like this:

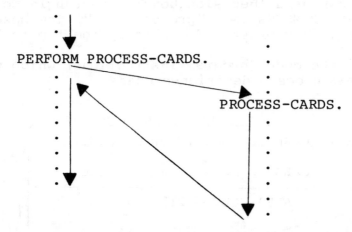

The computer knows where PROCESS-CARDS ends because it
either runs out of instructions to execute (as in the case
of SAMPLE-1) or it finds another package of code labelled
with a procedure-name.  (We'll define "procedure-name" in
more detail in Chapter 3.)

More commonly, we want to perform a block of statements
many times.  For example, the block of statements called
PROCESS-CARDS in SAMPLE-1 (statements 47 through 58) is
executed once for every card read in.  If there are 30,000
cards to be processed, this block of code will be executed
30,000 times.  The great strength of computer programming
lies in our ability to specify instructions once that are
eventually executed possibly millions of times.

We can arrange for this repeated processing by tagging an

" ..... UNTIL some condition is true"

on to the PERFORM.

Thus:    PERFORM PROCESS-CARDS
           UNTIL CARDS-LEFT IS EQUAL TO 'NO '.


means "do a test to see if the field named CARDS-LEFT has the
literal 'NO 'in it.  If not, execute the block of code named
PROCESS-CARDS.  When you have finished, go back to the PERFORM
statement and do the test again.  If the condition is still
not true, execute the block again.  Repeat until the condition
is true, then go on to the next statement after the PERFORM."


    This "PERFORM procedure UNTIL condition is true" enables
us to set up loops, where the computer tirelessly does some
operation over and over, until it has done what we want.

    Q.    Write a statement which will repeatedly carry
          out a procedure called READ-A-CARD, reading
          our name-and-address cards and stopping when
          one is found with a missing address.

    A.    PERFORM READ-A-CARD
             UNTIL ADDRESS IN CARD IS EQUAL TO SPACES.


The PERFORM loop can be shown graphically:

```
+------------------------------------------------+
|  PERFORM UNTIL CARDS-LEFT = 'NO '              |
|  +------+----------------------------------+   |
|  | P    |                                  |   |
|  | R    |    MOVE ....                      |   |
|  | O    |      .                            |   |
|  | C    |      .                            |   |
|  | E    |      .                            |   |
|  | S    |      .                            |   |
|  | S    |      .                            |   |
|  | -    |                                   |   |
|  | C    |      .                            |   |
|  | A    |                                   |   |
|  | R    |                                   |   |
|  | D    |                                   |   |
|  | S    |                                   |   |
|  +------+----------------------------------+   |
+------------------------------------------------+
```

If the condition tested is not true, the procedure in the inner
box is carried out and then the condition is tested again.  Only
when the condition is made true does control go down the left-
hand side into the box below.

- 25 -

Q. What happens if the procedure never makes the
   condition true?

A. The computer will perform the procedure over
   and over again forever, unless something happens
   to stop it.  The computer operator or the operating
   system will eventually halt your program.


Q. Use the process, decision, and loop boxes to
   show the structure of SAMPLE-1.

A.
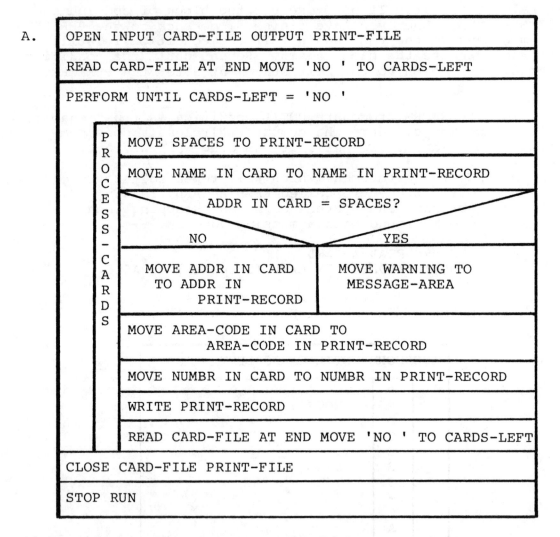

If not identical, your answer should be very similar to
this.

    A diagram like this is called a structured flow-
chart.  It shows the flow of control in a program.
As you see, it is normal to have decisions within loops,
process boxes within decisions, every combination of
structure nested within other structures.

- 26 -

As coupons asking for catalogs continue to come in, it becomes apparent that some people are including their addresses, but leaving off their phone numbers. Some people are even giving their addresses and phone numbers, leaving off their names! Here are some examples of the sort of cards you have to process:

You are asked to write a slightly more complex program, to be named SAMPLE-2, which will deal with the following possibilities:

1)   Name only missing:  Print  **** NAME MISSING ****

2)   Address only missing:
              Print  **** ADDRESS MISSING ****

3)   Whole phone number missing:
              Print  **** PHONE MISSING ****

No other combination of mistakes occurs.

Q.   Given that three warning messages are set up in Working Storage and called WARNING-1, WARNING-2, etc., redraw the structured flowchart to show the logic.

A.

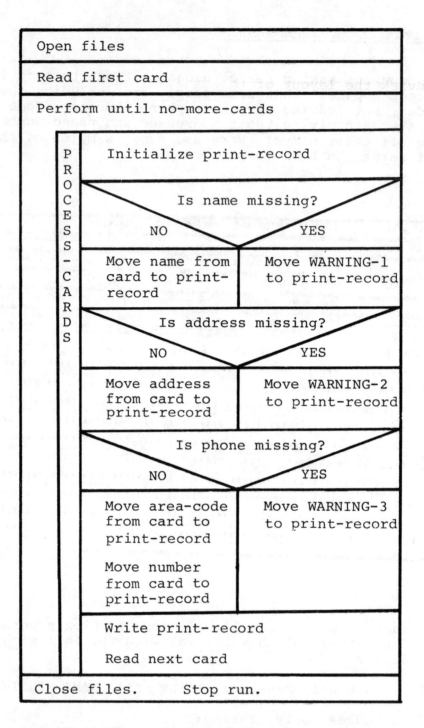

Note that we have used a precise shorthand description
for some of the boxes, especially those that we
already know how to code from SAMPLE-1.

Review the layout of the handwritten version of SAMPLE-1. You will notice it is written on special COBOL coding sheets; use a pad of COBOL coding sheets to write out your version of SAMPLE-2 from the structured flowchart you have just developed. Be sure to follow the format and punctuation used in the handwritten SAMPLE-1; note that most statements begin in column 12, except for certain names and headings, which begin in column 8. Most coding sheets have the statements already numbered for you; all you do is add the page number in column 3. The compiler will give numbers to your statements on the listing, so the main reason for numbering the cards is in case you drop the deck. Columns 73-80 on the coding pad are reserved for the program name. Don't bother about that at this stage.

Find out what your installation requires you to put in SELECT statements, in the Environment Division.

When you have finished, compare your solution with the model solution on the next page. Get someone to review your code before you key-punch and compile it; other people are better at finding errors in what you have written than you are, just as you are better at finding errors in what they have written. It is always worthwhile to take the time to have a walk-through of your code with someone else, and it's a good way to learn fast, as well.

You will find a compiled listing and a sample report on the following pages.

PROGRAM  SAMPLE-2

COBOL STATEMENT

```
101    IDENTIFICATION DIVISION.
102    PROGRAM-ID. SAMPLE-2.
103    ENVIRONMENT DIVISION.
104    INPUT-OUTPUT SECTION.
105    FILE-CONTROL.
106        SELECT CARD-FILE  ASSIGN TO SYS031-UR-2540R-S.
107        SELECT PRINT-FILE ASSIGN TO SYS033-UR-1403-S.
108    DATA DIVISION.
109    FILE SECTION.
110    FD CARD-FILE
111       LABEL RECORDS ARE OMITTED.
112    01 CARD.
113        05 NAME                PICTURE    X(20).
114        05 ADDR                PICTURE    X(40).
115        05 PHONE.
116            10 AREA-CODE        PICTURE    9(3).
117            10 NUMBR            PICTURE    X(8).
118        05 FILLER              PICTURE    X(9).
119    FD PRINT-FILE
120       LABEL RECORDS ARE OMITTED.
121    01 PRINT-RECORD.
122        05 FILLER              PICTURE    X(3).
123        05 NAME                PICTURE    X(20).
124        05 FILLER              PICTURE    X(5).


201        05 ADDR                PICTURE    X(40).
202        05 FILLER              PICTURE    X(5).
203        05 PHONE.
204            10 AREA-CODE        PICTURE    9(3).
205            10 FILLER           PICTURE    X.
206            10 NUMBR            PICTURE    X(8).
207        05 FILLER              PICTURE    X(10).
208        05 MESSAGE-AREA        PICTURE    X(25).
209        05 FILLER              PICTURE    X(12).
210    WORKING-STORAGE SECTION.
211    01 WARNING-1 PICTURE X(25) VALUE '**** NAME MISSING ****'.
212    01 WARNING-2 PICTURE X(25) VALUE '**** ADDRESS MISSING ****'.
213    01 WARNING-3 PICTURE X(25) VALUE '**** PHONE MISSING ****'.
214    01 CARDS-LEFT PICTURE X(3).
215    PROCEDURE DIVISION.
216        OPEN INPUT  CARD-FILE
217             OUTPUT PRINT-FILE.
218        MOVE 'YES' TO CARDS-LEFT.
219        READ CARD-FILE
220          AT END MOVE 'NO ' TO CARDS-LEFT.
221        PERFORM PROCESS-CARDS
222          UNTIL CARDS-LEFT IS EQUAL TO 'NO '.
223        CLOSE CARD-FILE PRINT-FILE.
224        STOP RUN.


301    PROCESS-CARDS.
302        MOVE SPACES TO PRINT-RECORD.
303        IF NAME IN CARD IS EQUAL TO SPACES
304            MOVE WARNING-1 TO MESSAGE-AREA
305        ELSE
306            MOVE NAME IN CARD TO NAME IN PRINT-RECORD.
307        IF ADDR IN CARD IS EQUAL TO SPACES
308            MOVE WARNING-2 TO MESSAGE-AREA
309        ELSE
310            MOVE ADDR IN CARD TO ADDR IN PRINT-RECORD.
311        IF PHONE IN CARD IS EQUAL TO SPACES
312            MOVE WARNING-3 TO MESSAGE-AREA
313        ELSE
314            MOVE AREA-CODE IN CARD TO AREA-CODE IN PRINT-RECORD
315            MOVE NUMBR IN CARD TO NUMBR IN PRINT-RECORD.
316        WRITE PRINT-RECORD.
317        READ CARD-FILE
318          AT END MOVE 'NO ' TO CARDS-LEFT.
```

Figure 2.1   Handwritten SAMPLE-2, on COBOL coding sheet

```
00001            IDENTIFICATICN DIVISION.
00002            PROGRAM-ID. SAMPLE-2.
00003            ENVIRONMENT DIVISION.
00004            INPUT-OUTPUT SECTION.
00005            FILE-CONTROL.
00006                SELECT CARD-FILE  ASSIGN TO SYS031-UR-2540R-S.
00007                SELECT PRINT-FILE ASSIGN TO SYS033-UR-1403-S.
00008            DATA DIVISICN.
00009            FILE SECTION.
00010            FD  CARD-FILE
00011                LABEL RECORDS ARE OMITTED.
00012            01  CARD.
00013                05  NAME               PICTURE   X(23).
00014                05  ADDR               PICTURE   X(40).
00015                05  PHONE.
00016                    10  AREA-CODE       PICTURE   9(3).
00017                    10  NUMBR           PICTURE   X(8).
00018                05  FILLER             PICTURE   X(9).
00019            FD  PRINT-FILE
00020                LABEL RECORDS ARE OMITTED.
00021            01  PRINT-RECORD.
00022                05  FILLER             PICTURE   X(3).
00023                05  NAME               PICTURE   X(20).
00024                05  FILLER             PICTURE   X(5).
00025                05  ADDR               PICTURE   X(40).
00026                05  FILLER             PICTURE   X(5).
00027                05  PHONE.
00028                    10  AREA-CODE       PICTURE   9(3).
00029                    10  FILLER          PICTURE   X.
00030                    10  NUMBR           PICTURE   X(8).
00031                05  FILLER             PICTURE   X(10).
00032                05  MESSAGE-AREA       PICTURE   X(25).
00033                05  FILLER             PICTURE   X(12).
00034            WORKING-STORAGE SECTION.
00035            01  WARNING-1 PICTURE X(25) VALUE '**** NAME MISSING ****'.
00036            01  WARNING-2 PICTURE X(25) VALUE '**** ADDRESS MISSING ****'.
00037            01  WARNING-3 PICTURE X(25) VALUE '**** PHONE MISSING ****'.
00038            01  CARDS-LEFT PICTURE X(3).
00039            PROCEDURE DIVISION.
00040                OPEN INPUT  CARD-FILE
00041                     OUTPUT PRINT-FILE.
00042                MOVE 'YES' TO CARDS-LEFT.
00043                READ CARD-FILE
00044                  AT END MOVE 'NO ' TO CARDS-LEFT.
00045                PERFORM PROCESS-CARDS
00046                  UNTIL CARDS-LEFT IS EQUAL TO 'NO '.
00047                CLOSE CARD-FILE
00048                      PRINT-FILE.
00049                STOP RUN.
00050            PROCESS-CARDS.
00051                MOVE SPACES TO PRINT-RECORD.
00052                IF NAME IN CARD IS EQUAL TO SPACES
00053                    MOVE WARNING-1 TO MESSAGE-AREA
00054                ELSE
00055                    MOVE NAME IN CARD TO NAME IN PRINT-RECORD.
00056                IF ADDR IN CARD IS EQUAL TO SPACES
00057                    MOVE WARNING-2 TO MESSAGE-AREA
00058                ELSE
00059                    MOVE ADDR IN CARD TO ADDR IN PRINT-RECORD.
00060                IF PHONE IN CARD IS EQUAL TO SPACES
00061                    MOVE WARNING-3 TO MESSAGE-AREA
00062                ELSE
00063                    MOVE AREA-CODE IN CARD TO AREA-CODE IN PRINT-RECORD
00064                    MOVE NUMBR IN CARD TO NUMBR IN PRINT-RECORD.
00065                WRITE PRINT-RECORD.
00066                READ CARD-FILE
00067                  AT END MOVE 'NO ' TO CARDS-LEFT.
```

Figure 2.2  Compiled listing for SAMPLE-2

|  |  |  |  |  |  |
|---|---|---|---|---|---|
| VICTOR S GRASPER | 990 GAUNTLET AVENUE | BURLINGAME | CA94010 | 415 243-7022 | |
| DR P.QUACKENBUSH | | | | 502 852-4822 | **** ADDRESS MISSING **** |
| FRANCES PAISANO | 2521 EDGE STREET | FORT LEE | NJ07324 | 201 614-7525 | |
| IAN S INKERMAN | 59 PECAN VALLEY RD | MONTVALE | NJ07645 | 201 103-6061 | |
| BARBARA DIGIACOMO | | | | 918 726-4401 | **** ADDRESS MISSING **** |
| C. ENCHAINE | 212 SLEEPY HOLLOW DR | GREENWICH | CT06830 | 203 886-7431 | |
| SARALEE JAMES | PARTHENON COURT | ATHENS | MO64065 | 816 542-0535 | |
| SCARLETT O'HARA | STE 414 NAT BANK | NEW ORLEANS | LA70012 | 504 815-1147 | |
| LUCY LAKESHORE | 7328 MAIN STREET | CHICAGO | IL60619 | 312 838-9903 | |
| SUSAN KRUPMAN | 131 W 32ND STREET | NEW YORK | NY10001 | 212 465-0330 | |
| I. MORRIS GOOD | 1313 PORPOISE | DALLAS | TX75219 | 214 225-7013 | |
| FREDERICK QUACK | | | | 408 244-6444 | **** ADDRESS MISSING **** |
| MEL HARRISON | 4 NEWTOWN PLAZA | SYRACUSE | NY13210 | 315 747-2121 | |
| DIGITAL DATAGRAB | APT 4R, 400 JOHN ST | CHICAGO | IL60611 | 312 494-1014 | |
| B. HUGH THOMPSON | 1111 SUTTER | SAN FRANCISCO | CA94103 | 415 263-4857 | |
| NATHAN DETROIT | 246 PEACHTREE ST | ATLANTA | GA30303 | | **** PHONE MISSING **** |
| C. P. FOSTER INC | 8TH & CHESTNUT | PHILADELPHIA | PA77055 | 215 229-5575 | |
| STARLET Q. FREEBODY | 12277 SUNSET BLVD | LOS ANGELES | CA90024 | 213 574-2179 | |
| | 405 PARK AVENUE | NEW YORK | NY10017 | 212 688-0214 | **** NAME MISSING **** |
| B BUCHWALD | | | | 202 936-1212 | **** ADDRESS MISSING **** |
| FRANCIS T. NORD | 1905 N. COUNTY ROAD | MINNEAPOLIS | MN55436 | 612 501-0631 | |
| JOHN WCODSIDE | 12074 MILAM | HOUSTON | TX77023 | 713 292-8996 | |
| Z. ROBERTSKI | 12 JEFFERSON ROAD | NEWTON | MA02163 | 517 569-8505 | |
| | 6 RIVERSIDE DRIVE | WASHINGTON | DC20202 | 202 755-4136 | **** NAME MISSING **** |
| PATSY PANCAKE | 4900 WESTERLY PLACE | NEWPORT BEACH | CA92660 | 714 338-8703 | |
| JOHN JOHNSON | 1201 SUPERIOR AVE | CLEVELAND | OH44114 | | **** PHONE MISSING **** |

Figure 2.3    Specimen print-out from SAMPLE-2

# CHAPTER 3:   DEFINING DATA TO THE COMPUTER

Having taken a look at how to make the computer manipulate data the way you want, let's take a first look at how you define this data to the computer.

## 3.1   THE COBOL CHARACTER SET

COBOL uses 51 characters:

the letters A thru Z and ⌀     27 (⌀ stands for blank or space)

the digits ⌀ thru 9     10

the special characters

$$+ - * / = \$ , ; . ' ( ) > <$$     14
___
51

Note that, except in non-numeric literals, and unless you are working with a computer that permits it, you can't use characters like @ or !.  As you know,

the letters A - Z and ⌀ are <u>alphabetic</u> characters (A)

the digits ⌀ - 9 are <u>numeric</u> characters (9)

A field that contains only digits, with maybe a decimal point embedded in the field, and maybe a plus or minus sign, is <u>numeric</u>.

A field which is not purely alphabetic or purely numeric, i.e., contains a mixture, maybe with some special characters, is <u>alphanumeric</u> (X).

Thus, to take some examples:

ACCT NUM is an A type field (alphabetic), even though it contains a blank.

3.14159 is a 9 type field, even though it contains a decimal point.

$132435 is an X type field because it contains a dollar sign.

-27.49 is a 9 type field, even though it contains a - used as a minus sign.

27-49 is an X type field because the - appears as a special character, not a minus sign.

With this in mind, let's take another look at our card layout.  What is the most detailed way in which we could describe the fields which make up the names, addresses, and phone numbers?

All the cards are of the format:

| Card Columns | Data | Length of field | Type of field | |
|---|---|---|---|---|
| cc  1 - 20 | Name | 20 | A | |
| cc 21 - 40 | Street Address | 20 | X | ⎫ |
| cc 41 - 53 | City | 13 | A | These fields make up "Address" |
| cc 54 - 55 | State | 2 | A | |
| cc 56 - 60 | Zip Code | 5 | 9 | ⎭ |
| cc 61 - 63 | Area-Code | 3 | 9 | ⎫ |
| cc 64 - 66 | Exchange | 3 | 9 | These fields make up "Phone" |
| cc 67 | Hyphen | 1 | X | |
| cc 68 - 71 | Local Number | 4 | 9 | ⎭ |
| cc 72 - 80 | Blank | 9 | A | |

Make sure you agree with this table, and that you understand why each field is given its particular field type.

Most records you will deal with are like this:  Several fields are grouped together into one or more group items. Each field which cannot be broken down further is called an elementary item.

    Q.    Suppose we defined a field called "name-and-address."  Would that be a group item?

    A.    Yes:  It would be composed of the elementary item "Name" and the group item "Address."

Whenever a file is going to be used in a COBOL program, it must have a File Definition (FD) in the Data Division. Here is the layout of a detailed FD for CARD-FILE:

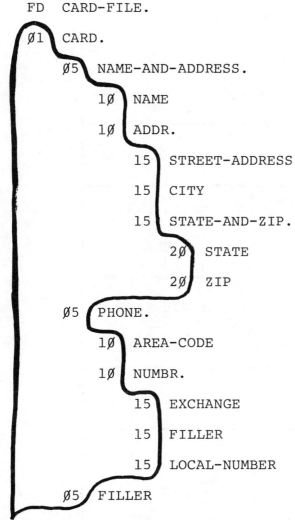

```
FD  CARD-FILE.
Ø1  CARD.
    Ø5  NAME-AND-ADDRESS.
        1Ø  NAME
        1Ø  ADDR.
            15  STREET-ADDRESS
            15  CITY
            15  STATE-AND-ZIP.
                2Ø  STATE
                2Ø  ZIP
    Ø5  PHONE.
        1Ø  AREA-CODE
        1Ø  NUMBR.
            15  EXCHANGE
            15  FILLER
            15  LOCAL-NUMBER
    Ø5  FILLER
```

These are the <u>level numbers</u>; starting with Ø1 for the name of the whole <u>record,</u> they increase for each level of subdivision of a group item, up to a level of 49 as a maximum.   They don't have to go Ø1, Ø5, 1Ø, 15, etc.,as shown above; you could have Ø1, Ø2, Ø3, etc., in fact, any ascending order.


However, it's convenient to leave some gaps in case you want to interpose some levels later on, and we recommend the scheme shown above.

The rule is: <u>Only elementary items have a PIC clause.</u>

Q.   Bearing in mind that in a PIC

           A means only alphabetic
           9 means only numeric
           X means alphanumeric

       work out the PICs for the card as defined on
       the previous page.

A.   FD   CARD-FILE.

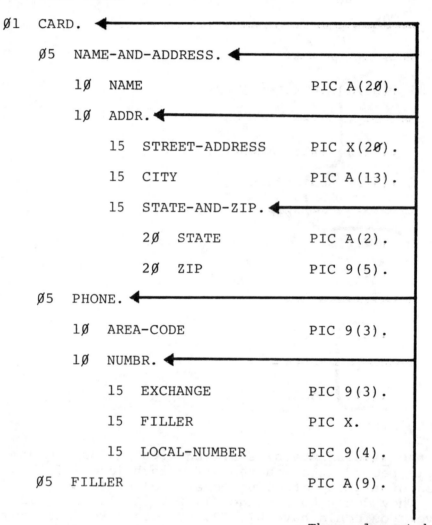

     Ø1   CARD.

         Ø5   NAME-AND-ADDRESS.

             1Ø   NAME                    PIC A(2Ø).

             1Ø   ADDR.

                 15   STREET-ADDRESS      PIC X(2Ø).

                 15   CITY                PIC A(13).

                 15   STATE-AND-ZIP.

                     2Ø   STATE           PIC A(2).

                     2Ø   ZIP             PIC 9(5).

         Ø5   PHONE.

             1Ø   AREA-CODE               PIC 9(3).

             1Ø   NUMBR.

                 15   EXCHANGE            PIC 9(3).

                 15   FILLER              PIC X.

                 15   LOCAL-NUMBER        PIC 9(4).

         Ø5   FILLER                      PIC A(9).

                                          These do not have
                                          PICs because they
                                          are group items
                                          and are further
                                          divided.

Q.    Why would you want to have this degree of
       grouping and subdivision?

A.    So that you could refer to any part or
       reasonable combination of parts of the
       record, as a unit in the Procedure Division.


    For example, if you had a 60-position field called
NAMADD in the print-line, you could write:

        MOVE NAME-AND-ADDRESS TO NAMADD.

and the whole 60 characters would be moved.    At the same
time, you could test the state by writing,

        IF STATE = 'NY'
            MOVE 'NEW YORK STATE' TO MESSAGE-AREA
        ELSE
            MOVE 'OUT OF STATE' TO MESSAGE-AREA.


Q.    Suppose you wanted to test the zip code, digit by
       digit, to check that the zip code and state
       matched (all zip codes beginning with 15 are
       in Pennsylvania, and so on).   Code the part
       of the FD that would enable you to do this,
       making ZIP a group item.

A.              .
                .
                .

            20  ZIP.
                25  FIRST-DIGIT           PIC 9.
                25  SECOND-DIGIT          PIC 9.
                25  THIRD-DIGIT           PIC 9.
                25  FOURTH-DIGIT          PIC 9.
                25  FIFTH-DIGIT           PIC 9.
        05  PHONE.
                .
                .
                .

        or similar structure.

We have used a lot of names for data fields and procedures, such as AREA-CODE and PROCESS-CARDS; there are
different sorts of names and strict rules must be followed
in coding them, or the compiler will reject them.

The four divisions of COBOL all have names which must be
coded exactly as we have already seen them.  Each division
consists of one or more sections.  Section names must also
be coded exactly as we have seen them, for example, INPUT-
OUTPUT SECTION or WORKING-STORAGE SECTION.  Note that the
names of the sections are hyphenated, and that the word
SECTION is followed by a period.

Sections consist of one or more paragraphs; in turn,
paragraphs consist of sentences, each followed by a period.
Each sentence consists of one or more statements, containing
verbs and data-names.  Each paragraph in the Procedure Division is a procedure and its name is a procedure-name.  You
can see how this works by looking at the skeleton of SAMPLE-1,
shown in Fig. 3.1 opposite.

Programmer-defined names:

- can be up to 30 characters long
- can be any combination of A-Z, Ø-9, and hyphens,
    but may not begin or end with a hyphen
- must have at least one alphabetic character if
    they are to be data-names
- should always have a mnemonic meaning

Here are some data-names.  Decide if they are OK, and
if not, why not.

| | |
|---|---|
| MESSAGE-AREA-FOR-WARNING-MESSAGES | Wrong; 3 characters too long |
| MSGØ6Ø | OK |
| NUMBERS-OF-$ | Wrong; $ is a special charac-ter and not allowed |
| 64083 | Wrong; data-names must have one alpha character, or the computer will think it is a numeric literal |
| MFACNO | OK; but cryptic |
| MAST-FILE-AC-NO- | Meaningful but ends with hyphen |

## COBOL Coding Form

SYSTEM _____  
PROGRAM _____  
PROGRAMMER _____  

GRAPHIC ___ PUNCH ___ DATE ___  
PUNCHING INSTRUCTIONS  
PAGE ___ OF ___   CARD FORM ___

| SEQUENCE | A | B | COBOL STATEMENT | IDENTIFICATION |
|---|---|---|---|---|
| 01 | IDENTIFICATION DIVISION. | | division name | |
| 02 | PROGRAM-ID. | | paragraph name | The program name goes here in → SAMPLE-1 every card. |
| 03 | | | | |
| 04 | ENVIRONMENT DIVISION. | | division name | |
| 05 | INPUT-OUTPUT SECTION. | | section name | |
| 06 | FILE-CONTROL. | | paragraph name | |
| 07 | SELECT...... | | statement | |
| 08 | | | | |
| 09 | DATA DIVISION. | | division name | All these division and section names must appear on a line of their own, be coded exactly as shown, and be followed by a period. |
| 10 | FILE SECTION. | | section name | |
| 11 | FD | | | |
| 12 | | | | |
| 13 | | | | |
| 14 | | | | |
| 15 | | | | |
| 16 | WORKING-STORAGE SECTION. | | section name | |
| 17 | | | | |
| 18 | PROCEDURE DIVISION. | | division name | |
| 19 | | | | |
| 20 | PROCESS-CARDS. | | | A paragraph with a procedure-name made up by the programmer. Provided you follow it with at least one space, you are allowed to have a statement on the same line. We prefer to have it on a line of its own. |
| 21 | MOVE SPACES TO PRINT-RECORD. | | | |
| 22 | | | | |

A statement must start in column 12 or further right.

Figure 3.1    Skeleton of a COBOL program

Here are some procedure-names:

1234567890123456789Ø    This is legal; procedure-names
                                may be all digits.  Once again,
                                pretty meaningless.

UPDATE-MASTER-FILE     OK

Programmer-defined names must not be the same as any
of the standard words reserved for special use in COBOL,
such as ADDRESS, NUMBER, SPACES, FILE-CONTROL, MOVE, DATA,
etc.  (This is why we have used ADDR instead of ADDRESS
and NUMBR instead of NUMBER.)  A list of these reserved
words is given in Appendix B.  Don't bother to memorize
them all at this stage; just note the ones that have hyphens
in them, and steer clear of them.  Then, if you are in
doubt, make up a name with a hyphen in it (which will help
to make it more readable and meaningful anyway) and you'll
have no problem.

Of course, once you have chosen a name, and defined it
in the Data Division, it is essential to spell it exactly
the same throughout the program.  To the computer,
MAST-FILE-AC-NO and MAS-FILE-AC-NO are totally different
data-names, and if you write one when you mean another,
you will get a rude message, telling you the computer
doesn't understand what you mean.

In general, you should make the names you define as
meaningful as possible, without making them so long you get
writer's cramp when you're coding.

### 3.4.1  Naming the Same Data in Different Places

In SAMPLE-1 we have the fields NAME and ADDR in CARD and
also in PRINT-RECORD.  As you saw, we can make use of these
names by writing NAME IN CARD, etc.  Using qualified data-
names to get unique definitions gets clumsy when the names
are long and you refer to them a lot.

A good practice instead is to put a suffix on the data-
name; -IN for an input field, and -OUT for an output field.
Thus, if we defined the card fields as NAME-IN, ADDRESS-IN,
and PHONE-IN, we could define the printer fields as NAME-OUT,
ADDRESS-OUT, and so on.

You can see at a glance that NAME-IN and NAME-OUT contain the same data, and you can write

        MOVE NAME-IN TO NAME-OUT
instead of

        MOVE NAME IN CARD TO NAME IN PRINT-RECORD

We will use this technique in the sample programs in the rest of this book.


### 3.5    PUNCTUATION, LAYOUT, AND COMMENTS


The period . tells the compiler where a sentence ends, and since we normally write one statement per sentence, we will have a period at the end of every complete statement.


The period must also be used:

- at the end of the definition of each FD statement or group item statement or elementary item definition in the Data Division

- after every division, section, or paragraph name.

Each period must be followed by one or more spaces; while it is legal to have several statements on one line, we recommend that you always start a new line after each period. This makes your program much more readable.


    Q.    Put the periods where they belong in the code below:

```
DATA DIVISION
FILE SECTION
FD  RECORD-IN
    LABEL RECORDS ARE OMITTED
01  REC
    02  PERSONNEL-NO                PIC 9{6}
    02  JOB-DESCRIP
        03  DEPT
            04  FACTORY             PIC X{3}
            04  SHOP-NO             PIC 9{3}
PROCEDURE DIVISION
    MOVE PERSONNEL-NO TO WAGE-ACCT
    IF FACTORY IS EQUAL TO CODE-FOR-PODUNK
        MOVE SHOP-NO TO SHOP-NO-WS
    ELSE
        PERFORM OTHER-GROUP-ROUTINE
```

A.

```
      DATA DIVISION.
      FILE SECTION.
      FD   RECORD-IN
           LABEL RECORDS ARE OMITTED.
      01   REC.
           02   PERSONNEL-NO                    PIC 9(6).
           02   JOB-DESCRIP.
                03   DEPT.
                     04   FACTORY             PIC X(3).
                     04   SHOP-NO             PIC 9(3).
      PROCEDURE DIVISION.
           MOVE PERSONNEL-NO TO WAGE-ACCT.
           IF FACTORY IS EQUAL TO CODE-FOR-PODUNK
                MOVE SHOP-NO TO SHOP-NO-WS
           ELSE
                PERFORM OTHER-GROUP-ROUTINE.
```

Notice that the FD does not have a period until it is completed by the LABEL RECORDS clause, and there is only one period in the whole IF statement, right at the end.


### 3.5.1  Avoiding Confusion with Handwriting


As you have seen, we are using the convention of writing number zero as Ø to avoid confusion with the letter O. You may find the convention reversed in some installations.

The other pairs of characters that are sometimes confused are I and 1, S and 5, Z and 2, U and V.


So, stick to this convention:

| | |
|---|---|
| Zero | Ø |
| Letter O for orange | O |
| Letter I for India | I |
| Number 1 | 1 |
| Letter S for sugar | S |
| Number 5 | 5 |
| Letter Z for zebra | Z |
| Number 2 | 2 |
| Letter U for uncle | U |
| Letter V for Victor | V |

When you write a program that is more than a few statements long, and then come back to it after a few months, you
will find that you have forgotten what the various statements
do.  If you have to check or change the program for any
reason, you will have to work through the logic of the program
and figure out afresh what each statement is for.

You may frequently be asked to modify programs written
by other people, either because the situation for which they
were written has changed, or they didn't do what they were
supposed to do in the first place.

So you must aim to write code that is easy for anyone
who knows COBOL to read and understand; if you think any
statement or group of statements is going to be hard to understand, and you can see no way to simplify them, write an
explanatory comment.  You do this by putting an * in column
7 of the line of code as shown below; everything else on this
line will be part of the program but will not be executed by
the computer.

| SEQUENCE | CONT | A | B | | | | | | | | |
|---|---|---|---|---|---|---|---|---|---|---|---|
| 3 4   6 | 7 | 8 | 12   16   20   24   28   32   36   40 | | | | | | | | |
| 01 | | PROCEDURE DIVISION. | | | | | | | | | |
| 02 | | MOVE PERSONNEL-NO TO WAGE-ACCT. | | | | | | | | | |
| 03 | | IF FACTORY IS EQUAL TO PODUNK-CODE | | | | | | | | | |
| 04 | | MOVE SHOP-NO TO SHOP-NO-WS | | | | | | | | | |
| 05 | | ELSE | | | | | | | | | |
| 06 | | PERFORM OTHER-GROUP-ROUTINE. | | | | | | | | | |
| 07 | * | THIS PROGRAM ONLY DEALS WITH STAFF AT | | | | | | | | | |
| 08 | * | THE PODUNK FACTORY | | | | | | | | | |
| 09 | | IF SHOP-NO-WS IS....... | | | | | | | | | |
| 10 | | | | | | | | | | | |

As we saw with the IF statement in SAMPLE-2, you can write a statement over several lines, with the separate parts (clauses) of the statement starting in column 14 or 16 of each line (or further to the right if you need to indent for clarity).  You should always break the sentence at a <u>key</u> <u>word</u> such as UNTIL or TO.  For example, do not write

```
PERFORM COMPUTE-PROCEDURE UNTIL CARDS-LEFT IS
          EQUAL TO 'NO '.
```

While this will work, your program will be much more readable if you always break the statement in a standard place, thus:

```
PERFORM COMPUTE-PROCEDURE
    UNTIL CARDS-LEFT IS EQUAL TO 'NO '.
```

By putting a <u>hyphen</u> in column 7, you can split <u>words</u> between lines; while this is legal, it is a poor practice except in the case of long non-numeric literals.  A non-numeric literal can be up to 120 characters long (for example, in a report heading), so it would have to be split over at least two lines.

Q.   Define in Working Storage a field called ASTERISK-DELIMITER, which is 120 characters long and consists of alternating asterisks and hyphens, thus *-*-*-*-*- etc.

A.

```
     WORKING-STORAGE SECTION.
     01   ASTERISK-DELIMITER              PIC X(120)
          VALUE '*-*-*-*-*-*-*-*-*-*-*-*-*-*-*-*-*-*-*-*-
   -      '*-*-*-*-*-*-*-*-*-*-*-*-*-*-*-*-*-*-*-*-*-*-*-
   -      '*-*-*-'.
```

Note that in this case the continuation cards must also begin with a single quote to identify what follows as a non-numeric literal.

As we saw in SAMPLE-1 and SAMPLE-2, you must have an FD (File Definition) for each <u>external</u> <u>file</u> (e.g., cards, printer) that is going to provide data to the program (input) or accept data from the program (output).


The FD does two things:

- tells the computer what the layout of the data record will be, and what data-names will be used for the various parts.

- tells the compiler to reserve an area of storage which will be used to hold each data record while the program deals with it.

So we can draw a diagram of computer storage like this:

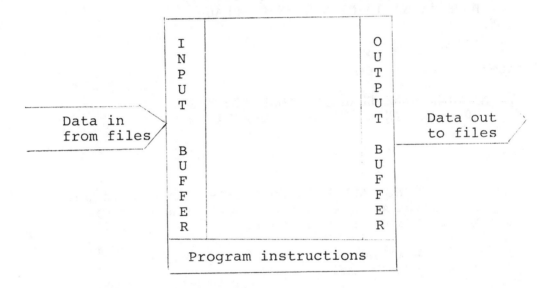

These reserved input/output work areas, called <u>buffers</u>, hold the data for each record.


The input buffer holds the data from the most recently read card; when we issue an instruction like:

    MOVE NAME IN CARD TO NAME IN PRINT-RECORD.

what is actually happening is that the computer is moving data from the input buffer to the output buffer, as specified by the appropriate FDs.  Then the instruction

    WRITE PRINT-RECORD.

transfers data from the output buffer to the printer.

As well as defining the files and reserving space for buffers, we need to reserve other positions in storage, for work areas in the program, for setting up messages and constants as is done in WARNING-1, WARNING-2, etc., and for all other storage of intermediate data between input and output. Storage is set up for these purposes in the Working Storage Section, which, as you have seen, follows the File Section.

A common use for Working Storage is the setting up of flags. A flag is a field, which can be set to 'YES' or 'NO ', as a signal that something has or has not happened.

For instance, in a more complex version of SAMPLE-1, we might want to defer processing of a card with a missing name until later in the program.

In this case we would write:

```
IF NAME IN CARD IS EQUAL TO SPACES
    MOVE 'YES' TO MISSING-NAME-FLAG
ELSE
    ...
```

and later in the program

```
IF MISSING-NAME-FLAG IS EQUAL TO 'YES'
    MOVE WARNING-1 TO MESSAGE-AREA
ELSE
    ...
```

Setting MISSING-NAME-FLAG to 'YES' allows us to delay handling the situation. We set a flag in one part of the program, and test for it in another.

Q.  Code a Working Storage Section entry to set up MISSING-NAME-FLAG.

A.  01  MISSING-NAME-FLAG            PIC X {3}.

Q.  With MISSING-NAME-FLAG HAVING PIC X(3), what is its contents if

    MOVE 'NO' TO MISSING-NAME-FLAG is executed.

A.  NOβ;  since the literal 'NO' is too short, the remaining position is filled with a blank. While this is quite adequate, we prefer to be doubly sure by moving 'NOβ' to flags.

As we said in Chapter 2, it is important that you know the contents of all work areas before you use them; so you have to initialize them to some value that you are sure of.

### 3.7.1    Initializing Constants with VALUE

Suppose you wanted to print a heading in the middle of a 132-position print-line, saying

SALES REPORT

The words consist of 12 characters, so you want 60 blanks on either side.  You would use the VALUE clause to set up this print-line in Working Storage by coding:

```
WORKING-STORAGE SECTION.
01  HEADING-1.
    05  FILLER          PIC X(60) VALUE SPACES.
    05  FILLER          PIC X(12) VALUE 'SALES REPORT'.
    05  FILLER          PIC X(60) VALUE SPACES.
```

As you have seen, we use FILLER to give a name to a field that will not be referred to, though it may be filled with blanks. Later, in the Procedure Division, you would write:

```
        .
        .
        MOVE HEADING-1 TO PRINT-LINE.
        WRITE PRINT-LINE.                    Note that these
                                             two are
    or                                       equivalent.

        WRITE PRINT-LINE FROM HEADING-1.
```

Use VALUE to set up any field which is a constant, that is not changed throughout the execution of the program.

The general format of the VALUE clause has three options:

VALUE { numeric literal / 'non-numeric literal' / figurative constant }    The braces show that these three are alternatives.

As well as the figurative constant SPACES, you might want to use ZERO or ZEROS to initialize a long numeric field, in much the same way as you use SPACES to initialize an alphabetic field.

Where a field is going to be used as a flag, like MISSING-NAME-FLAG in the previous section, its contents will vary from time to time as the program is executed.  Similarly, if a field is used to count the number of cards processed, its value would also change.  Working Storage fields like these must be initialized to a starting value before they are used for the first time. While this <u>could</u> be done with the VALUE clause, it is better practice to reserve VALUE for constants, and initialize flags and counters with a MOVE statement.

As you saw in SAMPLE-1 and SAMPLE-2, immediately before READing the card file, we wrote

MOVE 'YES' TO CARDS-LEFT.

CARDS-LEFT is a flag, whose value will be changed to 'NO ', when the program tries to read a card and finds there are no more cards left to be read.

So, to complete the previous picture of the storage inside the computer, visualize it as consisting of four areas:

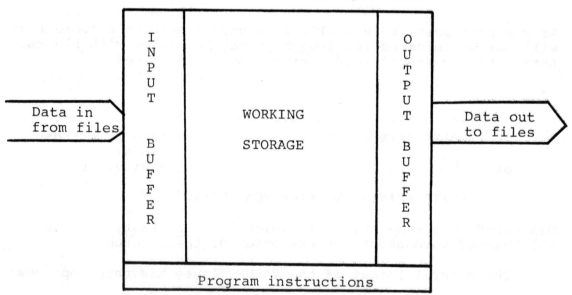

Data is read into the input buffer, moved to Working Storage for processing, then moved to the output buffer for printing.

The size and format of each buffer is automatically specified by the size and format of the corresponding FD; Working Storage must be defined separately according to your needs.

Suppose one column on a card was used to indicate the person's marital status:  S for single, M for married, D for divorced, and W for widowed.   We might describe the field as:

```
01  CARD.
        .
        .
    05  MARITAL-STATUS              PIC X.
```

Often we want to perform different operations depending on what is in that column of the card, so we would have to write:

```
IF MARITAL-STATUS = 'S' PERFORM SINGLE-ROUTINE.
IF MARITAL-STATUS = 'M' PERFORM MARRIED-ROUTINE.
IF MARITAL-STATUS = 'D' PERFORM DIVORCED-ROUTINE.
IF MARITAL-STATUS = 'W' PERFORM WIDOWED-ROUTINE.
```

To simplify this coding, we can set up condition names for each of the possible card entries.  This involves using the special level number 88, as illustrated below:

```
01  CARD.
        .
        .
    05  MARITAL-STATUS              PIC X.
        88  SINGLE      VALUE 'S'.
        88  MARRIED     VALUE 'M'.
        88  DIVORCED    VALUE 'D'.
        88  WIDOWED     VALUE 'W'.
```

Then we would code:

```
IF SINGLE PERFORM SINGLE-ROUTINE.
IF MARRIED PERFORM MARRIED-ROUTINE.
```

and so on.

The condition name, e.g., DIVORCED, takes the place of the condition MARITAL STATUS = 'D'.

Q.   A one-column field in CARD, called SEX, contains M for males and F for females.  Set up condition names.

A.
```
01  CARD.
        .
        .
    05  SEX                         PIC X.
        88  MALE    VALUE 'M'.
        88  FEMALE  VALUE 'F'.
```

1.    Which of the characters shown in the specimen card on
      page 6 are <u>not</u> in the COBOL character set?

2.    What is wrong with this FD?

```
      FD   OUT-PRINT
      01   LINE                        PIC X{132}
           05  FILLER                  PIC X{60}.
           05  FILLER                  PIC X{12}  VALUE REPORT
           05  FILLER                  PIC X{60}.        HEADING.
```

3.    What is wrong with this FD?

```
      FD   CARD-FILE
      01   CARD
           02  NAME.                   PIC A {20}.
           02  ADDRESS
               03  STREET.             PIC X {20}.
               03  CITY.               PIC A {20}.
               03  STATE-ZIP.          PIC X {20}.
```

4.    Here are some programmer-defined names.  Decide if they
      are OK   a)  as data-names,  b)  as procedure-names,  and
      if not, why not:

      4.1      MASTER-FILE-INVENTORY-CODE
      4.2      M9999
      4.3      HEADING-
      4.4      -TITLE-
      4.5      111X
      4.6      LINE-COUNTER
      4.7      ZIP CODE
      4.8      ZIP.CODE
      4.9      POSITION
      4.10     666

5.    What is wrong with this Working Storage Section?

```
      01   CARDS-LEFT-FLAG             PIC 999.
      01   PRINT-LINE-WS        VALUE SPACES.
           05  FILLER.
           05  FILLER     PIC X{24}
                          VALUE 'MONTHLY PRODUCTION REPORT'.
           05  FILLER.
```

6.    Write the FD entries to set up meaningful condition-names
      for a one-column card code called JOB-CODE with the
      following meanings:

               T  Trainee           P  Programmer
               J  Junior Programmer  A  Systems Analyst

*   *Answers are in Appendix D.*

7.  Rewrite the Working Storage Section specified in question 5, using correct COBOL, and changing the print-line to read REPORT OF MONTHLY SALES, PRODUCTION AND PROFITABILITY, centered in a 132-position print-line.

The mail-order firm for which you work sent catalogs to the names and addresses that were processed in SAMPLE-1 and SAMPLE-2, and has received back a number of orders together with applications to open credit accounts.  Applicants for credit accounts must fill in a form giving family income, years employed at the current job, sex, marital status, number of dependents, whether home-owner or renter, what rent or mortgage is paid monthly, and what other payments are made regularly.

For instance, Victor Grasper's form shows that he is a single male earning $15,700 per annum in a job where he has been for four years.  He has no dependents and owns an apartment on which he pays $250 per month.  His other debt payments are $40 per month.

This information is entered into the computer on a second card for each person.  Each person is given a six-digit number which is punched in cc 75-80 of the first name/address/phone card.  Victor Grasper's and Ian Inkerman's cards are shown below.

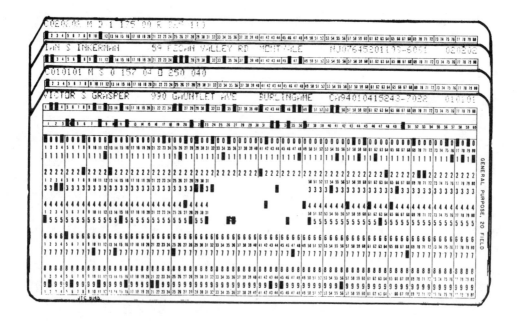

The layout of the second card is:

| cc | Data | Field Length | Field Type | Remarks |
|---|---|---|---|---|
| 1 | A letter 'C' for continuation | 1 | X | |
| 2-7 | 6-digit account number | 6 | 9 | |
| 8 | blank | 1 | X | |
| 9 | Sex | 1 | X | M for male, F for female |
| 1Ø | blank | 1 | X | |
| 11 | Marital status | 1 | X | S for single, etc. |
| 12 | blank | 1 | X | |
| 13 | Number of dependents | 1 | 9 | Number of people supported from Ø-9. More than 9 coded as 9. |
| 14 | blank | 1 | X | |
| 15-17 | Income in hundreds of dollars | 3 | 9 | e.g., 157 means $15,7ØØ |
| 18 | blank | 1 | X | |
| 19-2Ø | Years employed in this job | 2 | 99 | e.g., Ø1 means 1 year. Less than 1 year coded as ØØ. |
| 21 | blank | 1 | X | |
| 22 | Own-or-rent | 1 | X | O for own; R for rent |
| 23 | blank | 1 | X | |
| 24-26 | Monthly payments on mortgage or rent | 3 | 999 | |
| 27 | blank | 1 | X | |
| 28-3Ø | Monthly payments on other debts | 3 | 999 | |

```
VICTOR S GRASPER      PHONE (415) 243-7022    MALE          INCOME          $15700 PER YEAR;  IN THIS EMPLOY 04 YEARS
990 GAUNTLET AVE                               SINGLE        MORTGAGE:         $250 PER MTH
BURLINGAME    CA 94010  A/C: 010101            0 DEPENDENTS  OTHER PAYMENTS    $040 PER MTH


IAN S INKERMAN        PHONE (201) 103-6061     MALE          INCOME          $17500 PER YEAR;  IN THIS EMPLOY LESS THAN 1 YEAR
59 PECAN VALLEY RD                             DIVORCED      RENTAL:           $325 PER MTH
MONTVALE      NJ 07645  A/C: 020202            1 DEPENDENTS  OTHER PAYMENTS    $110 PER MTH


SARALEE JAMES         PHONE (816) 542-0535     FEMALE        INCOME          $21000 PER YEAR;  IN THIS EMPLOY 03 YEARS
PARTHENON COURT                                DIVORCED      MORTGAGE:         $275 PER MTH
ATHENS        MO 64065  A/C: 050505            1 DEPENDENTS  OTHER PAYMENTS  $ 75 PER MTH


SCARLETT O'HARA       PHONE (504) 815-1147     FEMALE        INCOME          $09500 PER YEAR;  IN THIS EMPLOY 26 YEARS
SUITE 414 NAT BANK                             WIDOWED       RENTAL:           $110 PER MTH
NEW ORLEANS   LA 70012  A/C: 060606            2 DEPENDENTS  OTHER PAYMENTS  $ 20 PER MTH


SUSAN KRUPMAN         PHONE (212) 354-0330     FEMALE        INCOME          $12900 PER YEAR;  IN THIS EMPLOY 01 YEARS
131 WEST 32ND ST                               SINGLE        RENTAL:           $150 PER MTH
NEW YORK      NY 10001  A/C: 040404            0 DEPENDENTS  OTHER PAYMENTS  $ 30 PER MTH


I. MORRIS GOOD        PHONE (214) 225-7013     MALE          INCOME          $27300 PER YEAR;  IN THIS EMPLOY 11 YEARS
1313 PORPOISE                                  MARRIED       MORTGAGE:         $400 PER MTH
DALLAS        TX 75219  A/C: 030303            4 DEPENDENTS  OTHER PAYMENTS    $150 PER MTH
```

Figure 3.2    Specimen print-out of profiles for
credit applicants

We want to read in the name-and-address and credit information cards in pairs, for one applicant at a time, and produce a report listing the details of the application (the application profile) in an easy-to-read form. To simplify the problem, we will assume that all the fields are present and correctly punched; in any program you write for your organization you would have to check for this.

Figure 3.2 shows what the profile is to look like for the first six applicants. Study the details of the layout and compare the data printed with the data on the cards. You will notice that the print-out is a bit clumsy; in places it says 1 DEPENDENTS and 04 YEARS, etc. This is to simplify your programming work. We'll clean up these finer points in a later chapter.

As a first step, produce a printer spacing chart to correspond with the report layout; check carefully that the spacing between fields is correct.

Now, how are we to get from the card data to the report giving a profile of each person? We obviously have to read in a pair of cards, somehow transform the data on them into correctly formatted print-lines, write the print-lines, move the paper up four lines, and repeat the process until we run out of cards.

Graphically, we can show the general process like this:

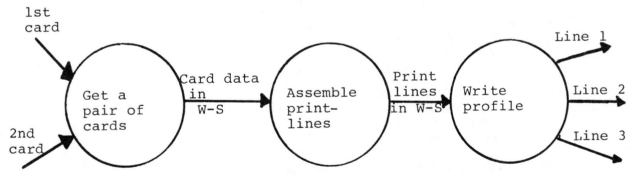

This is called a <u>program graph</u>; the circles show the basic data manipulations, and the lines connecting them represent the form that the data takes as it goes from input to output. Drawing a program graph is the first step in designing a program.

We can see from the program graph that there are three basic procedures which must be controlled in some way; so we now draw a <u>structure</u> <u>chart</u> (not a flowchart) which shows how the function of the overall program (to print profiles) breaks down:

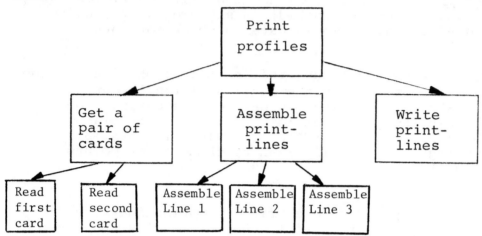

This chart shows that the overall function breaks down into three subfunctions such as "Get a pair of cards into Working Storage" (which in turn breaks down into "Read first card" and "Read second card"). The structure of this program is fairly simple; the structure chart becomes very important when the program gets complex, as we shall see later.


We want to keep on printing profiles until we run out of cards, so the heart of the program will be in shorthand form:

```
        Initialize (open files, read first card)
        PERFORM PRINT-PROFILES
           UNTIL no-more-cards.
        Terminate (close files, stop-run)
```

PRINT-PROFILES will contain
```
        PERFORM GET-A-PAIR-OF-CARDS-INTO-WS.
        PERFORM ASSEMBLE-PRINT-LINES.
        PERFORM WRITE-PRINT-LINES.
```

GET-A-PAIR-OF-CARDS must read in two cards, and move their contents to appropriate Working Storage areas.

Q. Since COBOL normally provides only one input buffer for each FD, what would happen if the first card was not moved to Working Storage before reading the second card?

A. The data in the second card would over-write the data from the first card in the buffer, and the data from the first card would be lost.

ASSEMBLE-PRINT-LINES must move data from the card holding areas in Working Storage to print-line holding areas, also in Working Storage, ready for printing.

So the Data Division must consist of:

- an FD for the card file providing for reading in cards with two formats

- an FD for the printer file

- a holding area for the card data

- three holding areas for the formatted information in each print-line.

Before going further, write the Data Division for this program, to be called SAMPLE-3. Remember to use 88 levels for condition-names. You deal with several types of records in one file (two types of cards in this case) by giving each Ø1 entry a different name and then writing in the FD:

DATA RECORDS ARE name-1 name-2, etc.

In this case, if the first card was described with an Ø1 called NAME-ADDRESS-AND-PHONE-IN, and the second card of each pair was described with an Ø1 called CREDIT-INFORMATION, the FD might read:

```
FD    APPLICATION-CARDS
          LABEL RECORDS ARE OMITTED
          DATA RECORDS ARE NAME-ADDRESS-AND-PHONE-IN
                           CREDIT-INFORMATION.
```

When you have coded the Data Division, compare it with the sample on the next page. If your answer differs in any significant way, be sure you understand why.

```
00001          IDENTIFICATION DIVISION.
00002          PROGRAM-ID. SAMPLE-3.
00003
00004          ENVIRONMENT DIVISION.
00005          INPUT-OUTPUT SECTION.
00006          FILE-CONTROL.
00007              SELECT APPLICATION-CARDS-FILE ASSIGN TO SYS031-UR-2540R-S.
00008              SELECT PROFILE-LISTING          ASSIGN TO SYS033-JR-1403-S.
00009
00010          DATA DIVISION.
00011          FILE SECTION.
00012
00013          FD   APPLICATION-CARDS-FILE
00014                   LABEL RECORDS ARE OMITTED
00015                   DATA RECORDS ARE NAME-ADDRESS-AND-PHONE-IN
00016                                   CREDIT-INFORMATION-IN.
00017          01   NAME-ADDRESS-AND-PHONE-IN.
00018               05   NAME-IN                      PIC X(20).
00019               05   ADDRESS-IN                   PIC X(40).
00020               05   PHONE-IN                     PIC X(11).
00021               05   FILLER                       PIC X(3).
00022               05   ACCT-NUM-IN1                 PIC 9(6).
00023          01   CREDIT-INFORMATION-IN.
00024               05   CARD-TYPE-IN                 PIC X.
00025               05   ACCT-NUM-IN2                 PIC 9(6).
00026               05   FILLER                       PIC X.
00027               05   CREDIT-INFO-IN               PIC X(22).
00028               05   FILLER                       PIC X(50).
00029
00030          FD   PROFILE-LISTING
00031                   LABEL RECORDS ARE OMITTED.
00032          01   PRINT-LINE-OUT                    PIC X(132).
00033
00034          WORKING-STORAGE SECTION.
00035          01   CARDS-LEFT                        PIC X(3).
00036
00037          01   APPLICATION-DATA.
00038               05   NAME-AND-ADDRESS-WS.
00039                    10   NAME-WS                 PIC X(20).
00040                    10   ADDRESS-WS.
00041                         15   STREET-WS          PIC X(20).
00042                         15   CITY-WS            PIC X(13).
00043                         15   STATE-WS           PIC XX.
00044                         15   ZIP-WS             PIC X(5).
00045               05   PHONE-WS.
00046                    10   AREA-CODE-WS            PIC 9(3).
00047                    10   NUMBR-WS               PIC X(8).
00048               05   FILLER                       PIC X(3).
00049               05   ACCT-NUM-WS                  PIC 9(6).
00050               05   CREDIT-INFO-WS.
00051                    10   SEX-WS                  PIC X.
00052                         88   MALE       VALUE 'M'.
00053                         88   FEMALE     VALUE 'F'.
00054                    10   FILLER                  PIC X.
00055                    10   MARITAL-STATUS-WS        PIC X.
00056                         88   SINGLE     VALUE 'S'.
00057                         88   MARRIED    VALUE 'M'.
00058                         88   DIVORCED   VALUE 'D'.
00059                         88   WIDOWED    VALUE 'W'.
00060                    10   FILLER                  PIC X.
```

Figure 3.3    SAMPLE-3    – 58 –

```
00061          10   NUMBER-DEPENS-WS           PIC 9.
00062          10   FILLER                     PIC X.
00063          10   INCOME-HUNDREDS-WS         PIC 9(3).
00064          10   FILLER                     PIC X.
00065          10   YEARS-EMPLOYED-WS          PIC 99.
00066          10   FILLER                     PIC X.
00067          10   CWN-OR-RENT-WS             PIC X.
00068             88   OWNED       VALUE 'O'.
00069             88   RENTED      VALUE 'R'.
00070          10   FILLER                     PIC X.
00071          10   MORTGAGE-OR-RENTAL-WS      PIC 9(3).
00072          10   FILLER                     PIC X.
00073          10   CTHER-PAYMENTS-WS          PIC 9(3).
00074
00075      01   LINE-1-WS.
00076          05   FILLER                     PIC X(5)     VALUE SPACES.
00077          05   NAME-L1                    PIC X(20).
00078          05   FILLER                     PIC X(11)
00079                             VALUE '    PHONE ('.
00080          05   AREA-CODE-L1               PIC 9(3).
00081          05   FILLER                     PIC XX       VALUE ') '.
00082          05   NUMBR-L1                   PIC X(8).
00083          05   FILLER                     PIC X(3)     VALUE SPACES.
00084          05   SEX-L1                     PIC X(6).
00085          05   FILLER                     PIC X(9)     VALUE SPACES.
00086          05   FILLER                     PIC X(14)
00087                             VALUE 'INCOME        $'.
00088          05   INCOME-HUNDREDS-L1         PIC 9(3).
00089          05   FILLER                     PIC X(28)
00090                             VALUE '00 PER YEAR; IN THIS EMPLOY '.
00091          05   YEARS-EMPLOYED-L1.
00092             10   YEARS-L1                PIC XX.
00093             10   DESCN-L1                PIC X(16).
00094
00095      01   LINE-2-WS.
00096          05   FILLER                     PIC X(5)     VALUE SPACES.
00097          05   STREET-L2                  PIC X(20).
00098          05   FILLER                     PIC X(27)    VALUE SPACES.
00099          05   MARITAL-STATUS-L2          PIC X(8).
00100          05   FILLER                     PIC X(7)     VALUE SPACES.
00101          05   OUTGO-DESCN                PIC X(16).
00102          05   MORTGAGE-OR-RENTAL-L2      PIC 9(3).
00103          05   MESSAGE-L2                 PIC X(46)    VALUE ' PER MTH'
00104
00105      01   LINE-3-WS.
00106          05   FILLER                     PIC X(5)     VALUE SPACES.
00107          05   CITY-L3                    PIC X(13).
00108          05   FILLER                     PIC X        VALUE SPACE.
00109          05   STATE-L3                   PIC XX.
00110          05   FILLER                     PIC X        VALUE SPACE.
00111          05   ZIP-L3                     PIC X(5).
00112          05   FILLER                     PIC X(7)     VALUE '  A/C: '.
00113          05   ACCT-NUM-L3                PIC 9(6).
00114          05   FILLER                     PIC X(12)    VALUE SPACES.
00115          05   NUMBER-DEPENS-L3           PIC 9.
00116          05   FILLER                     PIC X(14)
00117                             VALUE ' DEPENDENTS     '.
00118          05   FILLER                     PIC X(16)
00119                             VALUE 'OTHER PAYMENTS $'.
00120          05   OTHER-PAYMENTS-L3          PIC 9(3).
00121          05   MESSAGE-L3                 PIC X(46)    VALUE ' PER MTH'
```

Figure 3.3   continued      – 59 –

Now that we have the Data Division specified we can work
out the Procedure Division in detail.   We can imagine that
each box on the structure chart is a "mini-program" or "module"
with its own input and output.  For example, the input to
ASSEMBLE-PRINT-LINES is the data from the two cards stored in
APPLICATION-DATA; the output is the three lines formatted for
printing.  This data flow is shown on the structure chart by an
arrow with a circle on its tail, thus:

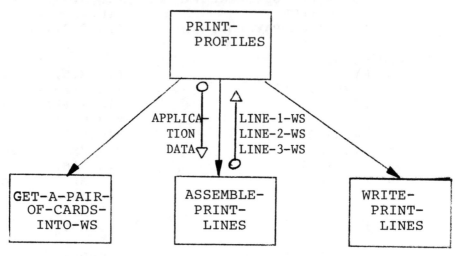

APPLICATION-DATA is, of course, the output of
GET-A-PAIR-OF-CARDS.  GET-A-PAIR-OF-CARDS also returns a
control variable, CARDS-LEFT, with a value of Ø at the end of
the card file.  Control variables are shown as an arrow with a
dark circle for a tail.

Q.  What is the input to WRITE-PRINT-LINES?

A.  The three formatted lines LINE-1-WS, LINE-2-WS, etc.

We also have to include the initialization and termination
functions, so the full structure chart looks like:

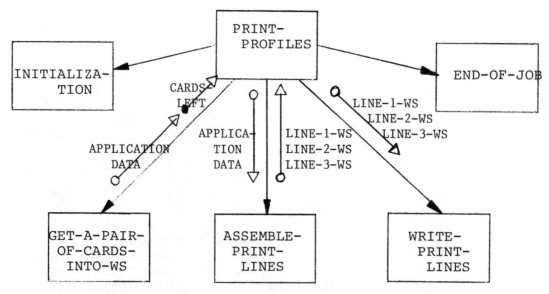

The structure chart doesn't show any of the detailed logic, nor does it show the fact that we want to set up a loop which will print profiles until we run out of cards, but it does show the major modules of the program, how they relate to one another, and what the main data flows are.

To see the loop logic, and the order in which the modules are executed, we need to draw a structured flowchart, thus:

```
+-------------------------------------------------+
| INITIALIZATION                                  |
|                                                 |
+-------------------------------------------------+
| PERFORM UNTIL CARDS-LEFT = 'NO '                |
|                                                 |
| +---+-----------------------------------------+ |
| | P |                                         | |
| | R |   GET-A-PAIR-OF-CARDS-                   | |
| | I |   INTO-WS                               | |
| | N |                                         | |
| | T +-----------------------------------------+ |
| | - |                                         | |
| | P |                                         | |
| | R |   ASSEMBLE-PRINT-LINES                   | |
| | O |                                         | |
| | F +-----------------------------------------+ |
| | I |                                         | |
| | L |   WRITE-PRINT-LINES                      | |
| | E |                                         | |
| | S |                                         | |
+---+---+-----------------------------------------+ |
| TERMINATION                                     |
|                                                 |
|                                                 |
+-------------------------------------------------+
```

In this SAMPLE-3, the initialization is more complicated than in SAMPLE-1 or SAMPLE-2. Before we can read cards or write reports, we have to instruct the computer to prepare the card file and printer file by coding an OPEN statement. In this case, the card file (APPLICATION-CARDS-FILE) will provide the input, and the printer file (PROFILE-LISTING) will receive the output, so we will code

```
OPEN INPUT APPLICATION-CARDS-FILE
     OUTPUT PROFILE-LISTING.
```

Note that there is only one period, right at the end of the statement, and that we line up the file names to make them easier to read. Every file that is OPENed must be included in a CLOSE statement, which will be part of program termination. You do not need to specify whether files are input or output in a CLOSE statement, just name the files.

As well as OPENing the files in INITIALIZATION, we need to read the first card of the card file into the input buffer. (You'll see why when we design the logic of GET-A-PAIR-OF-CARDS.) We will thus make INITIALIZATION into a separate paragraph.

When control goes to GET-A-PAIR-OF-CARDS-INTO-WS for the
first time, the first card is already in the buffer.  So you
have to move the card fields NAME-IN, etc., to Working Storage,
NAME-WS, etc., read in the second card, move its fields to
Working Storage, and then read in the first card of the next
pair of cards, so that a card is in the buffer next time the
program comes to perform GET-A-PAIR-OF-CARDS-INTO-WS.  We can
summarize the paragraph in shorthand thus:

        GET-A-PAIR-OF-CARDS-INTO-WS.
            Move fields from 1st card into fields in APPLICATION-DATA
            Read the second card of the pair
            Move fields from 2nd card into fields in APPLICATION-DATA
            Read the first card of the next pair.

This sort of shorthand summary is called "pseudocode"; it is not
quite COBOL, but can easily be translated into COBOL statements.
If we put the pseudocode for INITIALIZATION and GET-A-PAIR-OF-
CARDS into the flowchart, we will have:

```
 _____
|                                                                |
|  INITIALIZATION.                                               |
|       Open files                                               |
|       Initialize CARDS-LEFT                                    |
|       Read the first card                                      |
|_____|
|                                                                |
|  PERFORM UNTIL CARDS-LEFT = 'NO '                              |
|    _____|
|   |P |                                                         |
|   |R |  GET-A-PAIR-OF-CARDS-INTO-WS                            |
|   |I |      Move fields from 1st card into fields in          |
|   |N |          APPLICATION-DATA                              |
|   |T |      Read the second card of the pair                 |
|   |- |      Move fields from 2nd card into fields in         |
|   |P |          APPLICATION-DATA                              |
|   |R |      Read the first card of the next pair             |
|   |O |_____|
|   |F |                                                         |
|   |I |  ASSEMBLE-PRINT-LINES                                  |
|   |L |                                                         |
|   |E |_____|
|   |S |                                                         |
|   |  |  WRITE-PRINT-LINES                                     |
|   |__|_____|
|                                                                |
|  TERMINATION.                                                  |
|                                                                |
|_____|
```

ASSEMBLE-PRINT-LINES has to transfer the fields from
APPLICATION-DATA to the appropriate places in the print-lines.
So the pseudocode might start off:

                Move name to line 1.
                Move street to line 2.
                Move city, state, zip to line 3.
                Move area-code, number to line 1.
                Move account-number to line 3.
                IF male, set up MALE in line 1 sex field.
                IF female, set up FEMALE in line 1 sex field.

Q.    Complete the pseudocode for ASSEMBLE-PRINT-LINES.

A.            IF single, set up SINGLE in line 2 marital status.
                 (similarly for married, divorced, widowed)
              Move number of dependents to line 3.
              Move income to line 1 and format with last two zeros.
              IF years employed is Ø
                 Set up IN THIS EMPLOY LESS THAN 1 YEAR
                                         on line 1
              ELSE
                 Move years employed to line 1.
              IF owned, set up MORTGAGE on line 2.
              IF rented, set up RENTAL on line 2.
              Move mortgage/rental to line 2.
              Move other payments to line 3.

      or similar answer.

Note how we have capitalized the IFs and the ELSE, and lined
them up appropriately.

    When we come to write the print-lines, we want to move the
paper up four lines before printing the first time, then move
the paper up one time for the second and for the third lines.

    Termination will simply involve closing the files, and the
STOP RUN instruction which ends the execution of your program.

    Q.    Complete the structured flowchart, showing pseudocode
          for all the boxes.

A.

```
┌──────────────────────────────────────────────────────────────────┐
│ INITIALIZATION.                                                    │
│       Open files.                                                  │
│       Initialize CARDS-LEFT.                                       │
│       Read the first card.                                         │
├──────────────────────────────────────────────────────────────────┤
│ PERFORM UNTIL CARDS-LEFT = 'NO '                                   │
│  ┌───┬──────────────────────────────────────────────────────────┐ │
│  │ P │ GET-A-PAIR-OF-CARDS-INTO-WS                               │ │
│  │ R │     Move fields from 1st card into fields in             │ │
│  │ I │         APPLICATION-DATA.                                 │ │
│  │ N │     Read the second card of the pair.                    │ │
│  │ T │     Move fields from 2nd card into fields in             │ │
│  │ - │         APPLICATION-DATA.                                 │ │
│  │ P │     Read the first card of the next pair.                │ │
│  │ R ├──────────────────────────────────────────────────────────┤ │
│  │ O │                                                          │ │
│  │ F │ ASSEMBLE-PRINT-LINES                                     │ │
│  │ I │     Move name to line 1.                                 │ │
│  │ L │     Move street to line 2.                               │ │
│  │ E │     Move city, state, zip to line 3.                     │ │
│  │ S │     Move area-code, number to line 1.                    │ │
│  │   │     Move account-number to line 3.                       │ │
│  │   │     IF male, set up MALE in line 1 sex field.            │ │
│  │   │     IF female, set up FEMALE in line 1 sex field.        │ │
│  │   │     IF single, set up SINGLE in line 2 marital status    │ │
│  │   │         (similarly for married, divorced, widowed).      │ │
│  │   │     Move number of dependents to line 3.                 │ │
│  │   │     Move income to line 1 and format with last two zeros.│ │
│  │   │     IF years employed is Ø                               │ │
│  │   │         set up IN THIS EMPLOY LESS THAN 1 YEAR           │ │
│  │   │                                       on line 1          │ │
│  │   │     ELSE                                                  │ │
│  │   │         move years employed to line 1.                   │ │
│  │   │     IF owned, set up MORTGAGE on line 2.                 │ │
│  │   │     IF rented, set up RENTAL on line 2.                  │ │
│  │   │     Move mortgage/rental to line 2.                      │ │
│  │   ├──────────────────────────────────────────────────────────┤ │
│  │   │ WRITE-PRINT-LINES                                        │ │
│  │   │     Move paper up four lines; write line 1.              │ │
│  │   │     Move paper up 1 line; write line 2.                  │ │
│  │   │     Move paper up 1 line; write line 3.                  │ │
│  └───┴──────────────────────────────────────────────────────────┘ │
├──────────────────────────────────────────────────────────────────┤
│ TERMINATION                                                        │
│       Close files.                                                 │
│       Stop run.                                                    │
│                                                                    │
└──────────────────────────────────────────────────────────────────┘
```

or equivalent answer.

It is good practice to have the STOP RUN statement in the highest level module on the structure chart, so the Procedure Division will begin:

```
PROCEDURE DIVISION.
    PERFORM INITIALIZATION.
    PERFORM PRINT-PROFILES
        UNTIL CARDS-LEFT = 'NO '.
    PERFORM END-OF-JOB.
    STOP RUN.
```

Even though END-OF-JOB merely closes the files in this program, we will make it a separate module.

In INITIALIZATION we want to open the card file and the printer file, initialize CARDS-LEFT, and read the first card into the buffer.

Q.   Code the INITIALIZATION paragraph.

A.   INITIALIZATION.
```
        OPEN INPUT APPLICATION-CARDS-FILE
             OUTPUT PROFILE-LISTING.
        MOVE 'YES' TO CARDS-LEFT.
        READ APPLICATION-CARD
          AT END MOVE 'NO ' TO CARDS-LEFT.
    * THE FIRST CARD OF A PAIR IS NOW IN THE BUFFER
```

Note the comment to remind later readers of the program.

Q.   Code the PRINT-PROFILES paragraph and the END-OF-JOB paragraph.

A.   PRINT-PROFILES.
```
        PERFORM GET-A-PAIR-OF-CARDS-INTO-WS.
        PERFORM ASSEMBLE-PRINT-LINES.
        PERFORM WRITE-PRINT-LINES.

    END-OF-JOB.
        CLOSE APPLICATION-CARDS-FILE
              PROFILE-LISTING.
```

In WRITE-PRINT-LINES, you should clear the print-line by moving in spaces before each WRITE statement.  As we indicated in the pseudocode, you want to separate each profile by spacing four lines between the last line of one and the first line of the next.  This is done by adding AFTER ADVANCING to the WRITE statement.

```
        WRITE PRINT-LINE-OUT FROM LINE-1-WS
                            AFTER ADVANCING 4 LINES.
```

will move the paper up four lines before writing.  The only drawback is that, in some current versions of COBOL, if you use AFTER ADVANCING on one WRITE statement you have to use it on all the others.  This means that if you want to space one line, which is normally done automatically by a simple WRITE statement, you have to write AFTER ADVANCING 1 LINES.  This annoying lack of grammar will be removed on new versions of COBOL, but you may be stuck with it on your installation.

You now have all the information you need to code the Procedure Division for SAMPLE-3; when you have done so compare it with the solution below.

```
00122
00123          PROCEDURE DIVISION.
00124              PERFORM INITIALIZATION.
00125              PERFORM PRINT-PROFILES
00126                 UNTIL CARDS-LEFT IS EQUAL TO 'NO '.
00127              PERFORM END-OF-JOB.
00128              STOP RUN.
00129
00130          INITIALIZATION.
00131              OPEN INPUT  APPLICATION-CARDS-FILE
00132                   OUTPUT PROFILE-LISTING.
00133              MOVE 'YES' TO CARDS-LEFT.
00134              READ APPLICATION-CARDS-FILE
00135                 AT END MOVE 'NO ' TO CARDS-LEFT.
00136        * THE FIRST CARD OF A PAIR IS NOW IN THE BUFFER
00137
00138          PRINT-PROFILES.
00139              PERFORM GET-A-PAIR-OF-CARDS-INTO-WS.
00140              PERFORM ASSEMBLE-PRINT-LINES.
00141              PERFORM WRITE-PROFILE.
00142
00143          END-OF-JOB.
00144              CLOSE APPLICATION-CARDS-FILE
00145                    PROFILE-LISTING.
00146
00147          GET-A-PAIR-OF-CARDS-INTO-WS.
00148              MOVE NAME-IN TO NAME-WS.
00149              MOVE ADDRESS-IN TO ADDRESS-WS.
00150              MOVE PHONE-IN TO PHONE-WS.
00151              MOVE ACCT-NUM-IN1 TO ACCT-NUM-WS.
00152              READ APPLICATION-CARDS-FILE
00153                 AT END MOVE 'NO ' TO CARDS-LEFT.
00154        * THE SECOND CARD OF THE PAIR IS NOW IN THE BUFFER
00155              MOVE CREDIT-INFO-IN TO CREDIT-INFO-WS.
00156              READ APPLICATION-CARDS-FILE
00157                 AT END MOVE 'NO ' TO CARDS-LEFT.
00158        * THE FIRST CARD OF THE NEXT PAIR IS NOW IN THE BUFFER
00159
```

```
00160          ASSEMBLE-PRINT-LINES.
00161               MOVE NAME-WS TO NAME-L1.
00162               MOVE STREET-WS TO STREET-L2.
00163               MOVE CITY-WS TO CITY-L3.
00164               MOVE STATE-WS TO STATE-L3.
00165               MOVE ZIP-WS TO ZIP-L3.
00166               MOVE AREA-CODE-WS TO AREA-CODE-L1.
00167               MOVE NUMBR-WS TO NUMBR-L1.
00168               MOVE ACCT-NUM-WS TO ACCT-NUM-L3.
00169               IF MALE    MOVE 'MALE  ' TO SEX-L1.
00170               IF FEMALE MOVE 'FEMALE' TO SEX-L1.
00171               IF SINGLE    MOVE 'SINGLE  ' TO MARITAL-STATUS-L2.
00172               IF MARRIED   MOVE 'MARRIED ' TO MARITAL-STATUS-L2.
00173               IF DIVORCED MOVE 'DIVORCED' TO MARITAL-STATUS-L2.
00174               IF WIDOWED   MOVE 'WIDOWED ' TO MARITAL-STATUS-L2.
00175               MOVE NUMBER-DEPENS-WS TO NUMBER-DEPENS-L3.
00176               MOVE INCOME-HUNDREDS-WS TO INCOME-HUNDREDS-L1.
00177               IF YEARS-EMPLOYED-WS IS EQUAL TO 0
00178                   MOVE 'LESS THAN 1 YEAR' TO YEARS-EMPLOYED-L1
00179               ELSE
00180                   MOVE YEARS-EMPLOYED-WS TO YEARS-L1
00181                   MOVE ' YEARS        ' TO DESCN-L1.
00182               IF OWNED MOVE 'MORTGAGE:        $' TO OUTGO-DESCN.
00183               IF RENTED MOVE 'RENTAL:          $' TO OUTGO-DESCN.
00184               MOVE MORTGAGE-OR-RENTAL-WS TO MORTGAGE-OR-RENTAL-L2.
00185               MOVE OTHER-PAYMENTS-WS TO OTHER-PAYMENTS-L3.
00186
00187          WRITE-PROFILE.
00188               MOVE SPACES TO PRINT-LINE-OUT.
00189               WRITE PRINT-LINE-OUT FROM LINE-1-WS
00190                                    AFTER ADVANCING 4 LINES.
00191               MOVE SPACES TO PRINT-LINE-OUT.
00192               WRITE PRINT-LINE-OUT FROM LINE-2-WS
00193                                    AFTER ADVANCING 1 LINES.
00194               MOVE SPACES TO PRINT-LINE-OUT.
00195               WRITE PRINT-LINE-OUT FROM LINE-3-WS
00196                                    AFTER ADVANCING 1 LINES.
00197
```

Now that you have coded a substantial program, punch it into cards; it is preferable for you to do this yourself, so that you will get practice in the use of the key-punch.  If you cannot do the key-punching yourself, make sure that your writing on the coding sheet is completely accurate and clear before you submit the program to the key-punch department, and check every character on every card returned to you.

The "deck" of cards containing your program statements is called the "source deck," as it is the source from which the compiler will prepare the machine language or "object" program.  When you are satisfied that you have an accurately punched source deck, arrange to get the program compiled: Depending on the installation you are using, you will have to put two or three Job Control cards before and after your program deck for compilation.  This is because different installations use different operating systems; that is, special sets of programs supplied by the computer manufacturer which partly automate the job of the computer operations staff.

The Job Control cards give the operating system programs the information they need about how to process your job.  We will deal with Job Control later in detail, so don't bother about what needs to go on the Job Control cards now; just get someone who knows the installation to specify them for you.

Before compiling, check the cards again, making sure that all names are spelled correctly, that statements do not begin to the left of column 12, and, most importantly, that there is a period everywhere there should be, and nowhere else (e.g., in the middle of an IF statement).  Try to get into the habit of scanning through the deck for periods, which should be the last character on each card, except where the statement is split over two cards.  So if you do find a period, ask yourself, "Should it be there?" and if you don't find a period as the last character on a card, ask yourself, "Why isn't there a period here?"  Misplaced periods are one of the most common coding errors.

Now submit your job for compilation; you may be required to operate the computer yourself in a small installation, and that is outside the scope of this book.  More likely, you will take your deck of cards to someone responsible for Computer Operations, complete a form telling the computer operator what should be done with your job, and come back when the job has been run.  The Operations staff may hold your job until a number of similar jobs are ready for processing, to make the best use of the computer facility.

```
00001              IDENTIFICATION DIVISION.
00002              PROGRAM-ID. SAMPLE-1.
00003            * THIS VERSICN OF SAMPLE-1 HAS 3 DELIBERATE ERRORS
00004              ENVIRONMENT DIVISION.
00005              INPUT-OUTPUT SECTION.
00006              FILE-CONTROL.
00007                  SELECT CARD-FILE  ASSIGN TO SYS031-UR-2540R-S.
00008                  SELECT PRINT-FILE ASSIGN TO SYS033-UR-1403-S.
00009              DATA DIVISICN.
00010              FILE SECTION.
00011              FD  CARD-FILE
00012                  LABEL RECORDS ARE OMITTED.
00013              01  CARD.
00014                  05  NAME                    PICTJRE    X(20).
00015                  05  ADDR                    PICTURE    X(40).
00016                  05  PHONE.
00017                      10  AREA-CODE           PICTURE    9(3).
00018                      10  NUMBR               PICTJRE    X(8).
00019                  05  FILLER                  PICTJRE    X(9).
00020              FD  PRINT-FILE
00021                  LABEL RECORDS ARE OMITTED.
00022              01  PRINT-RECORD
00023                  05  FILLER                  PICTJRE    X(3).
00024                  05  NAME                    PICTJRE    X(20).
00025                  05  FILLER                  PICTURE    X(5).
00026                  05  ADDR                    PICTURE    X(40).
00027                  05  FILLER                  PICTURE    X(5).
00028                  J5  PHCNE.
00029                      10  AREA-CODE           PICTURE    9(3).
00030                      10  FILLER              PICTURE    X.
00031                      10  NUMBR               PICTURE    X(8).
00032                  05  FILLER                  PICTURE    X(10).
00033                  J5  MESSAGE-AREA            PICTURE    X(25).
00034                  05  FILLER                  PICTURE    X(12).
00035              WORKING-STORAGE SECTION.
00036              01  WARNING PICTURE X(25)  VALJE '**** ADDRESS MISSING ****'.
00037              01  CARDS-LEFT PICTURE 9(3).
00038              PROCEDURE DIVISION.
00039                  OPEN INPUT  CARD-FILE
00040                       OUTPUT PRINT-FILE.
00041                  MOVE 'YES' TO CARDS-LEFT.
00042                  READ CARD-FILE
00043                      AT END MOVE 'NO ' TO CARDS-LEFT.
00044                  PERFORM PROCESS-CARDS
00045                      UNTIL CARDS-LEFT IS EQUAL TO 'NO '.
00046                  CLOSE CARD-FILE
00047                        PRINT-FILE.
00048                  STOP RUN.
00049              PROCESS-CARDS.
00050                  MOVE SPACES TO PRINT-RECORD.
00051                  MOVE NAME IN CARD TO NAME IN PRINT-RECORD.
00052                  IF ADDR IN CARD IS EQUAL TO SPACES
00053                      MOVE WARNING TO MESSAGE AREA
00054                  ELSE
00055                      MOVE ADDR IN CARD TO ADDR IN PRINT-RECORD.
00056                  MOVE AREA-CODE IN CARD TO AREA-CODE IN PRINT-RECORD.
00057                  MOVE NUMBR IN CARD TO NUMBR IN PRINT-RECORD.
00058                  WRITE PRINT-RECORD.
00059                  READ CARD-FILE
00060                      AT END MOVE 'NC ' TO CARDS-LEFT.
```

| CARD | ERROR MESSAGE | |
|---|---|---|
| 23 | ILA1043I-W | END OF SENTENCE SHOULD PRECEDE 05 . ASSUMED PRESENT. |
| 41 | ILA4044I-C | ALPHANUMERIC LITERAL  (AN) SHOULD NOT BE MOVED TO NUMERIC FIELD. SUBSTITUTING ZERO . |
| 43 | ILA4044I-C | ALPHANUMERIC LITERAL  (AN) SHOULD NOT BE MOVED TO NUMERIC FIELD. SUBSTITUTING ZERO . |
| 53 | ILA3001I-E | MESSAGE NOT DEFINED. DISCARDED. |
| 53 | ILA4352I-E | AREA    MAY NOT BE TARGET FIELD FOR DNM=1-490  (AN) IN MOVE STATEMENT, AND IS DISCARDED. |
| 60 | ILA4044I-C | ALPHANUMERIC LITERAL  (AN) SHOULD NOT BE MOVED TO NUMERIC FIELD. SUBSTITUTING ZERO . |
| 60 | ILA4072I-W | EXIT FROM PERFORMED PROCEDURE ASSUMED BEFORE PROCEDURE-NAME . |
| 60 | ILA5029I-W | STOP RUN GENERATED AFTER LAST STATEMENT. |

Figure 3.4    Version of SAMPLE-1 showing three deliberate errors    - 69 -

When you get your program back from compilation, you will
see that, after the listing of the cards, there is a section
headed CARD and ERROR MESSAGE.  These messages are called
diagnostics.   Figure 3.4 on the previous page shows a listing
of SAMPLE-1 with some deliberate (but common) errors in it,
and the resulting diagnostics.  The codes under ERROR MESSAGE
are those for an IBM compiler, but all compilers produce
similar messages.  You will notice that the code is suffixed
by -W, -C, or -E; you may occasionally see a -D.


-W means a warning diagnostic on this compiler.  It flags
conditions which you should check out, but which do not
necessarily mean that anything is wrong.  For example, every
time you write a paragraph to be PERFORMed you will get the
warning

ILA4072I-W    EXIT FROM PERFORMED PROCEDURE ASSUMED
                                BEFORE PROCEDURE-NAME.

This means that the compiler is making the correct assumption
that you intend the procedure to terminate at the next
procedure-name (or at the end of the program, in this case)
and is quite OK.  But

ILA1043I-W    END OF SENTENCE SHOULD PRECEDE DS.   ASSUMED PRESENT.

arises because the period has been left out after Ø1 PRINT-RECORD;
while the compiler will assume in this case that you meant to
put a period, this is something that should be corrected.


-C means a conditional diagnostic; this is something that
you should correct because it will probably affect the
"object" program resulting from the compilation.

-E means an error diagnostic; the program will not run
until this has been corrected.  As you can see, leaving out
the hyphen from MESSAGE-AREA in statement 53 has caused the
compiler to look for a field called MESSAGE for which it can
find no Data Division entry, so it tells you

ILA3001I-E   MESSAGE NOT DEFINED. DISCARDED.

Then of course the compiler is really in trouble because it
finds the word AREA and has no idea what to do with it.


-D means a disaster diagnostic; usually an error within
the compiler itself.  If you ever come across this, get help.

Given the way we are writing COBOL, you will always get one or more

EXIT FROM PERFORMED PROCEDURE ASSUMED BEFORE PROCEDURE-NAME.

and one

STOP RUN GENERATED AFTER LAST STATEMENT.

If these are the only diagnostics you have, your program is ready for a test run.  If you have any others, work through the program diagnostic by diagnostic, checking the statement indicated to locate the error.

Always bear in mind:

- a single mistake may give rise to more than one diagnostic.  For example, if you fail to define a field, you will get a diagnostic for every statement in which that field is used.  In Fig. 3.4, the C level diagnostics for statements 41, 43, and 60 are all caused by giving CARDS-LEFT a PIC of 9(3) in statement 37.

- if you leave out a period, you may get some very strange messages, because the compiler tries to process everything up to the next period as though it were part of the original statement.

- Ø looks very much like 0 on a source listing and on a card.  If you define OWNER and punch ØWNER by mistake, you will get a lovely crop of diagnostics and may be unable to see why.  Be suspicious, check back to the punching of the original card.

When you have located as many errors as you can, and you still have some diagnostics that you cannot understand -- ask someone's advice, or recompile the program.  There are hundreds of possible diagnostic messages; sometimes an obscure diagnostic will go away when some quite simple things have been fixed in the program.

Bear in mind also that a compilation for a program of the size we are working with costs between $5 and $10; depending on how you value your time, it may be better to check out your corrections with a compile rather than scratch your head for an hour.  By the same token, though, don't burn up $10 worth of machine time to find out something that five minutes' quiet thought would have enabled you to see.

### 3.11.3 Executing the Program

When you have a compile with no serious errors
(a "clean" compile), test the program by running it with the
cards needed to produce the six profiles in Fig. 3.2 as input.
Be sure to punch the codes in the second card of each pair
in exactly the right columns. If the cards are punched
correctly, and your program is equivalent to the model solution,
you should get the report printed out. As we said, you will
need the Job Control cards that your installation requires
to execute the program with the test data.

If the report is printed out incorrectly, or if your
program fails to run for any reason, check the punching of the
test data cards carefully. If you still can't find anything
wrong, seek advice and help; we shall be dealing with testing
in Chapter 5.

# CHAPTER 4:   DOING ARITHMETIC

So far we have written useful programs without doing any arithmetic on our data, but for most kinds of problems we need to be able to add, subtract, multiply, and divide.  In this chapter, we will deal with the basic arithmetic statements.


## 4.1    ARITHMETIC STATEMENTS


### 4.1.1    ADD and SUBTRACT

There are two forms of the ADD instruction:

Form 1:          ADD FIELD-1 TO FIELD-2.

In this case the total of the contents of the two fields is stored in FIELD-2.  For example:

| Before addition | | After addition | |
|---|---|---|---|
| FIELD-1 | FIELD-2 | FIELD-1 | FIELD-2 |
| 1 2 3 4 | 5 4 3 2 | 1 2 3 4 | 6 6 6 6 |

The value that was in FIELD-2
is lost.


Form 2:    ADD FIELD-1 FIELD-2 GIVING FIELD-3.

As you would expect, the total is stored in FIELD-3.  For example:

| FIELD-1 | FIELD-2 | FIELD-3 | FIELD-1 | FIELD-2 | FIELD-3 |
|---|---|---|---|---|---|
| 1 2 3 4 | 5 4 3 2 | 1 1 1 1 | 1 2 3 4 | 5 4 3 2 | 6 6 6 6 |

Q.   Write a statement that will add MORTGAGE-OR-RENTAL and OTHER-PAYMENTS to produce a figure for TOTAL-OUTGO.

A.    ADD MORTGAGE-OR-RENTAL OTHER-PAYMENTS GIVING TOTAL-OUTGO.

Note that ADD FIELD-1 TO FIELD-2 GIVING FIELD-3 is wrong; you are not allowed to have TO and GIVING in the same statement.

There are also two forms of the SUBTRACT instruction:

Form 1:     SUBTRACT FIELD-1 FROM FIELD-2.

In this case the difference will appear in FIELD-2 after subtraction.

Form 2:     SUBTRACT FIELD-1 FROM FIELD-2 GIVING FIELD-3.

In this case FIELD-1 and FIELD-2 are undisturbed; the answer is in FIELD-3.

Q.    Code a statement which will reduce the value in COUNTER by 1.

A.    SUBTRACT 1 FROM COUNTER.

Q.    Code a statement taking TAXES away from GROSS-INCOME with NET-INCOME as the result.

A.    SUBTRACT TAXES FROM GROSS-INCOME GIVING NET-INCOME.

## 4.1.2   *MULTIPLY and DIVIDE*

Form 1:     MULTIPLY FIELD-1 BY FIELD-2.        Result is in
            DIVIDE FIELD-1 INTO FIELD-2.             FIELD-2

Form 2:

MULTIPLY FIELD-1 BY FIELD-2 GIVING FIELD-3.        Result is in
DIVIDE FIELD-1 INTO FIELD-2 GIVING FIELD-3.             FIELD-3

Q.    Code a statement to calculate GROSS-PAY by multiplying PAY-RATE by HOURS-WORKED.

A.    MULTIPLY PAY-RATE BY HOURS-WORKED GIVING GROSS-PAY.

Q.    Code a statement to calculate MONTHLY-SALARY from ANNUAL-SALARY.

A.    DIVIDE MONTHS-IN-YEAR INTO ANNUAL-SALARY
                      GIVING MONTHLY-SALARY.

Note that it is good practice never to code a numeric literal into a statement, with the possible exception of 0 and 1.  Even with a value such as 12 months in the year, which is very unlikely to change, you may forget what the 12 stands for.  With the data-name, MONTHS-IN-YEAR, initialized to 12 in Working Storage, it will always be perfectly clear.

In SAMPLE-3, we read in annual income: INCOME-HUNDREDS
and two lots of monthly-outgoings:
MORTGAGE-OR-RENTAL and OTHER-PAYMENTS.


Company policy is to base credit on discretionary income:
This is the amount of income left each month after deducting
all outgoings.


While everybody's tax bracket varies, it is your company's
practice to estimate by deducting a flat 25% of income to
get income-after-taxes.

Q. Write the code to calculate discretionary
income in SAMPLE-3 and check through it
with Victor Grasper's data (assume all the
fields you use are defined in the Data
Division).

A. MULTIPLY INCOME-HUNDREDS BY 100 GIVING INCOME.
MULTIPLY INCOME BY TAX-RATE GIVING ESTIMATED-TAX.
SUBTRACT ESTIMATED-TAX FROM INCOME GIVING NET-INCOME.
DIVIDE MONTHS-IN-YEAR INTO NET-INCOME
GIVING MONTHLY-NET.
SUBTRACT MORTGAGE-OR-RENTAL-WS OTHER-PAYMENTS-WS
FROM MONTHLY-NET
GIVING DISCRETIONARY-INCOME.

or equivalent answer.


Data for Victor Grasper:

| | |
|---|---|
| INCOME | 15,700 |
| ESTIMATED TAX | 3,925 |
| NET INCOME | 11,775 |
| MONTHLY-NET | 981.25 |
| MORTGAGE-OR-RENTAL | 250 |
| OTHER-PAYMENTS | 40 |
| DISCRETIONARY-INCOME | 691.25 |


Note that we have defined TAX-RATE in Working Storage,
rather than use a numeric literal in the program.  If the tax
rate is changed, we will only have to make one change to the
program.  If we had coded the literal 0.25 in several places
in the program, we would have had to hunt through to make
sure they all were changed.  However, since INCOME-HUNDREDS
needs, by definition, to be multiplied by 100 to give income,
it is acceptable to code 100 as a literal at this point.

When we discussed MOVEing numeric items in Chapter 2, we said that numeric items are lined up on their decimal points. The same is true with arithmetic operations, so if MONTHLY-NET had been defined with PIC 999 (with an assumed decimal point at the right) the .25 of $981.25 would be lost giving $981.  In this case, this may not matter so much, but what if the value had been $981.95?  You would have lost 95 cents.

You can avoid this problem by using the key-word ROUNDED. If ROUNDED is put on the end of an arithmetic statement then the computer will add 1 to the rightmost position retained if the next digit to its right would have been 5 or more.

For example, if we want to know what 563 divided by 5 to the nearest whole number equals, we would carry out the division, getting

112.6 —— *but the next digit is more than 5, so we add 1 to the rightmost position, getting 113.*

*this is the rightmost position of the whole number*

So, if RESULT is defined as PIC 99

DIVIDE 12 INTO 141 GIVING RESULT            gives 11 (losing .75)

DIVIDE 12 INTO 141 GIVING RESULT ROUNDED  gives 12

Note that, for the sake of clarity, we are breaking our own rules about using literals.

Q.    ANSWER is defined as PIC 99V99.  What appears in ANSWER with and without ROUNDED when DIVIDE DEN INTO NUM GIVING ANSWER, is executed with

      NUM : 23.986 and DEN : 3

A.    $\dfrac{23.986}{3}$   =   7.995333

Without ROUNDED, ANSWER is 07.99 losing 5333
With ROUNDED, ANSWER is 08.00

Q.    What about $\dfrac{23.984}{3}$  ?

A.    $\dfrac{23.984}{3}$   =   7.994666

Without ROUNDED, ANSWER is 07.99; with ROUNDED, ANSWER is 07.99. Since 4666 is less than 5000 the result is rounded down.

Where a formula must be worked out over several statements as with the DISCRETIONARY-INCOME calculation, it is often more conven- ient and easier to grasp if the whole calculation is condensed into one statement.  This can be done with the COMPUTE statement.  You use the symbols

$$
\begin{array}{ll}
= & \\
+ & \\
- & \\
/ & \text{for divide} \\
* & \text{for multiply}
\end{array}
$$

to make an algebraic expression, for example:

        COMPUTE ESTIMATED-TAX = INCOME-HUNDREDS * 100 * TAX-RATE.

                                            Note that a space
                                            must be left on each side.

When + or - are combined with * or / in an arithmetic expres- sion, parentheses should be used to make the meaning clear.  For example, does

                A + B * C          mean

        (A + B) * C or  A + (B * C)  ?

There's a lot of difference, as you'll see if you substitute values in each case.


If you leave the parentheses out for any reason, the computer will do multiplication and division before addition and subtraction, so in fact it would interpret A + B * C as A + (B * C).  But don't leave the parentheses out; even if you understand it and the com- puter understands it, someone else who someday reads your program may not.

    Q.  Code the computation of DISCRETIONARY-INCOME as
        five   COMPUTE statements.

    A.  COMPUTE ANNUAL-INCOME = INCOME-HUNDREDS * 100.
        COMPUTE ANNUAL-TAX = ANNUAL-INCOME * TAX-RATE.
        COMPUTE MONTHLY-NET =
                {ANNUAL-INCOME - ANNUAL-TAX} / MONTHS-IN-YEAR.
        COMPUTE MONTHLY-PAYMENTS = MORTGAGE-OR-RENTAL + OTHER-PAYMENTS.
        COMPUTE DISCRETIONARY-INCOME =
                MONTHLY-NET - MONTHLY-PAYMENTS.

    or similar answer.

Suppose AA, BB, and CC were all defined PIC 9(3).  You could code COMPUTE CC = AA + BB.  But what would happen if both AA and BB were more than 500?  The result will not fit into AA.

In this case the computer does not know what to do.  It will probably halt your program, printing a message to tell you that a field has overflowed.

So unless you are sure you have a result field big enough for any conceivable combination of input data, you should use the ON SIZE ERROR clause.  For example:

```
COMPUTE ANSWER = BIG-FIELD + LARGE-FIELD
    ON SIZE ERROR PERFORM OVERFLOW-ROUTINE.
```

You should code OVERFLOW-ROUTINE to deal with the condition, possibly by rejecting the current transaction and printing an error message.  In any case, code the routine to keep the program running if at all possible.

Q.    Suppose MONTHLY-NET and MONTHLY-PAYMENTS are both defined as 9(4) and DISCRETIONARY-INCOME is defined as 9(3).

Code a COMPUTE statement that will calculate DISCRETIONARY-INCOME, and set its value at $999 if the computed value is greater than that.

A.    COMPUTE DISCRETIONARY-INCOME =
            MONTHLY-NET - MONTHLY-PAYMENTS
        ON SIZE ERROR MOVE 999 TO DISCRETIONARY-INCOME.

Q.   Using the formula we coded previously, what is
the discretionary income of a person making
$16,000 a year, who is spending $750 per month
for rent and has other debt payments of $300 per month?

A.   -$50 per month; an outflow of $50.  Either this
person is understating his income, or he's in real
trouble.

DISCRETIONARY-INCOME is an example of a field that could have
a negative value, and the definition of its PICTURE should
reflect the fact by including an S for sign:  PIC S9 (3).
The S ensures that the computer will keep track of whether
the value is positive or negative.  It also allows us to
test for the sign of the value, and program accordingly,
by coding IF DISCRETIONARY-INCOME NEGATIVE....

A signed picture should be used wherever a numeric field
might be negative.  If you do not include a sign, the computer
will assume all numbers are positive, and in the case above,
the program will proceed happily, thinking the person has an
inflow of $50 per month, instead of the true situation.

Q.   Write the Data Division entries and the Procedure
Division code needed to take the quantity of an
item ordered away from the number in stock, and
perform the out-of-stock routine if the order
cannot be fully met.

A.   DATA DIVISION.
.
.
```
    ORDER-QUANTITY          PIC  9(3).
    STOCK-ON-HAND           PIC  S9(4).
.
.
PROCEDURE DIVISION.
.
.
    SUBTRACT ORDER-QUANTITY FROM STOCK-ON-HAND.

    IF STOCK-ON-HAND IS NEGATIVE
        PERFORM OUT-OF-STOCK-ROUTINE.
```

or similar answer.

1. Write the code to increase the value of VERMOUTH by the amount stored in GIN and store the new value in MARTINI.

2. Write the code to increase the value of LOOP-COUNT by 1.

3. If field TOTAL contains 480 and field NUMBR contains 24, what is in each field after executing

   DIVIDE NUMBR INTO TOTAL.

4. If RESULT is defined as PIC 9V99, what is in RESULT after execution of

   DIVIDE 8 INTO 9 GIVING RESULT ROUNDED.

5. If ABSOLUTE-VALUE is defined as PIC 9(3), what is in ABSOLUTE-VALUE after execution of

   SUBTRACT 1000 FROM 2 GIVING ABSOLUTE-VALUE.

6. Use the COMPUTE statement to write the code calculating the interest due on an amount up to $100,000 at a rate of interest which may be set to the nearest ¼% up to 20%, over a period to the nearest year, expressing the result to the nearest cent.  Include the Data Division entries for your data-names.

\*  *Answers are in Appendix D.*

# CHAPTER 5: DEVELOPING PROGRAMS

## 5.1 USING THE SOURCE STATEMENT LIBRARY

Before we apply the last chapter's arithmetic statements to a program, let us deal with an important feature which makes the programming job easier.

Very often, a program that you need to write has much in common with programs you have written before; you may use the same FDs time and time again or you may use a procedure like ASSEMBLE-PRINT-LINES in several programs.

To save having to code and key-punch the same statements, it is possible to catalog groups of statements on a special file kept by the computer known as the Source Statement Library (SSL). We will deal with how this SSL works, and how to catalog things in it in Chapter 11; for the moment all you need to know is how to use it.

### 5.1.1 The COPY Statement

Suppose the following statements have been cataloged and given the name FDCARDS,

```
            LABEL RECORDS ARE OMITTED
            DATA RECORDS ARE NAME-ADDRESS-AND-PHONE-IN
                            CREDIT-INFORMATION.
    01  NAME-ADDRESS-AND-PHONE-IN.
            05    NAME-IN                    PIC X(20).
            05    ADDRESS-IN                 PIC X(40).
            05    PHONE-IN                   PIC X(11).
            05    FILLER                     PIC X(3).
            05    ACCT-NUM-IN1               PIC 9(6).
    01  CREDIT-INFORMATION-IN.
            05    CARD-TYPE-IN               PIC X.
            05    ACCT-NUM-IN2               PIC 9(6).
            05    FILLER                     PIC X.
            05    CREDIT-INFO-IN             PIC X(22).
            05    FILLER                     PIC X(50).
```

You will recognize these as the statements making up the FD for APPLICATION-CARDS. Then, suppose you want to use this FD in a program. You simply write, in that program

```
    FD APPLICATION-CARDS-FILE COPY FDCARDS.
```

When the program is compiled, the compiler will fetch all the statements cataloged under the name FDCARDS and copy them into the program so that the listing will look like this:

```
        FD APPLICATION-CARDS-FILE COPY FDCARDS.
C               LABEL RECORDS ARE OMITTED
C               DATA RECORDS ARE NAME-ADDRESS-AND-PHONE-IN
C                               CREDIT-INFORMATION-IN.
C       01 NAME-ADDRESS-AND-PHONE-IN.
C           05   NAME-IN                        PIC X{20}.
C           05   ADDRESS-IN                     PIC X{40}.
C           05   PHONE-IN                       PIC X{11}.
C           05   FILLER                         PIC X{3}.
C           05   ACCT-NUM-IN1                   PIC 9{6}.
C       01 CREDIT-INFORMATION-IN.
C           05   CARD-TYPE-IN                   PIC X.
        and so on.
```

On IBM systems, copied statements are shown by a C to the left of each listed statement. If the group of statements you are cataloging is an 01 level with the statements following it, then the 01 statement itself must be cataloged. For example, if APPLICATION-DATA was cataloged with the name of CARDSWS, the library entry would have to begin

```
        01   APPLICATION-DATA.
             05   NAME-WS                       PIC X{20}.
             05   ADDRESS-WS                    PIC X{40}.
        and so on.
```

In your program you would write, for example:

```
        01   CARD-DATA-IN-WS COPY CARDSWS.
```

The compiler copies the library entry, changing APPLICATION-DATA to the name you supplied, so the listing becomes

```
        01   CARD-DATA-IN-WS COPY CARDSWS.
C       01   CARD-DATA-IN-WS.
C            05   NAME-WS                       PIC X{20}.
C            05   ADDRESS-WS                    PIC X{40}.
        and so on.
```

In the Procedure Division, the body of a paragraph is cataloged, so under the name WRITPRFL you might have

```
        MOVE SPACES TO PRINT-LINE-OUT.
        WRITE PRINT-LINE-OUT FROM LINE-1-WS
                        AFTER ADVANCING 4 LINES.
```

You would write in your program

```
        PRINT-APPLICATION-PROFILE. COPY WRITPRFL.
```

Note that there is a period after the procedure-name; this is only used in Procedure Division COPY statements.

Sometimes what is cataloged on the library may not be exactly what you want; you would like to make use of a library entry in your program but need to make some changes on it. For example, you might want to copy WRITPRFL but you need to call the three print-lines FIRST-LINE, SECOND-LINE, and THIRD-LINE.

You can do this with the REPLACING option of the COPY statement, thus:

```
PRINT-APPLICATION-PROFILE.  COPY WRITPRFL
                REPLACING LINE-1-WS BY FIRST-LINE
                          LINE-2-WS BY SECOND-LINE
                          LINE-3-WS BY THIRD-LINE.
```

Notice that REPLACING only appears once; also note the placing of the periods.

Q.   Given that WRITPRFL is the name in the library of the statements in the paragraph called WRITE-PROFILE in SAMPLE-3, what listing will result from the above COPY statement?

A.

```
C       MOVE SPACES TO PRINT-LINE-OUT.
C       WRITE PRINT-LINE-OUT FROM FIRST-LINE
C                       AFTER ADVANCING 4 LINES.
C       MOVE SPACES TO PRINT-LINE-OUT.
C       WRITE PRINT-LINE-OUT FROM SECOND-LINE
C                       AFTER ADVANCING 1 LINES.
C       MOVE SPACES TO PRINT-LINE-OUT.
C       WRITE PRINT-LINE-OUT FROM THIRD-LINE
C                       AFTER ADVANCING 1 LINES.
```

In most COBOL compilers, it is only possible to REPLACE one data-name by another data-name or by a literal. New compilers will enable you to REPLACE any group of characters by any other group; for example, to change -IN to -OUT on every data-name in a paragraph. Chapter 11 in Part II details the various options.

You have to specify to the compiler that you are using the SSL facility. This is done in various ways depending on the operating system you are using; the programs in this section were compiled under IBM's Disk Operating System (DOS), for which you have to put a card with CBL LIB, beginning in cc 2, immediately before the IDENTIFICATION DIVISION. Other operating systems are also dealt with in Part II, Chapter 11.

In a business situation, the development of a program normally begins with a <u>user request</u>; a manager says "I want a program (or a system) to do such and such." Often a <u>systems analyst</u> will then study the request and work with the user to understand exactly what he needs, what purpose it is to serve, and what information the user will supply to the computer department.

From this <u>systems study</u>, the systems analyst produces a <u>functional specification</u>, which sets out the form of the report(s) to be produced, the rules and policies to be used in producing them, and the nature of the input data. This is the point at which you, the programmer, should get involved. You should understand the functional specification, and from it be able to produce the <u>program graph</u> showing the data flow through the program.

From the program graph, you should produce a <u>structure chart</u> which breaks down the whole function of the <u>program into functional modules</u> as we have seen, and specifies the input and output of each module.

From the structure chart, you should be able to write the pseudocode for each module, and review the pseudocode to make sure that the logic you have written will do what you want. It is very helpful to get together with a group of your colleagues and walk them through the structure chart and the pseudocode, explaining what you have written, what it is supposed to do, and why you have done it this way. Many errors (bugs) are discovered in a <u>structured walk-through</u> of this type.

When you have written the COBOL code and gotten a clean compile, you may find it useful to walk-through the code again, to uncover any bugs that may have crept in during coding.

You are now ready to begin testing the program with some representative test data such as the cards we specified for SAMPLE-3. Almost certainly, the testing will reveal that your program is not perfect! You will find that the program either does not run at all, or runs but gives the wrong output. <u>Debugging</u> is the process of finding the cause of these faults and correcting them. You may need to go through several cycles of test, debug, test, debug; the more carefully you design and code your program, and the more carefully you review the structure chart, the pseudocode, and the COBOL, the less time you will need to spend in testing.

This is important, because debugging is extremely difficult
and people are not very good at it.  Your time is _much_ better
spent avoiding bugs than finding them.


When the program delivers good output on all tests, you
can hand it over to the user for user acceptance.  The user
will need your help to train his staff in the use of the
program, the correct preparation of the input data, and the
resolution of any problems.  You will also need to produce
operational instructions, which tells the computer operator

- how to set up the computer for this job
- how to respond to messages on the console typewriter
- how to recognize successful completion of the job
- what to do in case of error.

Before going on to the next programming problem, let us
look at the testing and debugging phase in more detail.


## 5.2.1  _Specifying Test Data_


If the program is at all complex, test it at first with
data you know to be reasonable and correctly punched.  When
the program correctly processes good data, you should start to
feed in data where

- the values of the fields are at the extreme ends
  of the possible range, e.g., income of $99,900 per annum
  and income of $0 per annum.

- all reasonable combinations of inputs are dealt with,
  e.g., we include applications which are both from
  males _and_ females, owners _and_ renters, etc.

- the values of fields are just out of range, or way
  out of range.

- data fields have been mispunched or are missing.


Every commercial system should edit the incoming data very
thoroughly, checking as far as possible that fields are present
and of reasonable value; in SAMPLE-2 we edited the cards for
the presence of name, address, and phone number.


As you can imagine, comprehensive editing can take a lot
of programming, so we shall not discuss it in detail until
later chapters.  The creation of thorough test data is also
very important and will be dealt with in Part II, Chapter 14.

When you run the program with the test data, it may fail the test for one of two reasons:

- the program runs OK, and comes to a normal end, but the output is incorrect, e.g., you get garbage in the print-lines because you did not initialize them correctly.

- the program "bombs," that is, comes to an abnormal end (abend).  You will get a message on the output saying, for example:

OS03I PROGRAM CHECK INTERRUPTION ........ DATA EXCEPTION

There will be some more detail in the middle of the message but it doesn't concern us at present.

If you get a program check, it means that the operating system has cancelled (terminated) your program because it tried to do something invalid.  There are several types of program checks, only three of which you will commonly meet:

1)   DATA EXCEPTION -- you have tried to do arithmetic on non-numeric data.  This might be because letters are punched in a card where there should be numbers.  More usually it happens because you have not initialized a Working Storage field.  For example, if you define in Working Storage

TOTAL-DISCR-INCOME                PIC 9{7}.

and later in the program write

ADD DISCRETIONARY-INCOME TO TOTAL-DISCR-INCOME.

your program will almost certainly bomb with a Data Exception when it tries to add the numeric DISCRETIONARY-INCOME to the uninitialized garbage in TOTAL-DISCR-INCOME.

Q.   How do you avoid this?

A.   By being sure to initialize every field that may have arithmetic done on it.  In this case you should add MOVE ZEROS TO TOTAL-DISCR-INCOME, before using TOTAL-DISCR-INCOME the first time.

2)   OVERFLOW EXCEPTION -- occurs when a result field is too large for its receiving field, and you have not specified ON SIZE ERROR.

3) DIVIDE EXCEPTION -- occurs when you try to divide a field by another field which is zero.

4) Other types of EXCEPTIONS may occur if something goes wrong inside the computer. This is rare; seek advice if it happens.

### 5.2.3 *Simple Debugging*

If your program abends, check to see what could have been the cause. If you cannot locate it by examining the date and the program, you must look more closely at what is happening during execution. There are several ways of doing this, discussed in detail in Part II, Chapter 14; the simplest way, which will enable you to locate most errors, is to use the TRACE and EXHIBIT statements.

Put a card bearing the command READY TRACE (starting in column 12) after the card with PROCEDURE DIVISION on it. This will invoke a facility which prints out all statement numbers of paragraph-names of paragraphs that actually get executed. Run the program again. The last number appearing on the print-out will be the paragraph causing the program check.

If you still cannot see what is wrong with this paragraph (Are all the data-names initialized? What should their values be during execution?), insert after each statement of the paragraph a card with EXHIBIT NAMED (starting in column 12) and a list of the data-names of which you would like to know the contents.

For example, suppose the last paragraph to be executed is

```
00113 CALCULATE-GROSS.
      ADD OVERTIME REGULAR GIVING TOTAL-HOURS.
      MULTIPLY TOTAL-HOURS BY RATE GIVING GROSS-PAY.
```

↑
*statement*
*number*

You insert three EXHIBIT statements thus:

```
   CALCULATE-GROSS                                    Exhibit all
1)      EXHIBIT NAMED OVERTIME REGULAR TOTAL-HOURS    data-names used
        ADD OVERTIME REGULAR GIVING TOTAL-HOURS.      in the paragraph
2)      EXHIBIT NAMED TOTAL-HOURS RATE GROSS-PAY
        MULTIPLY TOTAL-HOURS BY RATE GIVING GROSS-PAY.
3)      EXHIBIT NAMED GROSS-PAY
```

In each case include in the EXHIBIT statement the data-names that should have been changed by the previous program statement,

plus the ones that will be used by the next program statement.
(Note: no period after the READY TRACE statement or the
EXHIBIT statements.)

Run the program again.  You may get a print-out like this:

```
┌─────────113
│   ┌─────OVERTIME = 07     REGULAR = 38    TOTAL-HOURS = 000
│   ├─────TOTAL-HOURS = 45  RATE = &AC:     GROSS-PAY = 000.00
│   │
│   │     0S03I  PROGRAM CHECK INTERRUPTION.....DATA EXCEPTION
│   │
│   └  These are the first two EXHIBIT statements.
│
└  This is the statement number of the paragraph name.
```

The EXHIBIT NAMED statement has printed out the contents of
the data-names you specified, with their names in each case.

  Q.    What can we conclude from this print-out?

  A.    We know that abend was caused by the MULTIPLY
        statement because only the first two EXHIBIT
        statements were executed before the error message.
        We can see that RATE contains garbage instead of
        some reasonable figure like 11.25.  Clearly this
        is the cause of the data exception.  Where was
        this value &AC: loaded into RATE?  Maybe you
        left out the statement in which you were going
        to set up the value of RATE.

Of course, when you have fixed the bug, you will want
to take the READY TRACE and EXHIBIT statements out and recompile
the program.  It's a good idea to put them on two cards which
are different in color from the rest of the cards in the program,
making them easy to locate.

### 5.2.4   User Acceptance

Now you have a program which delivers valid output.  Compare
the output carefully with the data cards used as input.  Is the
output exactly what you intended?  If, for example, you have a
logic error which is causing the program to compute one person's
payroll check based on the salary of the previous person in the
file, the output is going to look right, but some people will
be very unhappy if you allow this program to be put into production.  When you can produce good output from good input and
reject bad transactions, in a well-chosen variety of cases, you
can take the program to the user who requested it, and get him
to try it out.

The normal method of user acceptance test is to use the
program with real data from the user's operation in parallel
with the current method, and check out the program output
compared with the product of the current, probably clerical,
operation.


When this <u>parallel</u> run has functioned satisfactorily,
the program can be <u>cut over</u>; used on a routine basis by
the user department.


Most programs need work on them after they have been
cut over, for a variety of reasons

> - the programmer did not test with a good enough range
>   of test data, and in use someone puts in data which
>   causes an unsuspected abend or incorrect output

> - the user's business needs change or he wants
>   <u>enhancements</u> to what the program does for him.


Whatever the reason, this sort of work is called program
<u>maintenance</u>, and can be very time-consuming.   You should
always write your programs to be easy to maintain; that is
with clear layout, meaningful data-names, and comments
about anything that is not evident from reading the listings.


If in doubt, imagine that you are someone else writing
the program, and that in two weeks time the real you will be
responsible for maintaining it.   Imagine that you get a
phone call at 1 a.m. from the night shift computer operator
telling you that the program has bombed with a data
exception, and will you please come in to fix it, because
the report has to be ready for the Board of Directors at 9 a.m.
Write programs you would be prepared to maintain in the
middle of the night.


## 5.3   ENHANCING SAMPLE-3


To give you a taste of maintenance, now that SAMPLE-3 is
working, the Marketing Manager would like you to modify it.
Each applicant's discretionary income should be calculated
as in Chapter 4 based on everyone being assumed to pay 25% tax.
This profile should print, on the second line, underneath
>           IN THIS EMPLOY
>           DISCRETIONARY INCOME $nnn PER MTH

(nnn standing for whatever the value is).
If any applicant's discretionary income works out to $1,000
or more, set it to $999.

```
VICTOR S GRASPER         PHONE (415) 243-7022   MALE              INCOME        $15700 PER YEAR:  IN THIS EMPLOY 04 YEARS
590 GAUNTLET AVE                                 SINGLE            MORTGAGE:       $250 PER MTH    DISCRETIONARY INCOME $691 PER MTH
BURLINGAME    CA 94010   A/C: 010101             0 DEPENDENTS      OTHER PAYMENTS $343 PER MTH


IAN S INKERMAN           PHONE (201) 103-6061    MALE              INCOME        $17500 PER YEAR:  IN THIS EMPLOY LESS THAN 1 YEAR
59 PECAN VALLEY RD                                DIVORCED          RENTAL:        $325 PER MTH    DISCRETIONARY INCOME $659 PER MTH
MONTVALE      NJ C7645    A/C: 020202             1 DEPENDENTS      OTHER PAYMENTS $110 PER MTH


SARALEE JAMES            PHONE (816) 542-3535    FEMALE            INCOME        $21000 PER YEAR:  IN THIS EMPLOY 03 YEARS
PARTHENON COURT                                  DIVORCED          MORTGAGE:      $275 PER MTH    DISCRETIONARY INCOME $963 PER MTH
ATHENS        MO 64065    A/C: 050505             1 DEPENDENTS      OTHER PAYMENTS $ 75 PER MTH


SCARLETT O'HARA          PHONE (504) 815-1147    FEMALE            INCOME        $09500 PER YEAR:  IN THIS EMPLOY 26 YEARS
SUITE 414 NAT BANK                               WIDOWED           RENTAL:        $110 PER MTH    DISCRETIONARY INCOME $464 PER MTH
NEW ORLEANS   LA 70012    A/C: 060606             2 DEPENDENTS      OTHER PAYMENTS $ 20 PER MTH


SUSAN KRUPMAN            PHONE (212) 354-3330    FEMALE            INCOME        $12900 PER YEAR:  IN THIS EMPLOY 01 YEARS
131 WEST 32ND ST                                 SINGLE            RENTAL:        $150 PER MTH    DISCRETIONARY INCOME $626 PER MTH
NEW YORK      NY 10001    A/C: 040404             0 DEPENDENTS      OTHER PAYMENTS $ 33 PER MTH


I. MORRIS GOOD           PHONE (214) 225-7013    MALE              INCOME        $27300 PER YEAR:  IN THIS EMPLOY 11 YEARS
1313 PORPOISE                                    MARRIED           MORTGAGE:      $400 PER MTH    DISCRETIONARY INCOME $999 PER MTH
DALLAS        TX 75219    A/C: 030303             4 DEPENDENTS      OTHER PAYMENTS $150 PER MTH
```

Figure 5.1   Output of SAMPLE-4

The resulting report should resemble Fig. 5.1.

From this functional specification, we can draw up the
structure chart for SAMPLE-4, as we will call the enhanced
program. For ease of reference in the body of the program,
we will prefix each module name with a letter and a number,
thus:

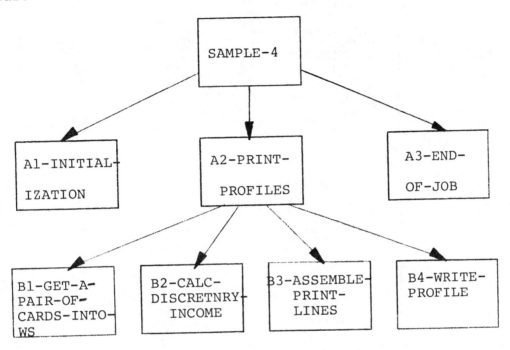

To make the problem simpler, you can assume that the
paragraphs and data definitions shown on the next two pages
have been cataloged on the Source Statement Library for your
use.

Further, the senior programmer in your group wishes you
to use COMPUTE statements for your calculation.

From this information, code SAMPLE-4, using COPY statements as far as possible. You can assume that the cards you
use for input are all correctly punched, and so you need not
worry about any further editing (although this would, of
course, be very important in the real world).

When you have completed your coding, compare it with the
model solution on the following pages. The code as you would
write it is given first, followed by the output from the compilation with the COPY statements expanded.

## Contents of Source Statement Library

<u>Library Name</u>

```
FILECONT ──────────  FILE-CONTROL.
                       SELECT APPLICATION-CARDS-FILE ASSIGN TO SYS031-UR-2540R-S.
                       SELECT PROFILE-LISTING        ASSIGN TO SYS033-UR-1403-S.

                     DATA DIVISION.
                     FILE SECTION.

                  FD  APPLICATION-CARDS-FILE
                         LABEL RECORDS ARE OMITTED
                         DATA RECORDS ARE NAME-ADDRESS-AND-PHONE-IN
                                          CREDIT-INFORMATION-IN.
                  01  NAME-ADDRESS-AND-PHONE-IN.
                      05  NAME-IN                     PIC X(20).
                      05  ADDRESS-IN                  PIC X(40).
                      05  PHONE-IN                    PIC X(11).
                      05  FILLER                      PIC X(3).
FDCARDS ─────────     05  ACCT-NUM-IN1                PIC 9(6).
                  01  CREDIT-INFORMATION-IN.
                      05  CARD-TYPE-IN                PIC X.
                      05  ACCT-NUM-IN2                PIC 9(6).
                      05  FILLER                      PIC X.
                      05  CREDIT-INFO-IN              PIC X(22).
                      05  FILLER                      PIC X(50).

                  FD  PROFILE-LISTING
                         LABEL RECORDS ARE OMITTED.
                  01  PRINT-LINE-OUT                  PIC X(132).

                     WORKING-STORAGE SECTION.
                  01  CARDS-LEFT                      PIC X(3).
                  01  APPLICATION-DATA.
                      05  NAME-AND-ADDRESS-WS.
                          10  NAME-WS                 PIC X(20).
                          10  ADDRESS-WS.
                              15  STREET-WS           PIC X(20).
                              15  CITY-WS .           PIC X(13).
                              15  STATE-WS            PIC XX.
                              15  ZIP-WS              PIC X(5).
                      05  PHONE-WS.
                          10  AREA-CODE-WS            PIC 9(3).
                          10  NUMBR-WS                PIC X(8).
                      05  FILLER                      PIC X(3).
                      05  ACCT-NUM-WS                 PIC 9(6).
                      05  CREDIT-INFO-WS.
                          10  SEX-WS                  PIC X.
                              88  MALE      VALUE 'M'.
                              88  FEMALE    VALUE 'F'.
                          10  FILLER                  PIC X.
CARDSWS ─────────         10  MARITAL-STATUS-WS       PIC X.
                              88  SINGLE    VALUE 'S'.
                              88  MARRIED   VALUE 'M'.
                              88  DIVORCED  VALUE 'D'.
                              88  WIDOWED   VALUE 'W'.
                          10  FILLER                  PIC X.
                          10  NUMBER-DEPENS-WS        PIC 9.
                          10  FILLER                  PIC X.
                          10  INCOME-HUNDRECS-WS      PIC 9(3).
                          10  FILLER                  PIC X.
                          10  YEARS-EMPLOYED-WS       PIC 99.
                          10  FILLER                  PIC X.
                          10  OWN-OR-RENT-WS          PIC X.
                              88  OWNED     VALUE 'O'.
                              88  RENTED    VALUE 'R'.
                          10  FILLER                  PIC X.
                          10  MORTGAGE-OR-RENTAL-WS   PIC 9(3).
                          10  FILLER                  PIC X.
                          10  OTHER-PAYMENTS-WS       PIC 9(3).

                  01  LINE-1-WS.
                      05  FILLER                      PIC X(5)   VALUE SPACES.
                      05  NAME-L1                     PIC X(20).
                      05  FILLER                      PIC X(11)
                                          VALUE '    PHONE ('.
                      05  AREA-CODE-L1                PIC 9(3).
                      05  FILLER                      PIC XX     VALUE ') '.
LINE1WS ─────────     05  NUMBR-L1                    PIC X(8).
                      05  FILLER                      PIC X(3)   VALUE SPACES.
                      05  SEX-L1                      PIC X(6).
                      05  FILLER                      PIC X(9)   VALUE SPACES.
                      05  FILLER                      PIC X(14)
                                          VALUE 'INCOME      $'.
                      05  INCOME-HUNDREDS-L1          PIC 9(3).
                      05  FILLER                      PIC X(28)
                                          VALUE '00 PER YEAR; IN THIS EMPLOY '.
                      05  YEARS-EMPLOYED-L1.
                          10  YEARS-L1                PIC XX.
                          10  DESCN-L1                PIC X(16).
```

```
          01  LINE-2-WS.
              05  FILLER                          PIC X(5)    VALUE SPACES.
LINE2WS       05  STREET-L2                       PIC X(20).
              05  FILLER                          PIC X(27)   VALUE SPACES.
              05  MARITAL-STATUS-L2               PIC X(8).
              05  FILLER                          PIC X(7)    VALUE SPACES.
              05  OUTGO-DESCN                     PIC X(16).
              05  MORTGAGE-OR-RENTAL-L2           PIC 9(3).
              05  MESSAGE-L2                      PIC X(46)   VALUE ' PER MTH'.


          01  LINE-3-WS.
              05  FILLER                          PIC X(5)    VALUE SPACES.
              05  CITY-L3                         PIC X(13).
              05  FILLER                          PIC X       VALUE SPACE.
              05  STATE-L3                        PIC XX.
              05  FILLER                          PIC X       VALUE SPACE.
              05  ZIP-L3                          PIC X(5).
              05  FILLER                          PIC X(7)    VALUE ' A/C: '.
LINE3WS       05  ACCT-NUM-L3                     PIC 9(6).
              05  FILLER                          PIC X(12)   VALUE SPACES.
              05  NUMBER-DEPENS-L3                PIC 9.
              05  FILLER                          PIC X(14)
                                          VALUE ' DEPENDENTS      '.
              05  FILLER                          PIC X(16)
                                          VALUE 'OTHER PAYMENTS $'.
              05  OTHER-PAYMENTS-L3               PIC 9(3).
              05  MESSAGE-L3                      PIC X(46)   VALUE ' PER MTH'.
```

```
          GET-A-PAIR-OF-CARDS-INTO-WS.
              MOVE NAME-IN TC NAME-WS.
              MOVE ADDRESS-IN TO ADDRESS-WS.
              MOVE PHONE-IN TC PHONE-WS.
              MOVE ACCT-NUM-IN1 TO ACCT-NUM-WS.
              READ APPLICATION-CARDS-FILE
GETPAIR           AT END MCVE 'NO ' TO CARDS-LEFT.
          * THE SECOND CARD OF THE PAIR IS NOW IN THE BUFFER
              MOVE CREDIT-INFO-IN TO CREDIT-INFO-WS.
              READ APPLICATICN-CARDS-FILE
                  AT END MOVE 'NO ' TO CARDS-LEFT.
          * THE FIRST CARD OF THE NEXT PAIR IS NOW IN THE BUFFER
```

```
          ASSEMBLE-PRINT-LINES.
              MOVE NAME-WS TO NAME-L1.
              MOVE STREET-WS TO STREET-L2.
              MOVE CITY-WS TO CITY-L3.
              MOVE STATE-WS TO STATE-L3.
              MOVE ZIP-WS TO ZIP-L3.
              MOVE AREA-CODE-WS TO AREA-CODE-L1.
              MOVE NUMBR-WS TO NUMBR-L1.
              MOVE ACCT-NUM-WS TO ACCT-NUM-L3.
              IF MALE    MOVE 'MALE '  TO SEX-L1.
              IF FEMALE MOVE 'FEMALE' TO SEX-L1.
              IF SINGLE   MOVE 'SINGLE ' TO MARITAL-STATUS-L2.
              IF MARRIED  MOVE 'MARRIED ' TO MARITAL-STATUS-L2.
              IF DIVORCED MOVE 'DIVORCED' TO MARITAL-STATUS-L2.
              IF WIDOWED  MOVE 'WIDOWED ' TO MARITAL-STATUS-L2.
              MOVE NUMBER-DEPENS-WS TO NUMBER-DEPENS-L3.
ASSMBLPR      MOVE INCOME-HUNDREDS-WS TO INCOME-HUNDREDS-L1.
              IF YEARS-EMPLOYED-WS IS EQUAL TO 0
                  MOVE 'LESS THAN 1 YEAR' TO YEARS-EMPLOYED-L1
              ELSE
                  MOVE YEARS-EMPLOYED-WS TO YEARS-L1
                  MOVE ' YEARS       ' TO DESCN-L1.
              IF OWNED MOVE 'MORTGAGE:     $' TO OUTGO-DESCN.
              IF RENTED MOVE 'RENTAL:       $' TO OUTGO-DESCN.
              MOVE MORTGAGE-OR-RENTAL-WS TO MORTGAGE-OR-RENTAL-L2.
              MOVE OTHER-PAYMENTS-WS TO OTHER-PAYMENTS-L3.
```

```
          WRITE-PROFILE.
              MOVE SPACES TO PRINT-LINE-OUT.
              WRITE PRINT-LINE-OUT FROM LINE-1-WS
                                  AFTER ADVANCING 4 LINES.
              MOVE SPACES TO PRINT-LINE-OUT.
WRITPRFL      WRITE PRINT-LINE-OUT FROM LINE-2-WS
                                  AFTER ADVANCING 1 LINES.
              MOVE SPACES TO PRINT-LINE-OUT.
              WRITE PRINT-LINE-OUT FROM LINE-3-WS
                                  AFTER ADVANCING 1 LINES.
```

```
CBL LIB
        IDENTIFICATION DIVISION.
        PROGRAM-ID. SAMPLE-4.

        ENVIRONMENT DIVISION.
        INPUT-OUTPUT SECTION.
        FILE-CONTROL. COPY FILECONT.

        DATA DIVISION.
        FILE SECTION.

        FD  APPLICATION-CARDS-FILE   COPY FDCARDS.

        FD  PROFILE-LISTING
                LABEL RECORDS ARE OMITTED.
        01  PRINT-LINE-OUT                      PIC X(132).

        WORKING-STORAGE SECTION.
        01  COMMON-WS.
            05  CARDS-LEFT                       PIC X(3).
        01  APPLICATION-DATA-WSB1 COPY CARDSWS.
        01  DISCR-INCOME-CALC-FIELDS-WSB2.
            05  ANNUAL-INCOME-WS                 PIC 9(5).
            05  ANNUAL-TAX-WS                    PIC 9(5).
            05  TAX-RATE-WS                      PIC 9V99      VALUE 0.25.
            05  MONTHS-IN-YEAR                   PIC 99        VALUE 12.
            05  MONTHLY-NET-INCOME-WS            PIC 9(4).
            05  MONTHLY-PAYMENTS-WS              PIC 9(4).
            05  DISCR-INCOME-WS                  PIC S9(3).
        01  LINE-1-WSB3 COPY LINE1WS.
        01  LINE-2-WSB3 COPY LINE2WS.
            05  FILLER                           PIC X(11)
            05  FILLER                           PIC X(22)
                                          VALUE 'DISCRETIONARY INCOME $'.
            05  DISCR-INCOME-L2                  PIC 9(3).
            05  FILLER                           PIC X(9)
                                          VALUE ' PER MTH '.
        01  LINE-3-WSB3 COPY LINE3WS.
```

Figure 5.2   SAMPLE-4 listing

```
PROCEDURE DIVISION.
    PERFORM A1-INITIALIZATION.
    PERFORM A2-PRINT-PROFILES
      UNTIL CARDS-LEFT = 'NO '.
    PERFORM A3-END-OF-JOB.
    STOP RUN.

A1-INITIALIZATION.
    OPEN INPUT APPLICATION-CARDS-FILE
         OUTPUT PROFILE-LISTING.
    MOVE ZEROES TO ANNUAL-INCOME-WS.
    MOVE ZEROES TO ANNUAL-TAX-WS.
    MOVE ZEROES TO MONTHLY-NET-INCOME-WS.
    MOVE ZEROES TO MONTHLY-PAYMENTS-WS.
    MOVE ZEROES TO DISCR-INCOME-WS.
    MOVE 'YES' TO CARDS-LEFT.
    READ APPLICATION-CARDS-FILE
        AT END MOVE 'NO ' TO CARDS-LEFT.
* THE FIRST CARD OF A PAIR IS NOW IN THE BUFFER

A2-PRINT-PROFILES.
    PERFORM B1-GET-A-PAIR-OF-CARDS-INTO-WS.
    PERFORM B2-CALC-DISCRETNRY-INCOME.
    PERFORM B3-ASSEMBLE-PRINT-LINES.
    PERFORM B4-WRITE-PROFILE.

A3-END-OF-JOB.
    CLOSE APPLICATION-CARDS-FILE
          PROFILE-LISTING.

B1-GET-A-PAIR-OF-CARDS-INTO-WS. COPY GETPAIR.

B2-CALC-DISCRETNRY-INCOME.
    COMPUTE ANNUAL-INCOME-WS = INCOME-HUNDREDS-WS * 100.
    COMPUTE ANNUAL-TAX-WS    = ANNUAL-INCOME-WS * TAX-RATE-WS.
    COMPUTE MONTHLY-NET-INCOME-WS ROUNDED
       = (ANNUAL-INCOME-WS - ANNUAL-TAX-WS) / MONTHS-IN-YEAR.
    COMPUTE MONTHLY-PAYMENTS-WS = MORTGAGE-OR-RENTAL-WS
                                  + OTHER-PAYMENTS-WS.
    COMPUTE DISCR-INCOME-WS = MONTHLY-NET-INCOME-WS
                              - MONTHLY-PAYMENTS-WS
       ON SIZE ERROR MOVE 999 TO DISCR-INCOME-WS.
*    DISCRETIONARY INCOMES OVER $999 PER MONTH ARE SET AT $999

B3-ASSEMBLE-PRINT-LINES. COPY ASSMBLPR.
    MOVE DISCR-INCOME-WS TO DISCR-INCOME-L2.

B4-WRITE-PROFILE. COPY WRITPRFL
        REPLACING LINE-1-WS BY LINE-1-WSB3
                  LINE-2-WS BY LINE-2-WSB3
                  LINE-3-WS BY LINE-3-WSB3.
```

Figure 5.2 continued.  SAMPLE-4 listing

```
      CBL LIB
      00001            IDENTIFICATION DIVISION.
      00002            PROGRAM-ID. SAMPLE-4.
      00003
      00004            ENVIRONMENT DIVISION.
      00005            INPUT-OUTPUT SECTION.
      00006            FILE-CONTROL. COPY FILECONT.
      00007 C              SELECT APPLICATION-CARDS-FILE ASSIGN TO SYS031-UR-2540R-S.
      00008 C              SELECT PROFILE-LISTING        ASSIGN TO SYS033-UR-1403-S.
      00009
      00010            DATA DIVISION.
      00011            FILE SECTION.
      00012
      00013            FD  APPLICATION-CARDS-FILE  COPY FDCARDS.
      00014 C                LABEL RECORDS ARE OMITTED
      00015 C                DATA RECORDS ARE NAME-ADDRESS-AND-PHONE-IN
      00016 C                            CREDIT-INFORMATION-IN.
      00017 C            01  NAME-ADDRESS-AND-PHONE-IN.
      00018 C                05  NAME-IN                  PIC X(20).
      00019 C                05  ADDRESS-IN               PIC X(40).
      00020 C                05  PHONE-IN                 PIC X(11).
      00021 C                05  FILLER                   PIC X(3).
      00022 C                05  ACCT-NUM-IN1             PIC 9(6).
      00023 C            01  CREDIT-INFORMATION-IN.
      00024 C                05  CARD-TYPE-IN             PIC X.
      00025 C                05  ACCT-NUM-IN2             PIC 9(6).
      00026 C                05  FILLER                   PIC X.
      00027 C                05  CREDIT-INFO-IN           PIC X(22).
      00028 C                05  FILLER                   PIC X(50).
      00029
      00030            FD  PROFILE-LISTING
      00031                    LABEL RECORDS ARE OMITTED.
      00032            01  PRINT-LINE-OUT               PIC X(132).
      00033
```

Figure 5.3   SAMPLE-4, full compilation, page 1 of 5

```
00034            WORKING-STORAGE SECTION.
00035            01   COMMON-WS.
00036                 05   CARDS-LEFT                    PIC X(3).
00037            01   APPLICATION-DATA-WSB1 COPY CARDSWS.
00038 C          01   APPLICATION-DATA-WSB1.
00039 C               05   NAME-AND-ADDRESS-WS.
00040 C                    10   NAME-WS                  PIC X(20).
00041 C                    10   ADDRESS-WS.
00042 C                         15   STREET-WS           PIC X(20).
00043 C                         15   CITY-WS             PIC X(13).
00044 C                         15   STATE-WS            PIC XX.
00045 C                         15   ZIP-WS              PIC X(5).
00046 C               05   PHONE-WS.
00047 C                    10   AREA-CODE-WS             PIC 9(3).
00048 C                    10   NUMBR-WS                 PIC X(8).
00049 C               05   FILLER                        PIC X(3).
00050 C               05   ACCT-NUM-WS                   PIC 9(6).
00051 C               05   CREDIT-INFO-WS.
00052 C                    10   SEX-WS                   PIC X.
00053 C                         88   MALE      VALUE 'M'.
00054 C                         88   FEMALE    VALUE 'F'.
00055 C                    10   FILLER                   PIC X.
00056 C                    10   MARITAL-STATUS-WS        PIC X.
00057 C                         88   SINGLE    VALUE 'S'.
00058 C                         88   MARRIED   VALUE 'M'.
00059 C                         88   DIVORCED  VALUE 'D'.
00060 C                         88   WIDOWED   VALUE 'W'.
00061 C                    10   FILLER                   PIC X.
00062 C                    10   NUMBER-DEPENS-WS         PIC 9.
00063 C                    10   FILLER                   PIC X.
00064 C                    10   INCOME-HUNDREDS-WS       PIC 9(3).
00065 C                    10   FILLER                   PIC X.
00066 C                    10   YEARS-EMPLOYED-WS        PIC 99.
00067 C                    10   FILLER                   PIC X.
00068 C                    10   CWN-OR-RENT-WS           PIC X.
00069 C                         88   OWNED     VALUE 'O'.
00070 C                         88   RENTED    VALUE 'R'.
00071 C                    10   FILLER                   PIC X.
00072 C                    10   MORTGAGE-OR-RENTAL-WS    PIC 9(3).
00073 C                    10   FILLER                   PIC X.
00074 C                    10   OTHER-PAYMENTS-WS        PIC 9(3).
00075            01   DISCR-INCOME-CALC-FIELDS-WSB2.
00076                 05   ANNUAL-INCOME-WS              PIC 9(5).
00077                 05   ANNUAL-TAX-WS                 PIC 9(5).
00078                 05   TAX-RATE-WS                   PIC 9V99     VALUE 0.25.
00079                 05   MONTHS-IN-YEAR                PIC 99       VALUE 12.
00080                 05   MONTHLY-NET-INCOME-WS         PIC 9(4).
00081                 05   MONTHLY-PAYMENTS-WS           PIC 9(4).
00082                 05   DISCR-INCOME-WS               PIC S9(3).
```

Figure 5.3 continued.   SAMPLE-4, full compilation, page 2 of 5

```
00083            01   LINE-1-WSB3 COPY LINE1WS.
00084 C          01   LINE-1-WSB3.
00085 C               05   FILLER                     PIC X(5)      VALUE SPACES.
00086 C               05   NAME-L1                    PIC X(20).
00087 C               05   FILLER                     PIC X(11)
00088 C                                    VALUE '    PHONE ('.
00089 C               05   AREA-CODE-L1               PIC 9(3).
00090 C               05   FILLER                     PIC XX        VALUE ') '.
00091 C               05   NUMBR-L1                   PIC X(8).
00092 C               05   FILLER                     PIC X(3)      VALUE SPACES.
00093 C               05   SEX-L1                     PIC X(6).
00094 C               05   FILLER                     PIC X(9)      VALUE SPACES.
00095 C               05   FILLER                     PIC X(14)
00096 C                                    VALUE 'INCOME        $'.
00097 C               05   INCOME-HUNDREDS-L1         PIC 9(3).
00098 C               05   FILLER                     PIC X(28)
00099 C                                    VALUE '00 PER YEAR; IN THIS EMPLOY '.
00100 C               05   YEARS-EMPLOYED-L1.
00101 C                    10   YEARS-L1              PIC XX.
00102 C                    10   DESCN-L1              PIC X(16).
00103            01   LINE-2-WSB3 COPY LINE2WS.
00104 C          01   LINE-2-WSB3.
00105 C               05   FILLER                     PIC X(5)      VALUE SPACES.
00106 C               05   STREET-L2                  PIC X(20).
00107 C               05   FILLER                     PIC X(27)     VALUE SPACES.
00108 C               05   MARITAL-STATUS-L2          PIC X(8).
00109 C               05   FILLER                     PIC X(7)      VALUE SPACES.
00110 C               05   OUTGO-DESCN        .       PIC X(16).
00111 C               05   MORTGAGE-OR-RENTAL-L2      PIC 9(3).
00112            05   FILLER                     PIC X(11)
00113                                  VALUE ' PER MTH   '.
00114            05   FILLER                     PIC X(22)
00115                                  VALUE 'DISCRETIONARY INCOME $'.
00116            05   DISCR-INCOME-L2            PIC 9(3).
00117            05   FILLER                     PIC X(9)
00118                                  VALUE ' PER MTH '.
00119            01   LINE-3-WSB3 COPY LINE3WS.
00120 C          01   LINE-3-WSB3.
00121 C               05   FILLER                     PIC X(5)      VALUE SPACES.
00122 C               05   CITY-L3                    PIC X(13).
00123 C               05   FILLER                     PIC X         VALUE SPACE.
00124 C               05   STATE-L3                   PIC XX.
00125 C               05   FILLER                     PIC X         VALUE SPACE.
00126 C               05   ZIP-L3                     PIC X(5).
00127 C               05   FILLER                     PIC X(7)      VALUE '   A/C: '.
00128 C               05   ACCT-NUM-L3                PIC 9(6).
00129 C               05   FILLER                     PIC X(12)     VALUE SPACES.
00130 C               05   NUMBER-DEPENS-L3           PIC 9.
00131 C               05   FILLER                     PIC X(14)
00132 C                                    VALUE ' DEPENDENTS    '.
00133 C               05   FILLER                     PIC X(16)
00134 C                                    VALUE 'OTHER PAYMENTS $'.
00135 C               05   OTHER-PAYMENTS-L3          PIC 9(3).
00136
```

Figure 5.3 continued.  SAMPLE-4, full compilation, page 3 of 5

```
00137          PROCEDURE DIVISION.
00138              PERFORM A1-INITIALIZATION.
00139              PERFORM A2-PRINT-PROFILES
00140                 UNTIL CARDS-LEFT = 'NO '.
00141              PERFORM A3-END-OF-JOB.
00142              STOP RUN.
00143
00144          A1-INITIALIZATION.
00145              OPEN INPUT APPLICATION-CARDS-FILE
00146                     OUTPUT PROFILE-LISTING.
00147              MOVE ZEROES TO ANNUAL-INCOME-WS.
00148              MOVE ZEROES TO ANNUAL-TAX-WS.
00149              MOVE ZEROES TO MONTHLY-NET-INCOME-WS.
00150              MOVE ZEROES TO MONTHLY-PAYMENTS-WS.
00151              MOVE ZEROES TO DISCR-INCOME-WS.
00152              MOVE 'YES' TO CARDS-LEFT.
00153              READ APPLICATION-CARDS-FILE
00154                 AT END MOVE 'NO ' TO CARDS-LEFT.
00155      * THE FIRST CARD OF A PAIR IS NOW IN THE BUFFER
00156
00157          A2-PRINT-PROFILES.
00158              PERFORM B1-GET-A-PAIR-OF-CARDS-INTO-WS.
00159              PERFORM B2-CALC-DISCRETNRY-INCOME.
00160              PERFORM B3-ASSEMBLE-PRINT-LINES.
00161              PERFORM B4-WRITE-PROFILE.
00162
00163          A3-END-OF-JOB.
00164              CLOSE APPLICATION-CARDS-FILE
00165                     PROFILE-LISTING.
00166
00167          B1-GET-A-PAIR-OF-CARDS-INTO-WS. COPY GETPAIR.
00168 C            MOVE NAME-IN TO NAME-WS.
00169 C            MOVE ADDRESS-IN TO ADDRESS-WS.
00170 C            MOVE PHONE-IN TO PHONE-WS.
00171 C            MOVE ACCT-NUM-IN1 TO ACCT-NUM-WS.
00172 C            READ APPLICATION-CARDS-FILE
00173 C                AT END MOVE 'NO ' TO CARDS-LEFT.
00174 C    * THE SECOND CARD OF THE PAIR IS NOW IN THE BUFFER
00175 C            MOVE CREDIT-INFO-IN TO CREDIT-INFO-WS.
00176 C            READ APPLICATION-CARDS-FILE
00177 C                AT END MOVE 'NO ' TO CARDS-LEFT.
00178 C    * THE FIRST CARD OF THE NEXT PAIR IS NOW IN THE BUFFER
```

Figure 5.3 continued.   SAMPLE-4, full compilation, page 4 of 5

```
00179
00180              B2-CALC-DISCRETNRY-INCOME.
00181                  COMPUTE ANNUAL-INCOME-WS = INCOME-HUNDREDS-WS * 100.
00182                  COMPUTE ANNUAL-TAX-WS    = ANNUAL-INCOME-WS * TAX-RATE-WS.
00183                  COMPUTE MONTHLY-NET-INCOME-WS ROUNDED
00184                     = (ANNUAL-INCOME-WS - ANNUAL-TAX-WS) / MONTHS-IN-YEAR.
00185                  COMPUTE MONTHLY-PAYMENTS-WS = MORTGAGE-OR-RENTAL-WS
00186                                            + OTHER-PAYMENTS-WS.
00187                  COMPUTE DISCR-INCOME-WS = MONTHLY-NET-INCOME-WS
00188                                          - MONTHLY-PAYMENTS-WS
00189                  ON SIZE ERROR MOVE 999 TO DISCR-INCOME-WS.
00190        *    DISCRETIONARY INCOMES OVER $999 PER MONTH ARE SET AT $999
00191
00192              B3-ASSEMBLE-PRINT-LINES. COPY ASSMBLPR.
00193 C               MOVE NAME-WS TO NAME-L1.
00194 C               MOVE STREET-WS TO STREET-L2.
00195 C               MOVE CITY-WS TO CITY-L3.
00196 C               MOVE STATE-WS TO STATE-L3.
00197 C               MOVE ZIP-WS TO ZIP-L3.
00198 C               MOVE AREA-CODE-WS TO AREA-CODE-L1.
00199 C               MOVE NUMBR-WS TO NUMBR-L1.
00200 C               MOVE ACCT-NUM-WS TO ACCT-NUM-L3.
00201 C               IF MALE   MOVE 'MALE  ' TO SEX-L1.
00202 C               IF FEMALE MOVE 'FEMALE' TO SEX-L1.
00203 C               IF SINGLE   MOVE 'SINGLE ' TO MARITAL-STATUS-L2.
00204 C               IF MARRIED  MOVE 'MARRIED ' TO MARITAL-STATUS-L2.
00205 C               IF DIVORCED MOVE 'DIVORCED' TO MARITAL-STATUS-L2.
00206 C               IF WIDOWED  MOVE 'WIDOWED ' TO MARITAL-STATUS-L2.
00207 C               MOVE NUMBER-DEPENS-WS TO NUMBER-DEPENS-L3.
00208 C               MOVE INCOME-HUNDREDS-WS TO INCOME-HUNDREDS-L1.
00209 C               IF YEARS-EMPLOYED-WS IS EQUAL TO 0
00210 C                   MOVE 'LESS THAN 1 YEAR' TO YEARS-EMPLOYED-L1
00211 C               ELSE
00212 C                   MOVE YEARS-EMPLOYED-WS TO YEARS-L1
00213 C                   MOVE ' YEARS        ' TO DESCN-L1.
00214 C               IF OWNED MOVE 'MORTGAGE:       $' TO OUTGO-DESCN.
00215 C               IF RENTED MOVE 'RENTAL:         $' TO OUTGO-DESCN.
00216 C               MOVE MORTGAGE-OR-RENTAL-WS TO MORTGAGE-OR-RENTAL-L2.
00217 C               MOVE OTHER-PAYMENTS-WS TO OTHER-PAYMENTS-L3.
00218 C               MOVE DISCR-INCOME-WS TO DISCR-INCOME-L2.
00219
00220              B4-WRITE-PROFILE. COPY WRITPRFL
00221                  REPLACING LINE-1-WS BY LINE-1-WSB3
00222                            LINE-2-WS BY LINE-2-WSB3
00223                            LINE-3-WS BY LINE-3-WSB3.
00224 C               MOVE SPACES TO PRINT-LINE-OUT.
00225 C               WRITE PRINT-LINE-OUT FROM LINE-1-WSB3
00226 C                               AFTER ADVANCING 4 LINES.
00227 C               MOVE SPACES TO PRINT-LINE-OUT.
00228 C               WRITE PRINT-LINE-OUT FROM LINE-2-WSB3
00229 C                               AFTER ADVANCING 1 LINES.
00230 C               MOVE SPACES TO PRINT-LINE-OUT.
00231 C               WRITE PRINT-LINE-OUT FROM LINE-3-WSB3
00232 C                               AFTER ADVANCING 1 LINES.
```

Figure 5.3 continued.   SAMPLE-4, full compilation, page 5 of 5

# CHAPTER 6: PROGRAM LOGIC

## 6.1    TESTING FOR CONDITIONS

There are a variety of useful tests that we can make in addition to the simple tests we have done up until now, for example, IF NAME IS EQUAL TO SPACES.  They are of five types:

Relational:          Is field-1 GREATER THAN, LESS THAN, OR EQUAL TO field-2?

Class:               Is field-1 NUMERIC or ALPHABETIC?

Condition name:      IF MARRIED ... (where MARRIED has previously been defined in an 88 level).

Sign:                Is field-1 POSITIVE, NEGATIVE, or ZERO?

Complex:             Is (condition-1 true) $\begin{Bmatrix} \text{AND} \\ \text{OR} \end{Bmatrix}$ (condition-2 true)?

Let us look at each of these types of test in turn.

### 6.1.1    Relational Tests

The general form is:

IF    field-1 $\begin{Bmatrix} \text{IS GREATER THAN} \\ \text{IS LESS THAN} \\ \text{IS EQUAL TO} \end{Bmatrix}$    field-2

statement-1

ELSE

statement-2.

Q.    Code a test to perform OK-ROUTINE if TOTAL-OUTGO is less than NET-INCOME and perform BANKRUPT-ROUTINE if TOTAL-OUTGO is more than or equal to NET-INCOME.

A.    IF TOTAL-OUTGO IS LESS THAN NET-INCOME
          PERFORM OK-ROUTINE
      ELSE
          PERFORM BANKRUPT-ROUTINE.

Q.    In the preceding question, what is wrong with:

```
IF TOTAL-OUTGO IS GREATER THAN NET-INCOME
    PERFORM BANKRUPT-ROUTINE
ELSE
    PERFORM OK-ROUTINE.
```

A.    This test gives the wrong result in the case where
TOTAL-OUTGO and NET-INCOME are exactly equal.

Most computers will allow you to use the characters

>     for IS GREATER THAN
<     for IS LESS THAN
=     for IS EQUAL TO

We prefer to stay away from > and < because some people
find them confusing and the printers of some computers can't
handle them.  We prefer to use = only in a COMPUTE statement
or when followed by a literal, e.g., IF CARDS-LEFT = 'NO '.


*6.1.2    Class Tests*


A field is NUMERIC when it contains only $\emptyset$ - 9 and decimal points, with a + sign, and ALPHABETIC when it contains
only A - Z and/or spaces.


Q.    FIELD-A contains 243-7022.  Which routine will
be performed when the statement below is
executed:

```
IF FIELD-A IS NUMERIC
    PERFORM NUMBER-ROUTINE
ELSE
    PERFORM GARBAGE-ROUTINE.
```

A.    GARBAGE-ROUTINE will be performed; FIELD-A
fails the test of being numeric because it
contains a hyphen.  So control goes to the
ELSE clause and the imperative statement
there is obeyed.


Q.    Given the format of PHONE-IN as we have used it,
how could you use class tests to make sure as
far as possible that the digits have been punched
correctly?

A.   Define the card with three fields, say EXCHANGE,
     HYPHEN, and NUMBER, and test EXCHANGE and NUMBER
     to make sure they are numeric.  This will not
     guarantee that the digits punched are the ones
     that should be there, but at least you will catch
     any spaces (which will fail the test), and any
     letters or other characters which got punched
     by accident.

Q.   If NAME-IN is blank, will it pass an
     ALPHABETIC test?

A.   Yes.  Blanks are alpha characters.
     So you need to test specifically for
     SPACES if you want to detect a
     missing field.

As you can see, class tests can be useful in editing:  If
you know a field contains a dollar amount, then test it for
NUMERIC.  If the test fails, something is wrong, and the
transactions should not be processed until the error is
corrected.

### 6.1.3   Condition Name Tests

We used condition names extensively in SAMPLE-3 and SAMPLE-4.
Provided MARRIED, SINGLE, OWNED, RENTED, etc., have been defined in 88 levels, you simply write

```
IF OWNED
     ...
ELSE ...
```

It is good practice, when a condition name can have one of
two values, to test for both, e.g.,

```
IF OWNED
     perform owned-routine
ELSE IF RENTED
     perform rented-routine
ELSE
     perform error-routine.
```

Note that we have now combined the two separate IF
statements used in SAMPLE-3 and SAMPLE-4, into this
IF ... ELSE IF ... form.

One advantage of this form is that it provides for the situation in which OWNED is not true and RENTED is not true. In this case you've got a problem, which you must deal with in "error-routine"; maybe something other than O or R is punched in the card. Anyway, don't assume that because OWNED is not true, RENTED is automatically true: Always test.

This is an example of defensive programming; trying to anticipate anything that might go wrong and dealing with it.

> Q. Code a defensive routine to add 1
> to MEN if MALE, and add 1 to WOMEN
> if FEMALE.

> A. IF MALE
>         ADD 1 TO MEN
>     ELSE IF FEMALE
>         ADD 1 TO WOMEN
>     ELSE
>         PERFORM SEX-ERROR-ROUTINE.

Note that where we have ELSE IF we prefer to continue on the same line, rather than our normal practice of leaving the ELSE on a line of its own.

## 6.1.4  Sign Tests

These allow you to test whether a field defined as numeric is positive, negative, or zero; e.g.,

```
    IF DISCRETIONARY-INCOME IS NEGATIVE
        PERFORM BANKRUPT-ROUTINE
    ELSE
        PERFORM OK-ROUTINE.
```

> Q. IF DISCRETIONARY-INCOME is defined
> PIC 9(3), will BANKRUPT-ROUTINE ever
> be performed?

> A. No, the field will always appear positive.
> Only signed fields, e.g., PIC S9(3), should
> be tested with a sign test.

You can combine various conditions in one test, using the logical operators AND, OR, and NOT.  For example, you may want to write:

```
        IF MALE AND MARRIED
              ADD 1 TO MARRIED-MEN
        ELSE
              ADD 1 TO OTHER-PEOPLE.
```

Or you might have occasion to write:

```
        IF SINGLE OR DIVORCED OR WIDOWED
           ADD 1 TO UNMARRIED-PERSONS.
```

First of all, let's see what the operators (AND, OR, NOT) really mean.  The AND operator, for example, forms expressions whose value is "true" if and only if <u>both</u> of the conditions ANDed together are individually true.

MALE AND INCOME-HUNDREDS IS GREATER THAN 150 is true only for people who are <u>both</u> men and also earn more than $15,000 per annum.  If the condition on either side of the AND is false, the whole expression is false.

We can put this formally by drawing up a <u>truth table</u>, which shows the various combinations of truth <u>and falsity</u>:

| X | Y | X AND Y |
|-------|-------|---------|
| True | True | True |
| True | False | False |
| False | True | False |
| False | False | False |

On the other hand, the operator OR creates expressions which are true if either one or both of the conditions either side of the OR is true.

Thus "FEMALE OR MARRIED" is true for men provided they are married, and also true for all women whether they are married or not, and certainly true for married women.

Q.   Draw up a truth table for the
     expression X or Y.

A.
| X | Y | X  OR  Y |
|---|---|----------|
| T | T | T |
| T | F | T |
| F | T | T |
| F | F | F |

The NOT operator allows us to form the logical negation, or
reversal of truth value, of a condition.  Thus, if condition
X is true, NOT-X is false; conversely, if X is false, NOT-X
is true.

Q.   Is NOT GREATER THAN 100 true or
     false for the number 101?

A.   False.  GREATER THAN 100 is true for
     101; so the negation must be false.

The human mind has a lot of difficulty with expressions in-
volving NOT; experiments suggest that they are about twice as
hard to follow as positive expressions.  The real trouble comes,
though, when we start to combine AND, OR, and NOT.  For example,
is NOT MARRIED OR AGE NOT GREATER THAN 21 true of a married
person aged 20?  It is difficult to evaluate this and get it
right without working through the truth table.

        NOT MARRIED is false

        AGE NOT GREATER THAN 21 is true
and the truth table shows that if X is false and Y is true,
X or Y is true.

    You would expect that NOT NOT MARRIED would be the same
as MARRIED, but COBOL does not allow you to have two NOT's
together.  You must enclose the inner NOT condition in
parentheses.  Thus, you can write:

```
        IF A NOT (NOT NUMERIC)
            PERFORM NUMBER-ROUTINE
        ELSE
            PERFORM ALPHA-ROUTINE
```

While you would rarely want to do this, the use of parentheses is vital whenever two or more different operators are used.

To see why this is so, try answering

Q.    Is MARRIED AND FEMALE OR AGE GREATER THAN 21
       true for a single man of 30?

A.    You will get a different answer depending on
       how you read the expression.

       If you read it as

       (MARRIED AND FEMALE) OR (AGE GREATER THAN 21)

       you have        False    OR           True

       which is True.

       If you read it as

       (MARRIED) AND (FEMALE OR AGE GREATER THAN 21) you have

         False    AND             True

       which is False.  The placing of the parentheses
       alters the meaning of the whole expression.


To put it another way, if A is false and C is true, then

       (A AND B) OR C  is always true, no matter what the

value of B, and

       A AND (B OR C)  is always false.

This problem of precedence of operators is something to watch out for in program specifications; if you read "If the person is married and lives in the state or is a veteran, apply a discount of 5%," you should be aware that this is an ambiguous sentence which can be programmed one of two ways.  You should make sure which of the two ways is the one that the user intends.


Complicating the issue is the fact that COBOL has its built-in rules for inserting parentheses if you leave them out; if you code A AND B OR NOT C, the compiler will treat it as though you had written  (A AND B) OR (NOT C).  So, always put parentheses in when you have two or more operands.  The only exception to this rule is when you have a string of expressions all connected by the same operand.

Thus, it's OK to write:

        IF MALE AND MARRIED AND OWNER AND INCOME GREATER THAN 10000

or

        AGE IS LESS THAN 21 OR INCOME IS LESS THAN 15000
                        OR RENTER
                        OR OUT-OF-STATE

    Once we have made proper use of parentheses to clearly
specify the intended precedence of logical operations, we are
still left with one problem:  When more than three operators
are involved, Boolean algebra (the rules for combining operators)
is not trivial.  That is, when we write the COBOL statement:

```
IF A OR {NOT {B OR {NOT {C AND D}}}}
    MOVE P TO Q
ELSE
    MOVE X TO Y.
```

even a competent mathematician would probably scratch his head for
a while to determine the conditions under which P was moved to Q.
We're tempted at this point to make the flat statement "you should
never write statements as complex as that" and that is true 95%
of the time.  If the situation is genuinely complex, you will
need to draw up a type of truth table known as a decision table;
these are dealt with in Section 6.3.


## 6.2    NESTED IF STATEMENTS


    Suppose we had occasion to count the number of people with
blue eyes, count separately the number of people with a height over
six feet, and count separately the number of people from California,
we could code (assuming appropriate definition of data-names).

```
IF COLOR-OF-EYES = 'BLUE' ADD 1 TO BLUE-EYES.
IF HEIGHT IS GREATER THAN HEIGHT-LIMIT
            ADD 1 TO SIX-FOOTERS.
IF HOME-STATE = 'CA' ADD 1 TO CALIFORNIANS.
```

If the program is processing data for a very tall, blue-eyed person
from San Francisco, all three of the counter fields will be incremented; for a short, black-eyed New Yorker, none of them would be
incremented.  You can imagine all combinations of counters being
incremented, because the conditions tested are independent of one
another; home state has nothing to do with having blue eyes or with
height.


    However, suppose we had occasion to count the number of people
who are married men, count separately the number of people who are
married women, and similarly count the number of single men and
single women; suppose further that we have defined the condition
names so that divorced and widowed people are considered single.
What sort of COBOL statements could we write to accomplish this?

One sequence of statements comes to mind immediately:

```
IF MALE AND MARRIED ADD 1 TO MARRIED-MEN.
IF FEMALE AND MARRIED ADD 1 TO MARRIED-WOMEN.
IF MALE AND SINGLE ADD 1 TO SINGLE-MEN.
IF FEMALE AND SINGLE ADD 1 TO SINGLE-WOMEN.
```

There is no question that this code is simple and straightforward; it can be understood by anyone who reads it.  On the other hand, this code is misleading; the separate IF statements imply the testing of independent conditions.

We know that the four combinations of conditions are very far from independent.  If we have discovered that a person is male and married, he cannot simultaneously be female and married, so there is no point even asking the question.  In other words, only one of the IF statements in the example above can have a value of "true" and yet all four IF statements will be tested.

Worse than this, though, is the clumsiness of the form once more than two conditions are involved.  For instance, suppose we wanted to take property ownership into account.  We would have to write:

```
IF MALE AND MARRIED AND OWNER ADD 1 TO MARRIED-MALE-OWNERS.
IF MALE AND MARRIED AND RENTER ADD 1 TO MARRIED-MALE-RENTERS.
.
. etc.
```

Q.    How many statements would be required to cover all
      the possible cases?

A.    8:  Each of the three conditions can have one of two
      values, and $2^3 = 8$.

This provides the motivation for another approach; the nested IF.  Consider, for example, our original problem of counting separate categories of single men, married men, single women, and married women.  We could accomplish this with the following COBOL statement:

```
IF MALE
    IF MARRIED
        ADD 1 TO MARRIED-MEN
    ELSE
        ADD 1 TO SINGLE-MEN
ELSE
    IF MARRIED
        ADD 1 TO MARRIED-WOMEN
    ELSE
        ADD 1 TO SINGLE-WOMEN.
```

This kind of statement does what we want to do, and also enables us to avoid most of the problems we noted with combinations of dependent conditions in the previous scheme. On the other hand, it requires clear thinking to use correctly, and if carelessly used, can get you into unbelievable trouble. Consequently, we must look closely at the nested IF to see how it works, and to see how to avoid the problems associated with it.

First of all, let's look more closely at how the nested IF works. The outer "layer" of logic expressed in our statement above could be written informally as:

```
IF MALE
     male-logic
ELSE
     female-logic.
```

From this point of view, it is clear that we have a very simple "either-or" binary situation; either MALE is true or it is not. What we must emphasize, though, is that if MALE is true, then we want to carry out "male-logic," whatever that is, and then proceed with the next COBOL sentence. That is, we want to "skip over" the ELSE clause, since it is obviously irrelevant to us. Let's keep that in mind as we investigate what "male-logic" entails. From the original statement of the problem, we see that it can be expressed as:

```
IF MARRIED
     ADD 1 TO MARRIED-MEN
ELSE
     ADD 1 TO SINGLE-MEN.
```

Thus, if it turns out that we are dealing with a married man, we will execute the statement that adds one to the MARRIED-MEN counter. What next? Well, we certainly don't want to execute the ELSE clause; that is, we don't want to add one to SINGLE-MEN, having just decided that we had a married man. In fact, we want to "skip over" the ELSE clause...and we recognize at this point that we are through with "male-logic."

What do we do next? We had decided before we got involved in the details of "male-logic" that, once it was accomplished, we wanted to proceed with the next COBOL statement. Thus, when we look at the full nested IF statement

```
IF MALE
     IF MARRIED
          ADD 1 TO MARRIED-MEN
     ELSE
          ADD 1 TO SINGLE-MEN
ELSE
     IF MARRIED
          ADD 1 TO MARRIED-WOMEN
     ELSE
          ADD 1 TO SINGLE-WOMEN.
```

it becomes clear that if MALE is true, we will then execute the first IF MARRIED ... clause. And if the object of our investigation is not only male but also married, then we will execute the statement ADD 1 TO MARRIED-MEN and then we will "skip over" the ELSE that matches the IF-MARRIED (since we have dispensed with "male-logic") and we will furthermore "skip over" the ELSE that matches the IF MALE (since we obviously have no interest in executing any statements associated with "female-logic").

We can generalize all of this by saying that an IF statement is of the form

```
IF logical-condition-1
    statement-1
ELSE
    statement-2.
```

where "statement-1" and "statement-2" can be any of the simple COBOL statements with which you are familiar, or a linear sequence of such statements, or another IF statement. Thus, it is possible that "statement-1" is a simple MOVE statement, and that "statement-2" is of the form

```
IF logical-condition-2
    statement-3
ELSE
    statement-4.
```

Sooner or later, the "statement-i's" will have been fully expanded into "simple" statements, or linear sequences of such statements. Keep in mind that, no matter how deeply nested, the IF statement is just one COBOL sentence; that is, there's only one period, and it's at the very end of the COBOL sentence.

By a "linear sequence" of simple statements, we mean that it is permissible to write such statements as:

```
IF logical-condition-1
    MOVE A TO B
    MOVE C TO D
    MOVE E TO F
ELSE
    IF logical-condition-2
        MOVE P1 TO Q1
        MOVE P2 TO Q2
    ELSE
        MOVE X1 TO Y1
        MOVE X2 TO Y2.
```

Once again, note that there is only one period in this structure!

Q.    What happens when the nested IF statement
      shown above is executed, assuming that
      "logical-condition-1" is false, and
      "logical-condition-2" is true?

A.    P1 will be moved to Q1 and P2 will be moved
      to Q2.  Nothing else will be moved anywhere
      and execution will continue at the statement
      following the IF.


Q.    Write out the nested IF which is equivalent
      to the eight sequential IFs started on
      page 109.

A.
```
IF MALE
    IF MARRIED
        IF OWNER
            ADD 1 TO MARRIED-MALE-OWNERS
        ELSE
            ADD 1 TO MARRIED-MALE-RENTERS
    ELSE
        IF OWNER
            ADD 1 TO SINGLE-MALE-OWNERS
        ELSE
            ADD 1 TO SINGLE-MALE-RENTERS
ELSE
    IF MARRIED
        IF OWNER
            ADD 1 TO MARRIED-FEMALE-OWNERS
        ELSE
            ADD 1 TO MARRIED-FEMALE-RENTERS
    ELSE
        IF OWNER
            ADD 1 TO SINGLE-FEMALE-OWNERS
        ELSE
            ADD 1 TO SINGLE-FEMALE-RENTERS.
```

## 6.2.1    Block Structures


Let's be very sure that we understand the consequences
of having multiple MOVE statements in linear sequences in
nested IFs.  We observed that the "outer layer" of the IF
statement was of the form

```
        IF logical-condition-1
            statement-1
        ELSE
            statement-2.
```

Suppose, as in the earlier example, that statement-1 consists of three MOVE statements. How does COBOL know when we've finished doing everything we wanted to do in statement-1? The answer is that statement-1 is terminated by the ELSE clause that matches the IF clause within which statement-1 is embedded. In more formal terms, statement-1 is known as a "block"; in some programming languages, blocks are delimited with the explicit words BEGIN and END, but in COBOL, blocks are delimited by the presence of an ELSE (in the case of statement-1), or by the period that ends the sentence (in the case of statement-2).

In case you think we're making a lot of noise about something relatively insignificant, we hasten to point out that it's a very significant issue -- and failure to understand it has caused enormous problems for a lot of COBOL programmers. To illustrate the potential problems, let's consider a slight variation to the original problem of counting categories of married men, single men, etc. Suppose we were required to make a cumulative count of all males and all females, as well as individual counts of the married males, married females, single males, and single females. We might be tempted to write the following IF statement:

```
IF MALE                          *
    IF MARRIED                   *
        ADD 1 TO MARRIED-MEN     *   THIS IS AN
    ELSE                         *
        ADD 1 TO SINGLE-MEN      *    EXAMPLE
    ADD 1 TO MALE-COUNTER        *
                                 *
ELSE                             *      OF
    IF MARRIED                   *
        ADD 1 TO MARRIED-WOMEN   *   INCORRECT
    ELSE                         *
        ADD 1 TO SINGLE-WOMEN    *     CODE
    ADD 1 TO FEMALE-COUNTER.     *
```

The intention of this code is fairly clear: Once we have determined that a person is male, we check further to see if he is married in order to increment MARRIED-MEN or SINGLE-MEN -- but in either case, the intention is to increment MALE-COUNTER. Obviously, the code is attempting to do the same thing with females.

Q. Does the code shown above achieve this?

If not, why not?

A.  No, because according to the formal definition
    of COBOL the statement ADD 1 TO MALE-COUNTER is
    included as part of a linear "block" of statements
    imbedded within the ELSE clause corresponding to
    non-married males.  Thus, if we discover that a
    person is male and is married, we will increment
    MARRIED-MEN, then skip around the next ELSE clause
    (since we aren't concerned with unmarried males)
    and skip around the outer level ELSE clause (since
    we aren't concerned with females of any variety).
    In other words, MALE-COUNTER is incremented only
    when we are dealing with unmarried males, which is
    not what we intended; similarly, FEMALE-COUNTER is
    incremented only when we are dealing with unmarried
    females.

So, how do we cope with the problem?  The simplest way in this
case is to accomplish the incrementing of MALE-COUNTER before we
determine whether the male is married or not; obviously, the same
applies to females.  Thus, we might write:

```
IF MALE
    ADD 1 TO MALE-COUNTER
    IF MARRIED
        ADD 1 TO MARRIED-MEN
    ELSE
        ADD 1 TO SINGLE-MEN
ELSE
    ADD 1 TO FEMALE-COUNTER
    IF MARRIED
        ADD 1 TO MARRIED-WOMEN
    ELSE
        ADD 1 TO SINGLE-WOMEN.
```

Q.  Is there any other easy way of accomplishing the
    incrementing of MALE-COUNTER and FEMALE-COUNTER?

A.  One way that comes to mind is to compute MALE-
    COUNTER and FEMALE-COUNTER separately, after
    the nested IF has been executed.  Thus, we
    would have:

```
IF MALE
    IF MARRIED
        ADD 1 TO MARRIED-MEN
    ELSE
        ADD 1 TO SINGLE-MEN
ELSE
    IF MARRIED
        ADD 1 TO MARRIED-WOMEN
    ELSE
        ADD 1 TO SINGLE-WOMEN.
ADD MARRIED-MEN SINGLE-MEN
        GIVING MALE-COUNTER.
ADD MARRIED-WOMEN SINGLE-WOMEN
        GIVING FEMALE-COUNTER.
```

While we're on the subject of minor issues that can become major problems, we should point out that it's not always practical to solve the block-structure problem by moving a statement back before the IF statement (as we did with the ADD 1 TO MALE-COUNTER in the example above).  For example, suppose we decided that MALE-COUNTER should be computed each time by adding MARRIED-MEN to SINGLE-MEN to produce the result.  Our initial attempt might be as follows:

```
IF MALE                                  *
    IF MARRIED                           *
        ADD 1 TO MARRIED-MEN             *    THIS IS AN
    ELSE                                 *
        ADD 1 TO SINGLE-MEN              *    EXAMPLE
    ADD MARRIED-MEN SINGLE-MEN           *
            GIVING MALE-COUNTER          *       OF
ELSE                                     *
    IF MARRIED                           *    INCORRECT
        ADD 1 TO MARRIED-WOMEN           *
    ELSE                                 *      CODE
        ADD 1 TO SINGLE-WOMEN            *
    ADD MARRIED-WOMEN SINGLE-WOMEN       *
            GIVING FEMALE-COUNTER.       *
```

However, as we've already discovered, this code will compute MALE-COUNTER only for unmarried males, and FEMALE-COUNTER only for unmarried females.  So, we could attempt to solve the problem as we did before, by moving the computational statement before the appropriate IF MARRIED clause; this would give us:

```
IF MALE                                  *
    ADD MARRIED-MEN SINGLE-MEN           *
            GIVING MALE-COUNTER          *    THIS IS AN
    IF MARRIED                           *
        ADD 1 TO MARRIED-MEN             *     EXAMPLE
    ELSE                                 *
        ADD 1 TO SINGLE-MEN              *       OF
ELSE                                     *
    ADD MARRIED-WOMEN SINGLE-WOMEN       *    INCORRECT
            GIVING FEMALE-COUNTER        *
    IF MARRIED                           *       CODE
        ADD 1 TO MARRIED-WOMEN           *
    ELSE                                 *
        ADD 1 TO SINGLE-WOMEN.           *
```

Unfortunately, this doesn't do what we want it to do either. The way we've coded things now, MALE-COUNTER is computed <u>before</u> we've incremented MARRIED-MEN (or SINGLE-MEN, as the case may be) ... which means that MALE-COUNTER is off by one. Assuming that this IF statement occurs in the middle of a loop that is executed once for each person in a large file, the result will be that the program concludes with MARRIED-MEN, SINGLE-MEN, MARRIED-WOMEN, and SINGLE-WOMEN computed correctly, but MALE-COUNTER and FEMALE-COUNTER computed incorrectly.

There is one remaining aspect of nested IFs that you must learn about: the "null" ELSE. It can be illustrated by suggesting still another variation on our original problem. Suppose we have decided to count only the married men and the married women; unmarried men and unmarried women are of no interest to us, and should not be counted. Our first attempt might result in the following code:

```
        IF MALE                         *   THIS IS AN
            IF MARRIED                   *
                ADD 1 TO MARRIED-MEN     *   EXAMPLE OF
        ELSE                             *
            IF MARRIED                   *   INCORRECT
                ADD 1 TO MARRIED-WOMEN.  *

                                             CODE
```

Sad to say, this code doesn't do what we wanted to accomplish. A general rule of COBOL is that ELSE clauses are matched with IF clauses much the way right parentheses are paired with left parentheses in an arithmetic expression; specifically, an ELSE is matched up with the last preceding unmatched IF clause in the statement.

Q.   Reformat the statement above to show this matching.

A.   IF MALE
         IF MARRIED
             ADD 1 TO MARRIED-MEN
         ELSE
             IF MARRIED
                 ADD 1 TO MARRIED-WOMEN.

In other words, this code says that if the subject is female, <u>no</u> counter is incremented; if the subject is male, then another <u>test</u> is made to see if he is married -- in which case MARRIED-MEN is incremented. If the subject is male but unmarried, the logic falls into the ELSE clause, in which another useless test is made to see if he is married!

So, how do we get the COBOL statements to do what we originally wanted to do -- count married men and married women, but ignore unmarried men and unmarried women?  It turns out that the ELSE NEXT SENTENCE clause is particularly appropriate for saying "otherwise, do nothing."  Our code now reads:

```
IF MALE
    IF MARRIED
        ADD 1 TO MARRIED-MEN
    ELSE
        NEXT SENTENCE
ELSE
    IF MARRIED
        ADD 1 TO MARRIED-WOMEN
    ELSE
        NEXT SENTENCE.
```

The first NEXT SENTENCE clause does just what we want:  It says, "There really isn't anything more to do -- processing should continue at the next COBOL sentence."  Its effect, then, is to allow us to skip around all of the logic pertaining to females.  The second NEXT SENTENCE clause has the same effect, but it turns out to be redundant; there is nothing left to skip around, since it occurred at the very end of the nested IF statement.  Then, we would accomplish the same thing by writing the code as:

```
IF MALE
    IF MARRIED
        ADD 1 TO MARRIED-MEN
    ELSE
        NEXT SENTENCE
ELSE
    IF MARRIED
        ADD 1 TO MARRIED-WOMEN.
```

We highly recommend that you use ELSE NEXT SENTENCE (where appropriate) to ensure that you have an ELSE to match each IF.  Once you have gone through this exercise, you can eliminate the redundant ELSE NEXT SENTENCEs at the end of the nested IF.

Suppose that we had defined "condition names" to allow us to separately distinguish the categories of single men, married men, single women, and married women.  In that case, the nested IF statement that we have been studying throughout this section could be rewritten in the following form:

```
IF SINGLE-MALE
    ADD 1 TO SINGLE-MALE-COUNTER
ELSE
    IF MARRIED-MALE
        ADD 1 TO MARRIED-MALE-COUNTER
    ELSE
        IF SINGLE-FEMALE
            ADD 1 TO SINGLE-FEMALE-COUNTER
        ELSE
            IF MARRIED-FEMALE
                ADD 1 TO MARRIED-FEMALE-COUNTER
            ELSE
                ADD 1 TO UNUSUAL-PERSON-COUNTER.
```

We can understand why such a logic structure has been termed a "case"; it simply asks, "Which case are we dealing with; a single male, a married male, a single female, a married female, or some other kind of person?"  Only one of these cases is presumed to be true, and the nested IF statement is simply trying to find out which one.


You can see that such a structure can be extended indefinitely without becoming too hard to read; that is, you should be able to write a "case" structure with 198 different cases, and someone else should be able to read it easily.  However, if we continue to indent each case by four spaces on our coding sheet, we shall obviously run out of room after eight or ten levels.  Moreover, since the logic is not really of the "level-within-level-within-level" type but rather of the "which-one-of-the-following-N-cases" type, there is really no need to indent each successive statement on the coding sheet.  The previous statement is just as readable if written:

```
IF      SINGLE-MALE
        ADD 1 TO SINGLE-MALE-COUNTER
ELSE IF MARRIED-MALE
        ADD 1 TO MARRIED-MALE-COUNTER
ELSE IF SINGLE-FEMALE
        ADD 1 TO SINGLE-FEMALE-COUNTER
ELSE IF MARRIED-FEMALE
        ADD 1 TO MARRIED-FEMALE-COUNTER
ELSE
        ADD 1 TO UNUSUAL-PERSON-COUNTER.
```

This case structure is shown in a structured flowchart like this:

| SINGLE-MALE | MARRIED-MALE | SINGLE-FEMALE | MARRIED-FEMALE | DEFAULT |
|---|---|---|---|---|
| ADD 1 TO SINGLE-MALE-COUNTER | ADD 1 TO MARRIED-MALE-COUNTER | ADD 1 TO SINGLE-FEMALE-COUNTER | ADD 1 TO MARRIED-FEMALE-COUNTER | ADD 1 TO UNUSUAL-PERSON-COUNTER |

The default case is handled by the trailing ELSE; it is obeyed if all the earlier tests fail.

Q. Write a case structure which tests a two-digit card code and writes the corresponding part-name as a literal in a field called PART-NAME, PIC X(15) according to the following table

| Code | Part-Name |
|---|---|
| 06 | 12 IN. RULER |
| 07 | 24 IN. RULER |
| 19 | PENCILS, GROSS |
| 21 | PENS, BALL-POINT |
| 27 | TEMPLATE |

A.
```
IF       CODE = 06
    MOVE '12 IN. RULER' TO PART-NAME
ELSE IF CODE = 07
    MOVE '24 IN. RULER' TO PART-NAME
ELSE IF CODE = 19
    MOVE 'PENCILS, GROSS' TO PART-NAME
etc.
```

The complexity of nested IFs arises mainly when the problem demands levels of IFs within IFs; that is by COBOL statements of the form

```
IF a
     IF b
          IF c
and so forth.
```

The reason this is complicated is that the person who reads your program has to keep several things in his head simultaneously; in the example above, he has to think about all possible combinations of a, b, and c at the same time. Naturally, you have also to worry about all combinations of a, b, and c when you write the code, which is equally difficult.

How can you circumvent this complexity?  The first answer, of course, is not to work on such complex problems!  Another, more serious solution, is to express some or all of such logic with the "complex tests" that we discussed in Section 6.1.5. That is, instead of writing three levels of nested IFs as we did just above, we may well be able to write

```
IF a AND b AND c
```

A dead giveaway in situations of this sort is the sequence of code

```
IF X
     IF Y
          IF Z
               MOVE A TO B
          ELSE NEXT SENTENCE
     ELSE NEXT SENTENCE
ELSE NEXT SENTENCE.
```

This should certainly be rewritten in the form

```
IF X AND Y AND Z
     MOVE A TO B.
```

Still another way of simplifying deeply nested IF structures is to break the job into smaller pieces, each one of which can be written and comprehended separately.  You may recall that earlier in this section, we paraphrased our nested IF example by writing

```
IF MALE
     male-logic
ELSE
     FEMALE-logic
```

- 120 -

There is a formal way of doing this in COBOL; we would
write

```
        IF MALE
            PERFORM MALE-LOGIC
        ELSE
            PERFORM FEMALE-LOGIC.
```

In some other part of our program, we would have the paragraph
of logic named MALE-LOGIC that would carry out the familiar
processing

```
        MALE-LOGIC.
            IF MARRIED
                ADD 1 TO MARRIED-MEN
            ELSE
                ADD 1 TO SINGLE-MEN.
```

This makes use of the concept of <u>subroutines</u> in which a large
complex structure can be tackled by breaking it into smaller
bite-sized chunks.


As we mentioned in the section on complex logic tests,
as soon as a nested IF becomes too complicated to handle
comfortably, you should analyze the problem with a decision
table, as described in the next section.

A decision table is an extension of the truth table we saw earlier, and is very valuable for analyzing problems. Suppose you have to write a program which deals with the following problem:

If a customer has placed an order which exceeds his credit limit, then the order should be sent to the credit department.  However, the order should always be accepted if it comes from one of our special customers, i.e., one who does business with us regularly and whose credit has been assured.  Also, if the order is less than the minimum shipping quantity, the order should be rejected and sent to the shipping manager.  However, the computer system should be capable of receiving "exceptions" to these rules, as there will be cases when a customer will insist that his order be shipped, even though it is too small.

There are four conditions, or variables, in this problem:

- the dollar order amount exceeds the credit limit

- the customer has special approval from the credit department

- the size of the order is less than the minimum allowed for shipping

- the shipping department has given special approval for shipment.

There are three possible actions that the program might be required to take:

- the order can be rejected and sent to the credit department

- the order can be rejected and sent to the shipping department

- the order can be processed normally.


We want to show the somewhat complicated relationship between conditions and actions as clearly as possible, and the best way of doing it is with a decision table as shown on the next page.

*This rule shows what to do with one particular*
*combination of conditions: If it is <u>true</u> that the*
*dollar amount of the order exceeds the credit limit*
*<u>and</u> the customer <u>does</u> <u>not</u> have special approval,*
*<u>and</u> the size of the order is <u>not</u> less than minimum,*
*<u>and</u> the customer <u>does</u> <u>not</u> have special approval*
*from the shipping department,*
*<u>then</u> reject the order and send it to the*
*credit department.*

Rules

| Conditions and actions | 1 | 2 | 3 | 4 | 5 | 6 | 7 | 8 | 9 | 10 | 11 | 12 | 13 | 14 | 15 | 16 |
|---|---|---|---|---|---|---|---|---|---|---|---|---|---|---|---|---|
| Dollar amount of order exceeds credit limit | F | F | F | F | F | F | F | F | T | T | T | T | T | T | T | T |
| Cust. has sp. approval from credit department | F | F | F | F | T | T | T | T | F | F | F | F | T | T | T | T |
| Size of order is less than minimum | F | F | T | T | F | F | T | T | F | F | T | T | F | F | T | T |
| Cust has sp. approval from shipping dept. | F | T | F | T | F | T | F | T | F | T | F | T | F | T | F | T |
| REJECT ORDER, SEND TO CREDIT DEPT. | | | | | | | | | X | X | X | X | | | | |
| REJECT ORDER, SEND TO SHIPPING DEPT. | | | X | | | | X | | | | X | | | | X | |
| PROCESS ORDER AND SHIP IT NORMALLY | X | X | | | X | X | | X | | | | | X | X | | X |

*These are the four conditions.*

*These are the three actions.*

*Note that this rule calls for two rejections;*
*we will assume that only Action 1 is necessary.*

The conditions, or variables, that form the top rows of the decision table are often referred to as <u>condition stubs</u>; we shall just call them conditions. In our example we have four conditions.

Similarly, our example contains three actions, often called <u>action stubs</u>. Note that the action stubs form the lower rows of <u>the decision</u> table, and that they represent computations to be performed, or in a general sense, procedures to be executed.

The most important part of the decision table is the <u>rules</u>. A rule is simply a specification that certain combinations of conditions should cause certain actions to be performed. Indeed, this is just what the narrative description of our order entry problem contains; but the rules in the narrative description are generally less precisely stated, more error-prone, and more subject to misinterpretation. The rules form the columns of the diagram; note that they are numbered at the top, but that this is done just as a convenient way of referring to them.  The rules can be in a variety of orders, depending on the alternation of sequence of "True" and "False" for the conditions.


As you will see from the example, the way to be sure you have covered all possible combination of conditions is:

- start with the last condition (in this case "Customer has special approval from the Shipping Department") and alternate F T F T  (or T F T F)

- for the next-to-last condition, alternate F F T T (or T T F F)

- as you work up, alternate in groups which in each case are twice as large as for the condition immediately below them.


Q.  How do you know how many combinations of conditions (rules) to allow for?

A.  In this type of decision table (called <u>exhaustive</u> because it exhaustively covers all the possible combinations) there will be $2^C$ rules, where C is the number of conditions.


Q.  Redraw the decision table, with the conditions and actions in the same order, but alternating T F instead of F T

A.  Your decision table should look like this:

*Rules*

| Conditions and actions | 16 | 15 | 14 | 13 | 12 | 11 | 10 | 9 | 8 | 7 | 6 | 5 | 4 | 3 | 2 | 1 |
|---|---|---|---|---|---|---|---|---|---|---|---|---|---|---|---|---|
| Dollar amount of order exceeds credit limit | T | T | T | T | T | T | T | T | F | F | F | F | F | F | F | F |
| Cust. has sp. approval from credit department | T | T | T | T | F | F | F | F | T | T | T | T | F | F | F | F |
| Size of order is less than minimum | T | T | F | F | T | T | F | F | T | T | F | F | T | T | F | F |
| Cust. has sp. approval from shipping dept. | T | F | T | F | T | F | T | F | | | | | | | | |
| REJECT ORDER, SEND TO CREDIT DEPT | | | | | X | X | X | X | | | | | | | | |
| REJECT ORDER, SEND TO SHIPPING DEPT | | X | | | X | | | | | X | | | | X | | |
| PROCESS ORDER AND SHIP IT NORMALLY | X | | X | X | | | | | X | | X | X | X | | X | X |

Note that we have kept the original numbering of the rules.

- 124 -

This decision table deals with conditions which are either true or false; it is called a limited entry decision table.   You may sometimes meet extended entry decision tables in which the conditions can have three, four, or more values. Extended entry  tables are more awkward to work with and we will not deal with them until Chapter 13 , in Part II.


We have already said that ours is an exhaustive decision table; a selective decision table contains only those rules that you can find in the original specification of the problem. Imagine a programmer trying to develop a decision table from the simple order entry problem described earlier.   He might notice that there are only three unique situations mentioned in the narrative specification; if the customer has exceeded his limit and is not a special customer, then his order should be rejected; if the customer has placed an order too small for shipment and does not have special approval from the shipping department, then his order should be rejected; otherwise, his order should be filled.   This situation may be represented by the selective decision table below, which has only three rules:

| Dollar amount of order exceeds credit limit | T | - |     |
|---|---|---|---|
| Cust. has special approval from credit dept. | F | - | E |
| Size of order is less than minimum | - | T | S |
| Cust. has special approval from shipping dept. | - | F | L |
|  |  |  | E |
| REJECT ORDER, SEND TO CREDIT DEPT. | X |  |  |
| REJECT ORDER, SEND TO SHIPPING DEPT. |  | X |  |
| PROCESS ORDER AND SHIP NORMALLY |  |  | X |

Note that there are two items in this new decision table that did not appear in the original exhaustive table: the "-" entry for some of the rules and the "else" rule.


The "-", or "dash" entry represents a "don't care" situation; that is we don't care if the specified condition is true or false because the action is the same in either case.


The "else" rule has an effect similar to the ELSE in COBOL.   In the case of the decision table above, we see that if rule #1 is satisfied, we will perform action #1, if rule #2 is satisfied, we will perform action #2, otherwise, the "else" rule will take effect, and we will perform action #3. Note that in this case, using the "else" saves us several rules.

Q.   How many rules in the exhaustive decision table
     are replaced by the "else" rule in the selective
     table?

A.   Nine:   rules 1, 2, 4, 5, 6, 8, 13, 14, and 16.


The primary difference between the exhaustive decision
table and the selective decision table is one of emphasis and
orientation.  In the case of the exhaustive table, we <u>first</u>
write down all $2^C$ combinations of conditions, and <u>then</u> go back
to the narrative specification of the problem to determine
which action should accompany each combination of conditions
(note that we did not use the word "rule" in this sentence;
we don't have a rule until <u>after</u> we have associated an action
with a set of conditions).  In the case of the selective
table, we <u>first</u> look at the narrative description of the
problem, and <u>then</u> try to write down the rules that are, in
effect, a more precise restatement of the problem.


This difference of orientation is often overlooked because of more practical aspects of the selective or exhaustive
approach.  If we have only a small number of conditions --
perhaps 2, or 3, or 4 -- then it is quite easy to write down
all $2^C$ possible combinations, using the nice easy "binary
counting sequence" of T F T F, etc.  In any case, by forcing
ourselves to write down <u>all</u> possible rules, we know that
we haven't overlooked any, and this can be a major consideration.


On the other hand, the exhaustive approach can be
exhaust<u>ing</u>!  It is quite usual to find an order entry policy
with ten conditions.  Much as we might like to, it would
clearly be impractical to write down all $2^{10}$ (1,024) possible
combinations.  Hence, we may be forced to choose the selective
approach.

The Marketing Manager and Comptroller of the company you work for have decided that they will open credit accounts for the people who have applied, with a credit limit based on the following policy:

A person's credit ceiling is set at a certain multiple of their monthly discretionary income, computed as follows:

For married persons who own their homes and have been two years or more at their present job.............................5 times

For married persons who either own their own homes or have been two years or more in their present jobs......................4 times

For persons not now married who are home-owners and have been two years or more in their present jobs........................3 times

For married persons who rent homes and for unmarried home-owners who have less than two years' service in their jobs......2 times

For single, widowed, or divorced persons who rent their homes......................an amount
                                             equal to their
                                             discretionary
                                             income

Notwithstanding the above, no one will receive a credit limit of more than $2,500.

You are required to produce a program called CREDCALC, which is an upgrade of SAMPLE-4. As well as calculating monthly discretionary income, CREDCALC will calculate the credit limit for each person according to the above policy, and print out the credit limit on the third line of each profile.

As a first step to this, let us produce a decision table covering the credit limit policy above.

    Q.    How many conditions are there?
           How many actions are there?

A.    Three conditions:    Married -- yes or no
                           Owner -- yes or no
                           Two or more years
                           in present job -- yes or no

Five actions corresponding to multiples of
discretionary income from 1 to 5

Note that the upper limit of $2,500 should not be
considered as part of the decision table, but should
be applied once the credit limit is calculated as a
multiple of income.

Since there are three conditions, there will be eight
rules for an exhaustive table.  We can draw up an exhaustive
limited entry decision table to represent the credit policy:

| | | 1 | 2 | 3 | 4 | 5 | 6 | 7 | 8 |
|---|---|---|---|---|---|---|---|---|---|
| Married? | | Y | Y | Y | Y | N | N | N | N |
| Home-owner? | | Y | Y | N | N | Y | Y | N | N |
| 2 or more years in job? | | Y | N | Y | N | Y | N | Y | N |
| Credit limit is this multiple of discr. income. | 1 times | | | | | | | X | X |
| | 2 times | | | | X | | X | | |
| | 3 times | | | | | X | | | |
| | 4 times | | X | X | | | | | |
| | 5 times | X | | | | | | | |

Can we simplify this decision table?  Yes, a little.
Consider rules 7 and 8:  They both lead to the same action
and have the same combination of Y and N except for one condition.  This means that we can put in a - (meaning "don't care")
for this condition, and reduce the two rules to one rule:

| | 7 |
|---|---|
| | N |
| | N |
| | - |
| 1 times | X |

This is in accordance with the original policy; if the person
is not married, and not an owner, he/she gets a credit limit of
one multiple, no matter how long he/she has been in a job.

Q.  Using the 88 levels MARRIED, OWNED, and STABLE-JOB
    as the conditions, and MOVE 1 TO CREDIT-FACTOR, etc.,
    as the actions, code the decision table as a
    nested IF.

A.

```
IF MARRIED
    IF OWNED
        IF STABLE-JOB
            MOVE 5 TO CREDIT-FACTOR
        ELSE
            MOVE 4 TO CREDIT-FACTOR
    ELSE
        IF STABLE-JOB
            MOVE 4 TO CREDIT-FACTOR
        ELSE
            MOVE 2 TO CREDIT-FACTOR
ELSE
    IF OWNED
        IF STABLE-JOB
            MOVE 3 TO CREDIT-FACTOR
        ELSE
            MOVE 2 TO CREDIT-FACTOR
    ELSE
        MOVE 1 TO CREDIT-FACTOR.
```

Whenever you code a nested IF as complex as this, it is
good practice to include the decision table as a series
of comment lines.

```
VICTOR S GRASPER      PHONE (415) 243-7022    MALE         INCOME       $15700 PER YEAR; IN THIS EMPLOY 04 YEARS
990 GAUNTLET AVE                              SINGLE       MORTGAGE:      $250 PER MTH    DISCRETIONARY INCOME $691 PER MTH
BURLINGAME   CA 94010  A/C: 010101            0 DEPENDENTS OTHER PAYMENTS $040 PER MTH   CREDIT LIMIT IS $2073


IAN S INKERMAN        PHONE (201) 103-6061    MALE         INCOME       $17500 PER YEAR; IN THIS EMPLOY LESS THAN 1 YEAR
59 PECAN VALLEY RD                            DIVORCED     RENTAL:        $325 PER MTH    DISCRETIONARY INCOME $659 PER MTH
MONTVALE     NJ 07645  A/C: 020202            1 DEPENDENTS OTHER PAYMENTS $110 PER MTH   CREDIT LIMIT IS $0659


SARALEE JAMES         PHONE (816) 542-0535    FEMALE       INCOME       $21000 PER YEAR; IN THIS EMPLOY 03 YEARS
PARTHENON COURT                               DIVORCED     MORTGAGE:      $275 PER MTH    DISCRETIONARY INCOME $963 PER MTH
ATHENS       MO 64065  A/C: 050505            1 DEPENDENTS OTHER PAYMENTS $ 75 PER MTH   CREDIT LIMIT IS $2500


SCARLETT O'HARA       PHONE (504) 815-1147    FEMALE       INCOME       $09500 PER YEAR; IN THIS EMPLOY 26 YEARS
SUITE 414 NAT BANK                            WIDOWED      RENTAL:        $110 PER MTH    DISCRETIONARY INCOME $464 PER MTH
NEW ORLEANS  LA 70012  A/C: 060606            2 DEPENDENTS OTHER PAYMENTS $ 20 PER MTH   CREDIT LIMIT IS $0464


SUSAN KRUPMAN         PHONE (212) 354-0330    FEMALE       INCOME       $12900 PER YEAR; IN THIS EMPLOY 01 YEARS
131 WEST 32ND ST                              SINGLE       RENTAL:        $150 PER MTH    DISCRETIONARY INCOME $626 PER MTH
NEW YORK     NY 10001  A/C: 040404            0 DEPENDENTS OTHER PAYMENTS $ 30 PER MTH   CREDIT LIMIT IS $0626


I. MORRIS GOOD        PHONE (214) 225-7013    MALE         INCOME       $27300 PER YEAR; IN THIS EMPLOY 11 YEARS
1313 PORPOISE                                 MARRIED      MORTGAGE:      $400 PER MTH    DISCRETIONARY INCOME $999 PER MTH
DALLAS       TX 75219  A/C: 030303            4 DEPENDENTS OTHER PAYMENTS $150 PER MTH   CREDIT LIMIT IS $2500


FRANCES PAISANO       PHONE (201) 614-7525    FEMALE       INCOME       $96000 PER YEAR; IN THIS EMPLOY LESS THAN 1 YEAR
2521 EDGE STREET                              SINGLE       MORTGAGE:      $100 PER MTH    DISCRETIONARY INCOME $999 PER MTH
FORT LEE     NJ 07024  A/C: 070707            0 DEPENDENTS OTHER PAYMENTS $050 PER MTH   CREDIT LIMIT IS $1998


FIRST CARD  GOOD  STARLET Q. FREEBODY 12277 SUNSET BLVD  LOS ANGELES CA90024213574-2179   080808
SECOND CARD GOOD  C080807 F S 0 C60 00 R 350 100                                                    ACCOUNT NUMBERS DO NOT MATCH


FIRST CARD  BAD   DR P.QUACKENBUSH   **** ADDRESS MISSING ****        602852-4822   090909
SECOND CARD GOOD  C090909 M M 8 120 10 0 320 135


FIRST CARD  GOOD  C. ENCHAINE      212 SLEEPY HOLLOW DRGREENWICH    CT06830203886-7431   101010
SECONC CARD BAD   X101010 F S 1 130 08 R 240 050


FIRST CARD        B. HUGH THOMPSON   1111 SUTTER      SAN FRANCISCOCA94103413263-4857   111111
SECOND CARD       M S 0 065 00 R 360 110                                                     OUTGO EXCEEDS INCOME: REJECT


*********************************************************************************************************************
*                                                                                                                   *
*  TOTAL CREDIT GIVEN: $0010920    AVERAGE CREDIT GIVEN: $001545 ON 0007 ACCEPTED APPLICATIONS.    NUMBER REJECTED 004 *
*                                                                                                                   *
*********************************************************************************************************************
```

Figure 6.1   Applicant credit limit report

Now that we have the decision table and the essential logic, we can proceed to implement CREDCALC. Here is the full functional specification:

Main function. CREDCALC is to read in the same pairs of cards as SAMPLE-4, and print a similar report, with the exception that under DISCRETIONARY INCOME will be printed CREDIT LIMIT IS $nnnn, where nnnn is the amount determined by company policy as already stated.

Heading. The first page of this report is to be headed
          APPLICANT CREDIT LIMIT REPORT

Editing. CREDCALC should check the input cards for missing name, missing address, missing phone, and account numbers not matching. CREDCALC must also check to be sure that the second card of each pair has a 'C' in cc 1. If any of these errors is found, both cards should be rejected, and their contents written out, one card to a line, with a suitable error message indicating what is wrong. Similarly, if a pair of cards passes these editing tests, but the discretionary income turns out to be negative, both cards should be rejected.

Summary report. After all the cards have been read, calculate the average credit limit granted to each accepted applicant, and print out a one-line summary, with a border of asterisks, stating total credit granted, average credit granted per accepted applicant, number of applications accepted, number of applications rejected.


     Figure 6.1 on the opposite page shows a sample of the report required; four pairs of cards containing some error follow seven valid applications.


     From this functional specification, draw up a program graph showing the main flow of data and the main transformations. Don't show errors on the program graph. Then draw up a structure chart, breaking down the major functions into single independent ones, and indicating which modules will need to perform error-handling modules.


     Then compare your charts with the samples on the next page.

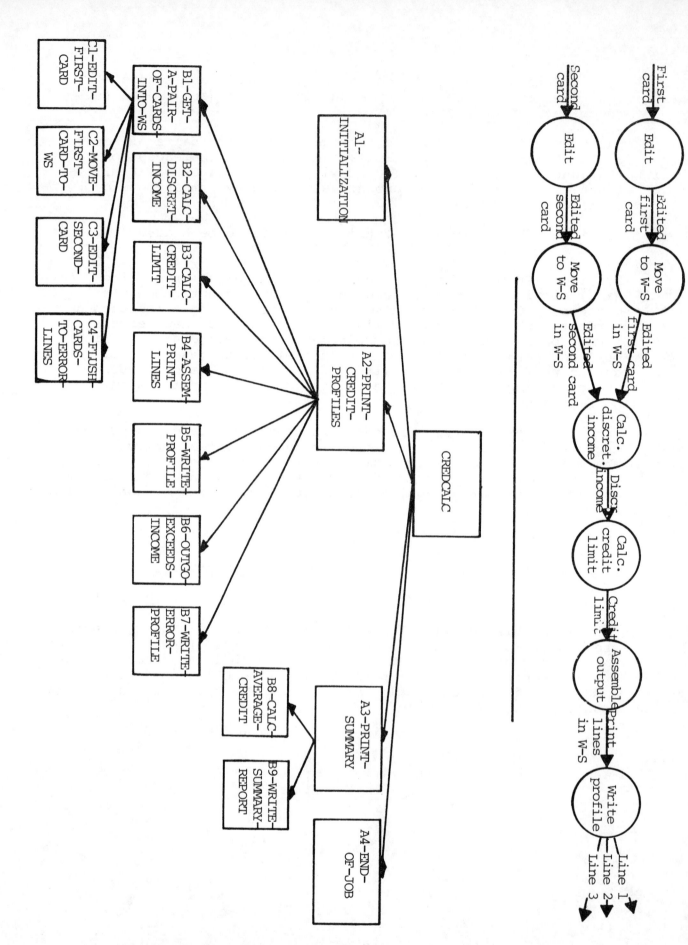

Figure 6.2   Sample program graph and structure chart

From the structure chart opposite, you can see that the key module is A2-PRINT-CREDIT-PROFILES. The highest-level "executive" module will PERFORM this until all the cards have been read, when it will go on to PERFORM A3-PRINT-SUMMARY.

The pseudocode for A2-PRINT-CREDIT-PROFILES is:

```
Get a pair of cards.
IF pair of cards passes the edit tests
    calculate discretionary income
    IF discretionary income is positive
        calculate credit limit
        assemble print lines
        write normal credit profile
    ELSE
        write the cards as an error profile with
            message OUTGO EXCEEDS INCOME
ELSE
    write the cards as an error profile with
        message indicating error.
```

Once again assume you have available to you in the SSL all the data structures and procedures which you used in SAMPLE-4, with the addition of

DISCR-INCOME-CALC-FIELDS (called DISIFLDS) and

CALC-DISCRETNRY-INCOME    (called DISCINCM)

You will need to set up Data Division entries for the fields used in calculating credit limit. It is good practice to set up data-names FACTOR1, FACTOR2, etc., for the various values of CREDIT-FACTOR, and for UPPER-LIMIT ($2,500), and to set these fields to the specified amounts with VALUE clauses.

Q.    What is the value of using data-names in this way? Why not code literals in the program?

A.    It is a safeguard in case of change; if the policy were to change, say to allow an upper limit of $3,000, you would only have to change the value once in Working Storage, and you would be sure the correct value would be used wherever you had referred to it.

You will also need to set up formats for the initial heading, for the error-lines, and for the summary report lines.

When you have done this, you will be ready to write the pseudocode for the whole of CREDCALC from the structure chart and from the suggestions already given. Get a colleague to walk-through your pseudocode with you, to see if he can spot any errors in logic, before you code the Data Division and the Procedure Division.

The model solution to CREDCALC given on the following pages is a listing of the cards as you would punch them (called an "80:80" listing because the 80 columns on the card are shown in the first 80 print positions).

Following that is a complete listing of the program with the COPY statements expended by the compiler.

```
IDENTIFICATION DIVISICN.
PRCGRAM-ID.  CREDCALC.

ENVIRONMENT DIVISICN.
INPUT-OUTPUT SECTION.
FILE-CCNTROL. COPY FILECONT.

DATA DIVISION.
FILE SECTION.

FD  APPLICATION-CARDS-FILE  COPY FDCARDS.

FD  PROFILE-LISTING
        LABEL RECORDS ARE OMITTED.
01  PRINT-LINE-OUT                    PIC X(132).
WORKING-STORAGE SECTICN.

01  COMMON-WS.
    05   CARDS-LEFT              PIC X(3).
    05   FIRST-CARD              PIC X(4).
    05   SECONC-CARD             PIC X(4).
    05   ACCT-NUM-MATCH          PIC X(4).
    05   PAIR-VALIDITY           PIC X(4).
    05   APPLICATICNS-ACCEPTED-ACCUM PIC 9(4).
    05   APPLICATIONS-REJECTED-ACCUM PIC 9(4).

01  HEADER-WS1.
    05   FILLER                  PIC X(52)     VALUE SPACES.
    05   TITLE                   PIC X(29)
                    VALUE 'APPLICANT CREDIT LIMIT REPORT'.
    05   FILLER                  PIC X(52)     VALUE SPACES.

01  APPLICATION-DATA-WSB1 COPY CARDSWS.

01  DISCR-INCCME-CALC-FIELDS-WSB2  COPY DISIFLDS.

01  CRED-LIMIT-CALC-FIELDS-WSB3.
    05   CREDIT-FACTOR           PIC 9.
    05   FACTOR1                 PIC 9        VALUE 1.
    05   FACTOR2                 PIC 9        VALUE 2.
    05   FACTOR3                 PIC 9        VALUE 3.
    05   FACTOR4                 PIC 9        VALUE 4.
    05   FACTOR5                 PIC 9        VALUE 5.
    05   CREDIT-LIMIT-WS         PIC 9(4).
    05   UPPER-LIMIT-WS          PIC 9(4)     VALUE 2500.
    05   TOTAL-CREDIT-GIVEN-WS   PIC 9(7).

01  LINE-1-WSB4 COPY LINE1WS.
```

Figure 6.3    CREDCALC, 80:80 listing, page 1 of 7

```
01   LINE-2-WSB4 COPY LINE2WS.
     05  FILLER                      PIC X(11)
                                     VALUE ' PER MTH    '.
     05  FILLER                      PIC X(22)
                                     VALUE 'DISCRETIONARY INCOME $'.
     05  DISCR-INCOME-L2             PIC 9(3).
     05  FILLER                      PIC X(9)
                                     VALUE ' PER MTH '.


01   LINE-3-WSB4 COPY LINE3WS.
     05  FILLER                      PIC X(8)     VALUE ' PER MTH'.
     05  FILLER                      PIC X(20)
                   VALUE '   CREDIT LIMIT IS $'.
     05  CREDIT-LIMIT-L3             PIC 9(4).


01   LINE-OF-ASTERISKS-WSB9.
     05  FILLER                      PIC X(6)     VALUE '      *'.
     05  FILLER                      PIC X(120)
         VALUE '************************************************************
         '************************************************************
         '**********'.
     05  FILLER                      PIC X(6)     VALUE '*      '.


01   SIDE-DELIMITER-WSB9.
     05  FILLER                      PIC X(6)     VALUE '      *'.
     05  FILLER                      PIC X(120)   VALUE SPACES.
     05  FILLER                      PIC X(6)     VALUE '*      '.


01   SUMMARY-LINE-WSB9.
     05  FILLER                      PIC X(6)     VALUE '      *'.
     05  FILLER                      PIC X(24)
                   VALUE '   TOTAL CREDIT GIVEN: $'.
     05  TOTAL-CREDIT-GIVEN          PIC 9(7).
     05  FILLER                      PIC X(27)
                   VALUE '     AVERAGE CREDIT GIVEN: $'.
     05  AVERAGE-CREDIT              PIC 9(6).
     05  FILLER                      PIC X(4)     VALUE ' ON '.
     05  APPLICATIONS-ACCEPTED       PIC 9(4).
     05  FILLER                      PIC X(24)
                   VALUE ' ACCEPTED APPLICATIONS. '.
     05  FILLER                      PIC X(20)
                   VALUE '   NUMBER REJECTED '.
     05  APPLICATIONS-REJECTED       PIC 9(3).
     05  FILLER                      PIC X(10)
                   VALUE ' *        '.
```

Figure 6.3 continued.   CREDCALC, 80:80 listing, page 2 of 7

```
01   CARD-ERROR-LINE1-WSC4.
     05  FILLER                       PIC X(5)      VALUE SPACES.
     05  FILLER                       PIC X(12)
                          VALUE 'FIRST CARD  '.
     05  FIRST-CARD-ERR1              PIC X(4).
     05  FILLER                       PIC XX        VALUE SPACES.
     05  NAME-ERR1                    PIC X(20).
     05  ADDRESS-ERR1                 PIC X(40).
     05  PHONE-ERR1                   PIC X(11).
     05  FILLER                       PIC X(3)      VALUE SPACES.
     05  ACCT-NUM-ERR1                PIC 9(6).

01   CARD-ERROR-LINE2-WSC4.
     05  FILLER                       PIC X(5)      VALUE SPACES.
     05  FILLER                       PIC X(12)
                          VALUE 'SECOND CARD '.
     05  SECOND-CARD-ERR2             PIC X(4).
     05  FILLER                       PIC X(2)      VALUE SPACES.
     05  CREDIT-INFO-ERR2             PIC X(80).
     05  MESSAGE-ERR-LINE-2           PIC X(29)     VALUE SPACES.
```

Figure 6.3 continued.   CREDCALC, 80:80 listing, page 3 of 7

```
      PROCEDURE DIVISION.
          PERFORM A1-INITIALIZATION.
          PERFORM A2-PRINT-CREDIT-PROFILES
            UNTIL CARDS-LEFT = 'NO '.
          PERFORM A3-PRINT-SUMMARY.
          PERFORM A4-END-OF-JOB.
          STOP RUN.
      A1-INITIALIZATION.
          OPEN INPUT APPLICATION-CARDS-FILE
                OUTPUT PROFILE-LISTING.
          WRITE PRINT-LINE-OUT FROM HEADER-WS1
                            AFTER ADVANCING 2 LINES.
          MOVE ZEROES TO APPLICATIONS-ACCEPTED-ACCUM.
          MOVE ZEROES TO APPLICATIONS-REJECTED-ACCUM.
          MOVE ZEROES TO ANNUAL-INCOME-WS.
          MOVE ZEROES TO ANNUAL-TAX-WS.
          MOVE ZEROES TO MONTHLY-NET-INCOME-WS.
          MOVE ZEROES TO MONTHLY-PAYMENTS-WS.
          MOVE ZEROES TO DISCR-INCOME-WS.
          MOVE ZEROES TO CREDIT-FACTOR.
          MOVE ZEROES TO CREDIT-LIMIT-WS.
          MOVE ZEROES TO TOTAL-CREDIT-GIVEN-WS.
          MOVE ZEROES TO TOTAL-CREDIT-GIVEN.
          MOVE ZEROES TO AVERAGE-CREDIT.
          MOVE ZEROES TO APPLICATIONS-ACCEPTED.
          MOVE ZEROES TO APPLICATIONS-REJECTED.
          MOVE SPACES TO FIRST-CARD.
          MOVE SPACES TO SECOND-CARD.
          MOVE SPACES TO ACCT-NUM-MATCH.
          MOVE SPACES TO PAIR-VALIDITY.
          MOVE 'YES' TO CARDS-LEFT.
          READ APPLICATION-CARDS-FILE
             AT END MOVE 'NO ' TO CARDS-LEFT.
    *  FIRST CARD IS NOW IN BUFFER


      A2-PRINT-CREDIT-PROFILES.
          PERFORM B1-GET-A-PAIR-OF-CARDS.
          IF PAIR-VALIDITY = 'GOOD'
              PERFORM B2-CALC-DISCRETNRY-INCOME
              IF DISCR-INCOME-WS IS POSITIVE
                  PERFORM B3-CALC-CREDIT-LIMIT
                  PERFORM B4-ASSEMBLE-PRINT-LINES
                  PERFORM B5-WRITE-PROFILE
              ELSE
                  PERFORM B6-OUTGO-EXCEEDS-INCOME
          ELSE
              PERFORM B7-WRITE-ERROR-PROFILE.

      A3-PRINT-SUMMARY.
          PERFORM B8-CALC-AVERAGE-CREDIT.
          PERFORM B9-WRITE-SUMMARY-REPORT.


      A4-END-OF-JOB.
          CLOSE APPLICATION-CARDS-FILE
                PROFILE-LISTING.
```

Figure 6.3 continued.   CREDCALC, 80:80 listing, page 4 of 7

```
B1-GET-A-PAIR-OF-CARDS.
    PERFORM C1-EDIT-FIRST-CARD.
    PERFORM C2-MOVE-FIRST-CARD-TO-WS.
    READ APPLICATION-CARDS-FILE
        AT END MOVE 'NO ' TO CARDS-LEFT.
* SECOND CARD OF PAIR IS NOW IN BUFFER
    PERFORM C3-EDIT-SECOND-CARD.
    IF      (FIRST-CARD = 'GOOD')
        AND (SECOND-CARD = 'GOOD')
        AND (ACCT-NUM-MATCH = 'GOOD')
            MOVE 'GOOD' TO PAIR-VALIDITY
            MOVE CREDIT-INFO-IN TO CREDIT-INFO-WS
    ELSE
        MOVE 'BAD ' TO PAIR-VALIDITY
        PERFORM C4-FLUSH-CARDS-TO-ERROR-LINES.
    READ APPLICATION-CARDS-FILE
        AT END MOVE 'NO ' TO CARDS-LEFT.
* FIRST CARD OF NEXT PAIR IS NOW IN BUFFER


B2-CALC-DISCRETNRY-INCOME. COPY DISCINCM.


B3-CALC-CREDIT-LIMIT.
*    MARRIED?            Y Y Y Y N N N N    THIS DECISION TABLE      *
*    OWNED?              Y Y N N Y Y N N    SETS OUT COMPANY POLICY  *
*    2 OR MORE YEARS?    Y N Y N Y N Y N    FOR DETERMINING CREDIT   *
*    ------------------------------------   LIMIT FROM DISCRETIONARY *
*    CREDIT   FACTOR1              X X      INCOME. FACTOR1 ETC ARE  *
*    LIMIT IS      2          X X           SET UP IN WSB3.          *
*    MULTIPLE      3            X                                    *
*    OF DISCR      4      X X                                        *
*    INCOME.       5 X                                               *


    IF MARRIED
        IF OWNED
            IF YEARS-EMPLOYED-WS NOT LESS THAN 02
                MOVE FACTOR5 TO CREDIT-FACTOR
            ELSE
                MOVE FACTOR4 TO CREDIT-FACTOR
        ELSE
            IF YEARS-EMPLOYED-WS NOT LESS THAN 02
                MOVE FACTOR4 TO CREDIT-FACTOR
            ELSE
                MOVE FACTOR2 TO CREDIT-FACTOR
    ELSE
        IF OWNED
            IF YEARS-EMPLOYED-WS NOT LESS THAN 02
                MOVE FACTOR3 TO CREDIT-FACTOR
            ELSE
                MOVE FACTOR2 TO CREDIT-FACTOR
        ELSE
            MOVE FACTOR1 TO CREDIT-FACTOR.
    COMPUTE CREDIT-LIMIT-WS = DISCR-INCOME-WS * CREDIT-FACTOR.
    IF CREDIT-LIMIT-WS IS GREATER THAN UPPER-LIMIT-WS
        MOVE UPPER-LIMIT-WS TO CREDIT-LIMIT-WS.
    ADD CREDIT-LIMIT-WS TO TOTAL-CREDIT-GIVEN-WS.
```

Figure 6.3 continued.   CREDCALC, 80:80 listing, page 5 of 7

```
B4-ASSEMBLE-PRINT-LINES.
    MOVE NAME-WS TO NAME-L1.
    MOVE STREET-WS TO STREET-L2.
    MOVE CITY-WS TO CITY-L3.
    MOVE STATE-WS TO STATE-L3.
    MOVE ZIP-WS TO ZIP-L3.
    MOVE AREA-CODE-WS TO AREA-CODE-L1.
    MOVE NUMBR-WS TO NUMBR-L1.
    MOVE ACCT-NUM-WS TO ACCT-NUM-L3.
    IF      MALE    MOVE 'MALE  ' TO SEX-L1
    ELSE IF FEMALE MOVE 'FEMALE' TO SEX-L1
    ELSE               MOVE '******' TO SEX-L1.
    IF       SINGLE   MOVE 'SINGLE  ' TO MARITAL-STATUS-L2
    ELSE IF MARRIED  MOVE 'MARRIED ' TO MARITAL-STATUS-L2
    ELSE IF DIVORCED MOVE 'DIVORCED' TO MARITAL-STATUS-L2
    ELSE IF WIDOWED  MOVE 'WIDOWED ' TO MARITAL-STATUS-L2
    ELSE               MOVE '********' TO MARITAL-STATUS-L2.
    MOVE NUMBER-DEPENS-WS TO NUMBER-DEPENS-L3.
    MOVE INCOME-HUNDREDS-WS TO INCOME-HUNDREDS-L1.
    IF YEARS-EMPLOYED-WS IS EQUAL TO 0
        MOVE 'LESS THAN 1 YEAR' TO YEARS-EMPLOYED-L1
    ELSE
        MOVE YEARS-EMPLOYED-WS TO YEARS-L1
        MOVE ' YEARS        ' TO DESCN-L1.
    IF      OWNED   MOVE 'MORTGAGE:      $' TO OUTGO-DESCN
    ELSE IF RENTED MOVE 'RENTAL:        $' TO OUTGO-DESCN
    ELSE               MOVE '***************' TO OUTGO-DESCN.
    MOVE MORTGAGE-OR-RENTAL-WS TO MORTGAGE-OR-RENTAL-L2.
    MOVE OTHER-PAYMENTS-WS TO OTHER-PAYMENTS-L3.
    MOVE DISCR-INCOME-WS TO DISCR-INCOME-L2.
    MOVE CREDIT-LIMIT-WS TO CREDIT-LIMIT-L3.

B5-WRITE-PROFILE. COPY WRITPRFL
        REPLACING LINE-1-WS BY LINE-1-WSB4
                  LINE-2-WS BY LINE-2-WSB4
                  LINE-3-WS BY LINE-3-WSB4.
    ADD 1 TO APPLICATIONS-ACCEPTED-ACCUM.

B6-OUTGO-EXCEEDS-INCOME.
    MOVE SPACES TO FIRST-CARD-ERR1.
    MOVE NAME-WS TO NAME-ERR1.
    MOVE ADDRESS-WS TO ADDRESS-ERR1.
    MOVE PHONE-WS TO PHONE-ERR1.
    MOVE ACCT-NUM-WS TO ACCT-NUM-ERR1.
    MOVE SPACES TO SECOND-CARD-ERR2.
    MOVE CREDIT-INFO-WS TO CREDIT-INFO-ERR2.
    MOVE 'OUTGO EXCEEDS INCOME: REJECT' TO MESSAGE-ERR-LINE-2.
    PERFORM B7-WRITE-ERROR-PROFILE.

B7-WRITE-ERROR-PROFILE.
    MOVE SPACES TO PRINT-LINE-OUT.
    WRITE PRINT-LINE-OUT FROM CARD-ERROR-LINE1-WSC4
                    AFTER ADVANCING 4 LINES.
    WRITE PRINT-LINE-OUT FROM CARD-ERROR-LINE2-WSC4
                    AFTER ADVANCING 1 LINES.
    ADD 1 TO APPLICATIONS-REJECTED-ACCUM.
```

Figure 6.3 continued.   CREDCALC, 80:80 listing, page 6 of 7

```
B8-CALC-AVERAGE-CREDIT.
    MOVE TOTAL-CREDIT-GIVEN-WS TO TOTAL-CREDIT-GIVEN.
    IF TOTAL-CREDIT-GIVEN = 0
        MOVE ZEROES TO AVERAGE-CREDIT
    ELSE
        DIVIDE APPLICATIONS-ACCEPTED-ACCUM
            INTO TOTAL-CREDIT-GIVEN
            GIVING AVERAGE-CREDIT  ROUNDED.
B9-WRITE-SUMMARY-REPORT.
    MOVE APPLICATIONS-ACCEPTED-ACCUM TO APPLICATIONS-ACCEPTED.
    MOVE APPLICATIONS-REJECTED-ACCUM TO APPLICATIONS-REJECTED.
    WRITE PRINT-LINE-OUT FROM LINE-OF-ASTERISKS-WSB9
                    AFTER ADVANCING 6 LINES.
    WRITE PRINT-LINE-OUT FROM SIDE-DELIMITER-WSB9
                    AFTER ADVANCING 1 LINES.
    WRITE PRINT-LINE-OUT FROM SUMMARY-LINE-WSB9
                    AFTER ADVANCING 1 LINES.
    WRITE PRINT-LINE-OUT FROM SIDE-DELIMITER-WSB9
                    AFTER ADVANCING 1 LINES.
    WRITE PRINT-LINE-OUT FROM LINE-OF-ASTERISKS-WSB9
                    AFTER ADVANCING 1 LINES.
C1-EDIT-FIRST-CARD.
    MOVE 'GOOD' TO FIRST-CARD.
    IF NAME-IN IS EQUAL TO SPACES
        MOVE '*** NAME MISSING ***' TO NAME-IN
        MOVE 'BAD ' TO FIRST-CARD.
    IF ADDRESS-IN IS EQUAL TO SPACES
        MOVE '**** ADDRESS MISSING ****' TO ADDRESS-IN
        MOVE 'BAD ' TO FIRST-CARD.
    IF PHONE-IN IS EQUAL TO SPACES
        MOVE 'NO PHONE **' TO PHONE-IN
        MOVE 'BAD ' TO FIRST-CARD.

C2-MOVE-FIRST-CARD-TO-WS.
    MOVE NAME-IN TO NAME-WS.
    MOVE ADDRESS-IN TO ADDRESS-WS.
    MOVE PHONE-IN TO PHONE-WS.
    MOVE ACCT-NUM-IN1 TO ACCT-NUM-WS.

C3-EDIT-SECOND-CARD.
    MOVE 'GOOD' TO SECOND-CARD.
    MOVE 'GOOD' TO ACCT-NUM-MATCH.
    IF CARD-TYPE-IN IS NOT EQUAL TO 'C'
        MOVE 'BAD ' TO SECOND-CARD.
    IF ACCT-NUM-IN2 IS NOT EQUAL TO ACCT-NUM-WS
        MOVE 'BAD' TO ACCT-NUM-MATCH.

C4-FLUSH-CARDS-TO-ERROR-LINES.
    MOVE FIRST-CARD TO FIRST-CARD-ERR1.
    MOVE NAME-WS TO NAME-ERR1.
    MOVE ADDRESS-WS TO ADDRESS-ERR1.
    MOVE PHONE-WS TO PHONE-ERR1.
    MOVE ACCT-NUM-WS TO ACCT-NUM-ERR1.
    MOVE SECOND-CARD TO SECOND-CARD-ERR2.
    MOVE CREDIT-INFO-WS TO CREDIT-INFO-ERR2.
    IF ACCT-NUM-MATCH = 'BAD '
        MOVE 'ACCOUNT NUMBERS DO NOT MATCH'
                        TO MESSAGE-ERR-LINE-2
    ELSE
        MOVE SPACES TO MESSAGE-ERR-LINE-2.
```

Figure 6.3 continued.   CREDCALC, 80:80 listing, page 7 of 7

```
CBL LIB
00001              IDENTIFICATICN DIVISION.
00002              PROGRAM-ID.  CREDCALC.
00003
00004              ENVIRONMENT DIVISION.
00005              INPUT-OUTPUT SECTION.
00006              FILE-CONTROL. COPY FILECONT.
00007 C                SELECT APPLICATION-CARDS-FILE ASSIGN TO SYS031-UR-2540R-S.
00008 C                SELECT PROFILE-LISTING          ASSIGN TO SYS033-UR-1403-S.
00009
00010              DATA DIVISION.
00011              FILE SECTION.
00012
00013              FD   APPLICATION-CARDS-FILE  COPY FDCARDS.
00014 C                    LABEL RECORDS ARE OMITTED
00015 C                    DATA RECORDS ARE NAME-ADDRESS-AND-PHONE-IN
00016 C                                     CREDIT-INFORMATION-IN.
00017 C            01   NAME-ADDRESS-AND-PHONE-IN.
00018 C                 05   NAME-IN                   PIC X(20).
00019 C                 05   ADDRESS-IN                PIC X(40).
00020 C                 05   PHONE-IN                  PIC X(11).
00021 C                 05   FILLER                    PIC X(3).
00022 C                 05   ACCT-NUM-IN1              PIC 9(6).
00023 C            01   CREDIT-INFORMATION-IN.
00024 C                 05   CARD-TYPE-IN              PIC X.
00025 C                 05   ACCT-NUM-IN2              PIC 9(6).
00026 C                 05   FILLER                    PIC X.
00027 C                 05   CREDIT-INFO-IN            PIC X(22).
00028 C                 05   FILLER                    PIC X(50).
00029
00030              FD   PROFILE-LISTING
00031                     LABEL RECORDS ARE OMITTED.
00032              01   PRINT-LINE-OUT                 PIC X(132).
00033              WORKING-STORAGE SECTION.
00034
00035              01   COMMON-WS.
00036                   05   CARDS-LEFT                PIC X(3).
00037                   05   FIRST-CARD                PIC X(4).
00038                   05   SECOND-CARD               PIC X(4).
00039                   05   ACCT-NUM-MATCH            PIC X(4).
00040                   05   PAIR-VALIDITY             PIC X(4).
00041                   05   APPLICATIONS-ACCEPTED-ACCUM PIC 9(4).
00042                   05   APPLICATIONS-REJECTED-ACCUM PIC 9(4).
00043
00044              01   HEADER-WS1.
00045                   05   FILLER                    PIC X(52)   VALUE SPACES.
00046                   05   TITLE                     PIC X(29)
00047                                    VALUE 'APPLICANT CREDIT LIMIT REPORT'.
00048                   05   FILLER                    PIC X(52)   VALUE SPACES.
00049
```

Figure 6.4     CREDCALC, full compilation, page 1 of 10

- 142 -

```
00050              01  APPLICATICN-DATA-WSB1 COPY CARDSWS.
00051 C            01  APPLICATION-DATA-WSB1.
00052 C                05  NAME-AND-ADDRESS-WS.
00053 C                    10   NAME-WS                    PIC X(20).
00054 C                    10   ADDRESS-WS.
00055 C                        15   STREET-WS              PIC X(20).
00056 C                        15   CITY-WS                PIC X(13).
00057 C                        15   STATE-WS               PIC XX.
00058 C                        15   ZIP-WS                 PIC X(5).
00059 C                05  PHONE-WS.
00060 C                    10   AREA-CODE-WS               PIC 9(3).
00061 C                    10   NUMBR-WS                   PIC X(8).
00062 C                05  FILLER                          PIC X(3).
00063 C                05  ACCT-NUM-WS                     PIC 9(6).
00064 C                05  CREDIT-INFO-WS.
00065 C                    10   SEX-WS                     PIC X.
00066 C                        88   MALE      VALUE 'M'.
00067 C                        88   FEMALE    VALUE 'F'.
00068 C                    10   FILLER                     PIC X.
00069 C                    10   MARITAL-STATUS-WS          PIC X.
00070 C                        88   SINGLE    VALUE 'S'.
00071 C                        88   MARRIED   VALUE 'M'.
00072 C                        88   DIVORCED  VALUE 'D'.
00073 C                        88   WIDOWED   VALUE 'W'.
00074 C                    10   FILLER                     PIC X.
00075 C                    10   NUMBER-DEPENS-WS           PIC 9.
00076 C                    10   FILLER                     PIC X.
00077 C                    10   INCOME-HUNDREDS-WS         PIC 9(3).
00078 C                    10   FILLER                     PIC X.
00079 C                    10   YEARS-EMPLOYED-WS          PIC 99.
00080 C                    10   FILLER                     PIC X.
00081 C                    10   CWN-OR-RENT-WS             PIC X.
00082 C                        88   OWNED     VALUE 'O'.
00083 C                        88   RENTED    VALUE 'R'.
00084 C                    10   FILLER                     PIC X.
00085 C                    10   MORTGAGE-OR-RENTAL-WS      PIC 9(3).
00086 C                    10   FILLER                     PIC X.
00087 C                    10   OTHER-PAYMENTS-WS          PIC 9(3).
00088
00089              01  DISCR-INCOME-CALC-FIELDS-WSB2  COPY DISIFLDS.
00090 C            01  DISCR-INCOME-CALC-FIELDS-WSB2.
00091 C                05  ANNUAL-INCOME-WS               PIC 9(5).
00092 C                05  ANNUAL-TAX-WS                  PIC 9(5).
00093 C                05  TAX-RATE-WS                    PIC 9V99    VALUE 0.25.
00094 C                05  MONTHS-IN-YEAR                 PIC 99      VALUE 12.
00095 C                05  MONTHLY-NET-INCOME-WS          PIC 9(4).
00096 C                05  MONTHLY-PAYMENTS-WS            PIC 9(4).
00097 C                05  DISCR-INCOME-WS                PIC S9(3).
00098
00099              01  CRED-LIMIT-CALC-FIELDS-WSB3.
00100                  05  CREDIT-FACTOR                  PIC 9.
00101                  05  FACTOR1                        PIC 9       VALUE 1.
00102                  05  FACTOR2                        PIC 9       VALUE 2.
00103                  05  FACTOR3                        PIC 9       VALJE 3.
00104                  05  FACTOR4                        PIC 9       VALUE 4.
00105                  05  FACTOR5                        PIC 9       VALUE 5.
00106                  05  CREDIT-LIMIT-WS                PIC 9(4).
00107                  05  UPPER-LIMIT-WS                 PIC 9(4)    VALUE 2500.
00108                  05  TOTAL-CREDIT-GIVEN-WS          PIC 9(7).
```

Figure 6.4 continued.   CREDCALC, full compilation, page 2 of 10

```
00109
00110           01   LINE-1-WSB4 COPY LINE1WS.
00111 C          01   LINE-1-WSB4.
00112 C              05   FILLER                        PIC X(5)     VALUE SPACES.
00113 C              05   NAME-L1                       PIC X(20).
00114 C              05   FILLER                        PIC X(11)
00115 C                                     VALUE '   PHONE ('.
00116 C              05   AREA-CODE-L1                  PIC 9(3).
00117 C              05   FILLER                        PIC XX       VALUE ') '.
00118 C              05   NUMBR-L1                      PIC X(8).
00119 C              05   FILLER                        PIC X(3)     VALUE SPACES.
00120 C              05   SEX-L1                        PIC X(6).
00121 C              05   FILLER                        PIC X(9)     VALUE SPACES.
00122 C              05   FILLER                        PIC X(14)
00123 C                                     VALUE 'INCOME        $'.
00124 C              05   INCOME-HUNDREDS-L1            PIC 9(3).
00125 C              05   FILLER                        PIC X(28)
00126 C                                     VALUE '00 PER YEAR; IN THIS EMPLOY '.
00127 C              05   YEARS-EMPLOYED-L1.
00128 C                  10   YEARS-L1                  PIC XX.
00129 C                  10   DESCN-L1                  PIC X(16).
00130
00131           01   LINE-2-WSB4 COPY LINE2WS.
00132 C          01   LINE-2-WSB4.
00133 C              05   FILLER                        PIC X(5)     VALUE SPACES.
00134 C              05   STREET-L2                     PIC X(20).
00135 C              05   FILLER                        PIC X(27)    VALUE SPACES.
00136 C              05   MARITAL-STATUS-L2             PIC X(8).
00137 C              05   FILLER                        PIC X(7)     VALUE SPACES.
00138 C              05   OUTGO-DESCN                   PIC X(16).
00139 C              05   MORTGAGE-OR-RENTAL-L2         PIC 9(3).
00140              05   FILLER                        PIC X(11)
00141                                 VALUE ' PER MTH    '.
00142              05   FILLER                        PIC X(22)
00143                                 VALUE 'DISCRETIONARY INCOME $'.
00144              05   DISCR-INCOME-L2               PIC 9(3).
00145              05   FILLER                        PIC X(9)
00146                                 VALUE ' PER MTH '.
00147
00148           01   LINE-3-WSB4 COPY LINE3WS.
00149 C          01   LINE-3-WSB4.
00150 C              05   FILLER                        PIC X(5)     VALUE SPACES.
00151 C              05   CITY-L3                       PIC X(13).
00152 C              05   FILLER                        PIC X        VALUE SPACE.
00153 C              05   STATE-L3                      PIC XX.
00154 C              05   FILLER                        PIC X.       VALUE SPACE.
00155 C              05   ZIP-L3                        PIC X(5).
00156 C              05   FILLER                        PIC X(7)     VALUE '   A/C: '.
00157 C              05   ACCT-NUM-L3                   PIC 9(6).
00158 C              05   FILLER                        PIC X(12)    VALUE SPACES.
00159 C              05   NUMBER-DEPENS-L3              PIC 9.
00160 C              05   FILLER                        PIC X(14)
00161 C                                     VALUE ' DEPENDENTS     '.
00162 C              05   FILLER                        PIC X(16)
00163 C                                     VALUE 'OTHER PAYMENTS $'.
00164 C              05   OTHER-PAYMENTS-L3             PIC 9(3).
00165              05   FILLER                        PIC X(8)     VALUE ' PER MTH'
00166              05   FILLER                        PIC X(20)
00167                                     VALUE '   CREDIT LIMIT IS $',
00168              05   CREDIT-LIMIT-L3               PIC 9(4).
00169
```

```
00170    01   LINE-OF-ASTERISKS-WSB9.
00171         05   FILLER                              PIC X(6)    VALUE '      *'.
00172         05   FILLER                              PIC X(120)
00173              VALUE '**********************************************************
00174    -        '**********************************************************
00175    -        '**********'.
00176         05   FILLER                              PIC X(6)    VALUE '*        '.
00177
00178    01   SIDE-DELIMITER-WSB9.
00179         05   FILLER                              PIC X(6)    VALUE '      *'.
00180         05   FILLER                              PIC X(120)  VALUE SPACES.
00181         05   FILLER                              PIC X(6)    VALUE '*        '.
00182
00183    01   SUMMARY-LINE-WSB9.
00184         05   FILLER                              PIC X(6)    VALUE '      *'.
00185         05   FILLER                              PIC X(24)
00186                             VALUE '   TOTAL CREDIT GIVEN: $'.
00187         05   TOTAL-CREDIT-GIVEN                  PIC 9(7).
00188         05   FILLER                              PIC X(27)
00189                             VALUE '   AVERAGE CREDIT GIVEN: $'.
00190         05   AVERAGE-CREDIT                      PIC 9(6).
00191         05   FILLER                              PIC X(4)    VALUE ' ON '.
00192         05   APPLICATIONS-ACCEPTED               PIC 9(4).
00193         05   FILLER                              PIC X(24)
00194                             VALUE ' ACCEPTED APPLICATIONS. '.
00195         05   FILLER                              PIC X(20)
00196                             VALUE '   NUMBER REJECTED '.
00197         05   APPLICATIONS-REJECTED               PIC 9(3).
00198         05   FILLER                              PIC X(10)
00199                             VALUE ' *        '.
00200
00201    01   CARD-ERROR-LINE1-WSC4.
00202         05   FILLER                              PIC X(5)    VALUE SPACES.
00203         05   FILLER                              PIC X(12)
00204                             VALUE 'FIRST CARD  '.
00205         05   FIRST-CARD-ERR1                     PIC X(4).
00206         05   FILLER                              PIC XX      VALUE SPACES.
00207         05   NAME-ERR1                           PIC X(20).
00208         05   ADDRESS-ERR1                        PIC X(40).
00209         05   PHONE-ERR1                          PIC X(11).
00210         05   FILLER                              PIC X(3)    VALUE SPACES.
00211         05   ACCT-NUM-ERR1                       PIC 9(6).
00212
00213    01   CARD-ERROR-LINE2-WSC4.
00214         05   FILLER                              PIC X(5)    VALUE SPACES.
00215         05   FILLER                              PIC X(12)
00216                             VALUE 'SECOND CARD '.
00217         05   SECOND-CARD-ERR2                    PIC X(4).
00218         05   FILLER                              PIC X(2)    VALUE SPACES.
00219         05   CREDIT-INFO-ERR2                    PIC X(80).
00220         05   MESSAGE-ERR-LINE-2                  PIC X(29)   VALUE SPACES.
```

Figure 6.4 continued.   CREDCALC, full compilation, page 4 of 10

```
00222          PROCEDURE DIVISION.
00223              PERFORM A1-INITIALIZATION.
00224              PERFORM A2-PRINT-CREDIT-PROFILES
00225                 UNTIL CARDS-LEFT = 'NO '.
00226              PERFORM A3-PRINT-SUMMARY.
00227              PERFORM A4-END-OF-JOB.
00228              STOP RUN.
00229          A1-INITIALIZATION.
00230              OPEN INPUT APPLICATION-CARDS-FILE
00231                   OUTPUT PROFILE-LISTING.
00232              WRITE PRINT-LINE-OUT FROM HEADER-WS1
00233                                AFTER ADVANCING 2 LINES.
00234              MOVE ZEROES TO APPLICATIONS-ACCEPTED-ACCUM.
00235              MOVE ZEROES TO APPLICATIONS-REJECTED-ACCUM.
00236              MOVE ZEROES TO ANNUAL-INCOME-WS.
00237              MOVE ZEROES TO ANNUAL-TAX-WS.
00238              MOVE ZEROES TO MONTHLY-NET-INCOME-WS.
00239              MOVE ZEROES TO MONTHLY-PAYMENTS-WS.
00240              MOVE ZEROES TO DISCR-INCOME-WS.
00241              MOVE ZEROES TO CREDIT-FACTOR.
00242              MOVE ZEROES TO CREDIT-LIMIT-WS.
00243              MOVE ZEROES TO TOTAL-CREDIT-GIVEN-WS.
00244              MOVE ZEROES TO TOTAL-CREDIT-GIVEN.
00245              MOVE ZEROES TO AVERAGE-CREDIT.
00246              MOVE ZEROES TO APPLICATIONS-ACCEPTED.
00247              MOVE ZEROES TO APPLICATIONS-REJECTED.
00248              MOVE SPACES TO FIRST-CARD.
00249              MOVE SPACES TO SECOND-CARD.
00250              MOVE SPACES TO ACCT-NUM-MATCH.
00251              MOVE SPACES TO PAIR-VALIDITY.
00252              MOVE 'YES' TO CARDS-LEFT.
00253              READ APPLICATION-CARDS-FILE
00254                  AT END MOVE 'NO ' TO CARDS-LEFT.
00255        *   FIRST CARD IS NOW IN BUFFER
00256
00257
00258          A2-PRINT-CREDIT-PROFILES.
00259              PERFORM B1-GET-A-PAIR-OF-CARDS.
00260              IF PAIR-VALIDITY = 'GOOD'
00261                  PERFORM B2-CALC-DISCRETNRY-INCOME
00262                  IF DISCR-INCOME-WS IS POSITIVE
00263                      PERFORM B3-CALC-CREDIT-LIMIT
00264                      PERFORM B4-ASSEMBLE-PRINT-LINES
00265                      PERFORM B5-WRITE-PROFILE
00266                  ELSE
00267                      PERFORM B6-OUTGO-EXCEEDS-INCOME
00268              ELSE
00269                  PERFORM B7-WRITE-ERROR-PROFILE.
00270
00271          A3-PRINT-SUMMARY.
00272              PERFORM B8-CALC-AVERAGE-CREDIT.
00273              PERFORM B9-WRITE-SUMMARY-REPORT.
00274
00275          A4-END-OF-JOB.
00276              CLOSE APPLICATION-CARDS-FILE
00277                    PROFILE-LISTING.
00278
```

Figure 6.4 continued.  CREDCALC, full compilation, page 5 of 10

```
00279          B1-GET-A-PAIR-OF-CARDS.
00280             PERFORM C1-EDIT-FIRST-CARD.
00281             PERFORM C2-MOVE-FIRST-CARD-TO-WS.
00282            'READ APPLICATION-CARDS-FILE
00283               AT END MOVE 'NO ' TO CARDS-LEFT.
00284      * SECOND CARD OF PAIR IS NOW IN BUFFER
00285             PERFORM C3-EDIT-SECOND-CARD.
00286             IF       (FIRST-CARD = 'GOOD')
00287                 AND (SECOND-CARD = 'GOOD')
00288                 AND (ACCT-NUM-MATCH = 'GOOD')
00289                   MOVE 'GOOD' TO PAIR-VALIDITY
00290                   MOVE CREDIT-INFO-IN TO CREDIT-INFO-WS
00291             ELSE
00292               MOVE 'BAD ' TO PAIR-VALIDITY
00293               PERFORM C4-FLUSH-CARDS-TO-ERROR-LINES.
00294             READ APPLICATION-CARDS-FILE
00295               AT END MOVE 'NO ' TO CARDS-LEFT.
00296      * FIRST CARD OF NEXT PAIR IS NOW IN BUFFER
00297
00298          B2-CALC-DISCRETNRY-INCOME. COPY DISCINCM.
00299 C          COMPUTE ANNUAL-INCOME-WS = INCOME-HUNDREDS-WS * 100.
00300 C          COMPUTE ANNUAL-TAX-WS     = ANNUAL-INCOME-WS * TAX-RATE-WS.
00301 C          COMPUTE MONTHLY-NET-INCOME-WS ROUNDED
00302 C             = (ANNUAL-INCOME-WS - ANNUAL-TAX-WS) / MONTHS-IN-YEAR.
00303 C          COMPUTE MONTHLY-PAYMENTS-WS = MORTGAGE-OR-RENTAL-WS
00304 C                                      + OTHER-PAYMENTS-WS.
00305 C          COMPUTE DISCR-INCOME-WS = MONTHLY-NET-INCOME-WS
00306 C                                  - MONTHLY-PAYMENTS-WS
00307 C          ON SIZE ERROR MOVE 999 TO DISCR-INCOME-WS.
00308 C      *   DISCRETIONARY INCOMES OVER $999 PER MONTH ARE SET AT $999
00309
```

Figure 6.4 continued.   CREDCALC, full compilation, page 6 of 10

```
00310          B3-CALC-CREDIT-LIMIT.
00311     *       MARRIED?           Y Y Y Y N N N N        THIS DECISION TABLE
00312     *       OWNED?             Y Y N N Y Y N N        SETS OUT COMPANY POLICY
00313     *       2 OR MORE YEARS?   Y N Y N Y N Y N        FOR DETERMINING CREDIT
00314     *       ----------------------------------        LIMIT FROM DISCRETIONARY
00315     *       CREDIT    FACTOR1            X X          INCOME. FACTOR1 ETC ARE
00316     *       LIMIT IS      2        X   X             SET UP IN WSB3.
00317     *       MULTIPLE      3          X
00318     *       OF DISCR      4    X X
00319     *       INCOME.       5 X
00320
00321          IF MARRIED
00322              IF OWNED
00323                  IF YEARS-EMPLOYED-WS NOT LESS THAN 02
00324                      MOVE FACTOR5 TO CREDIT-FACTOR
00325                  ELSE
00326                      MOVE FACTOR4 TO CREDIT-FACTOR
00327              ELSE
00328                  IF YEARS-EMPLOYED-WS NOT LESS THAN 02
00329                      MOVE FACTOR4 TO CREDIT-FACTOR
00330                  ELSE
00331                      MOVE FACTOR2 TO CREDIT-FACTOR
00332          ELSE
00333              IF OWNED
00334                  IF YEARS-EMPLOYED-WS NOT LESS THAN 02
00335                      MOVE FACTOR3 TO CREDIT-FACTOR
00336                  ELSE
00337                      MOVE FACTOR2 TO CREDIT-FACTOR
00338              ELSE
00339                  MOVE FACTOR1 TO CREDIT-FACTOR.
00340          COMPUTE CREDIT-LIMIT-WS = DISCR-INCOME-WS * CREDIT-FACTOR.
00341          IF CREDIT-LIMIT-WS IS GREATER THAN UPPER-LIMIT-WS
00342              MOVE UPPER-LIMIT-WS TO CREDIT-LIMIT-WS.
00343          ADD CREDIT-LIMIT-WS TO TOTAL-CREDIT-GIVEN-WS.
00344
```

Figure 6.4 continued.   CREDCALC, full compilation, page 7 of 10

```
0345            B4-ASSEMBLE-PRINT-LINES.
0346                MOVE NAME-WS TO NAME-L1.
0347                MOVE STREET-WS TO STREET-L2.
0348                MOVE CITY-WS TO CITY-L3.
0349                MOVE STATE-WS TO STATE-L3.
0350                MOVE ZIP-WS TO ZIP-L3.
0351                MOVE AREA-CODE-WS TO AREA-CODE-L1.
0352                MOVE NUMBR-WS TO NUMBR-L1.
0353                MOVE ACCT-NUM-WS TO ACCT-NUM-L3.
0354                IF        MALE   MOVE 'MALE  ' TO SEX-L1
0355                ELSE IF FEMALE MOVE 'FEMALE' TO SEX-L1
0356                ELSE              MOVE '******' TO SEX-L1.
0357                IF        SINGLE   MOVE 'SINGLE  ' TO MARITAL-STATUS-L2
0358                ELSE IF MARRIED  MOVE 'MARRIED ' TO MARITAL-STATUS-L2
0359                ELSE IF DIVORCED MOVE 'DIVORCED' TO MARITAL-STATUS-L2
0360                ELSE IF WIDOWED  MOVE 'WIDOWED ' TO MARITAL-STATUS-L2
0361                ELSE              MOVE '********' TO MARITAL-STATUS-L2.
00362              MOVE NUMBER-DEPENS-WS TO NUMBER-DEPENS-L3.
00363              MOVE INCOME-HUNDREDS-WS TO INCOME-HUNDREDS-L1.
00364              IF YEARS-EMPLOYED-WS IS EQUAL TO 0
00365                  MOVE 'LESS THAN 1 YEAR' TO YEARS-EMPLOYED-L1
00366              ELSE
00367                  MOVE YEARS-EMPLOYED-WS TO YEARS-L1
00368                  MOVE ' YEARS          ' TO DESCN-L1.
00369              IF        OWNED  MOVE 'MORTGAGE:        $' TO OUTGO-DESCN
00370              ELSE IF RENTED MOVE 'RENTAL:          $' TO OUTGO-DESCN
00371              ELSE              MOVE '*****************' TO OUTGO-DESCN.
00372              MOVE MORTGAGE-OR-RENTAL-WS TO MORTGAGE-OR-RENTAL-L2.
00373              MOVE OTHER-PAYMENTS-WS TO OTHER-PAYMENTS-L3.
00374              MOVE DISCR-INCOME-WS TO DISCR-INCOME-L2.
00375              MOVE CREDIT-LIMIT-WS TO CREDIT-LIMIT-L3.
00376
00377            B5-WRITE-PROFILE. COPY WRITPRFL
00378                    REPLACING LINE-1-WS BY LINE-1-WSB4
00379                              LINE-2-WS BY LINE-2-WSB4
00380                              LINE-3-WS BY LINE-3-WSB4.
00381  C           MOVE SPACES TO PRINT-LINE-OUT.
00382  C           WRITE PRINT-LINE-OUT FROM LINE-1-WSB4
00383  C                           AFTER ADVANCING 4 LINES.
00384  C           MOVE SPACES TO PRINT-LINE-OUT.
00385  C           WRITE PRINT-LINE-OUT FROM LINE-2-WSB4
00386  C                           AFTER ADVANCING 1 LINES.
00387  C           MOVE SPACES TO PRINT-LINE-OUT.
00388  C           WRITE PRINT-LINE-OUT FROM LINE-3-WSB4
00389  C                           AFTER ADVANCING 1 LINES.
00390              ADD 1 TO APPLICATIONS-ACCEPTED-ACCUM.
00391
00392            B6-OUTGO-EXCEEDS-INCOME.
00393              MOVE SPACES TO FIRST-CARD-ERR1.
00394              MOVE NAME-WS TO NAME-ERR1.
00395              MOVE ADDRESS-WS TO ADDRESS-ERR1.
00396              MOVE PHONE-WS TO PHONE-ERR1.
00397              MOVE ACCT-NUM-WS TO ACCT-NUM-ERR1.
00398              MOVE SPACES TO SECOND-CARD-ERR2.
00399              MOVE CREDIT-INFO-WS TO CREDIT-INFO-ERR2.
00400              MOVE 'OUTGO EXCEEDS INCOME: REJECT' TO MESSAGE-ERR-LINE-2.
00401              PERFORM B7-WRITE-ERROR-PROFILE.
00402
```

Figure 6.4 continued.   CREDCALC, full compilation, page 8 of 10   - 149 -

```
00403        B7-WRITE-ERROR-PROFILE.
00404            MOVE SPACES TO PRINT-LINE-OUT.
00405            WRITE PRINT-LINE-OUT FROM CARD-ERROR-LINE1-WSC4
00406                            AFTER ADVANCING 4 LINES.
00407            WRITE PRINT-LINE-OUT FROM CARD-ERROR-LINE2-WSC4
00408                            AFTER ADVANCING 1 LINES.
00409            ADD 1 TO APPLICATIONS-REJECTED-ACCUM.
00410
00411        B8-CALC-AVERAGE-CREDIT.
00412            MOVE TOTAL-CREDIT-GIVEN-WS TO TOTAL-CREDIT-GIVEN.
00413            IF TOTAL-CREDIT-GIVEN = 0
00414                MOVE ZEROES TO AVERAGE-CREDIT
00415            ELSE
00416                DIVIDE APPLICATIONS-ACCEPTED-ACCUM
00417                    INTO TOTAL-CREDIT-GIVEN
00418                    GIVING AVERAGE-CREDIT  ROUNDED.
00419
00420        B9-WRITE-SUMMARY-REPORT.
00421            MOVE APPLICATIONS-ACCEPTED-ACCUM TO APPLICATIONS-ACCEPTED.
00422            MOVE APPLICATIONS-REJECTED-ACCUM TO APPLICATIONS-REJECTED.
00423            WRITE PRINT-LINE-OUT FROM LINE-OF-ASTERISKS-WSB9
00424                            AFTER ADVANCING 6 LINES.
00425            WRITE PRINT-LINE-OUT FROM SIDE-DELIMITER-WSB9
00426                            AFTER ADVANCING 1 LINES.
00427            WRITE PRINT-LINE-OUT FROM SUMMARY-LINE-WSB9
00428                            AFTER ADVANCING 1 LINES.
00429            WRITE PRINT-LINE-OUT FROM SIDE-DELIMITER-WSB9
00430                            AFTER ADVANCING 1 LINES.
00431            WRITE PRINT-LINE-OUT FROM LINE-OF-ASTERISKS-WSB9
00432                            AFTER ADVANCING 1 LINES.
00433
```

Figure 6.4 continued.   CREDCALC, full compilation, page 9 of 10

```
00434          C1-EDIT-FIRST-CARD.
00435              MOVE 'GOOD' TO FIRST-CARD.
00436              IF NAME-IN IS EQUAL TO SPACES
00437                  MOVE '*** NAME MISSING ***' TO NAME-IN
00438                  MOVE 'BAD ' TO FIRST-CARD.
00439              IF ADDRESS-IN IS EQUAL TO SPACES
00440                  MOVE '**** ADDRESS MISSING ****' TO ADDRESS-IN
00441                  MOVE 'BAD ' TO FIRST-CARD.
00442              IF PHONE-IN IS EQUAL TO SPACES
00443                  MOVE 'NO PHONE **' TO PHONE-IN
00444                  MOVE 'BAD ' TO FIRST-CARD.
00445
00446          C2-MOVE-FIRST-CARD-TO-WS.
00447              MOVE NAME-IN TO NAME-WS.
00448              MOVE ADDRESS-IN TO ADDRESS-WS.
00449              MOVE PHONE-IN TO PHONE-WS.
00450              MOVE ACCT-NUM-IN1 TO ACCT-NUM-WS.
00451
00452          C3-EDIT-SECOND-CARD.
00453              MOVE 'GOOD' TO SECOND-CARD.
00454              MOVE 'GOOD' TO ACCT-NUM-MATCH.
00455              IF CARD-TYPE-IN IS NOT EQUAL TO 'C'
00456                  MOVE 'BAD ' TO SECOND-CARD.
00457              IF ACCT-NUM-IN2 IS NOT EQUAL TO ACCT-NUM-WS
00458                  MOVE 'BAD' TO ACCT-NUM-MATCH.
00459
00460          C4-FLUSH-CARDS-TO-ERROR-LINES.
00461              MOVE FIRST-CARD TO FIRST-CARD-ERR1.
00462              MOVE NAME-WS TO NAME-ERR1.
00463              MOVE ADDRESS-WS TO ADDRESS-ERR1.
00464              MOVE PHONE-WS TO PHONE-ERR1.
00465              MOVE ACCT-NUM-WS TO ACCT-NUM-ERR1.
00466              MOVE SECOND-CARD TO SECOND-CARD-ERR2.
00467              MOVE CREDIT-INFO-WS TO CREDIT-INFO-ERR2.
00468              IF ACCT-NUM-MATCH = 'BAD '
00469                  MOVE 'ACCOUNT NUMBERS DO NOT MATCH'
00470                                      TO MESSAGE-ERR-LINE-2
00471              ELSE
00472                  MOVE SPACES TO MESSAGE-ERR-LINE-2.
```

Figure 6.4 continued.    CREDCALC, full compilation, page 10 of 10

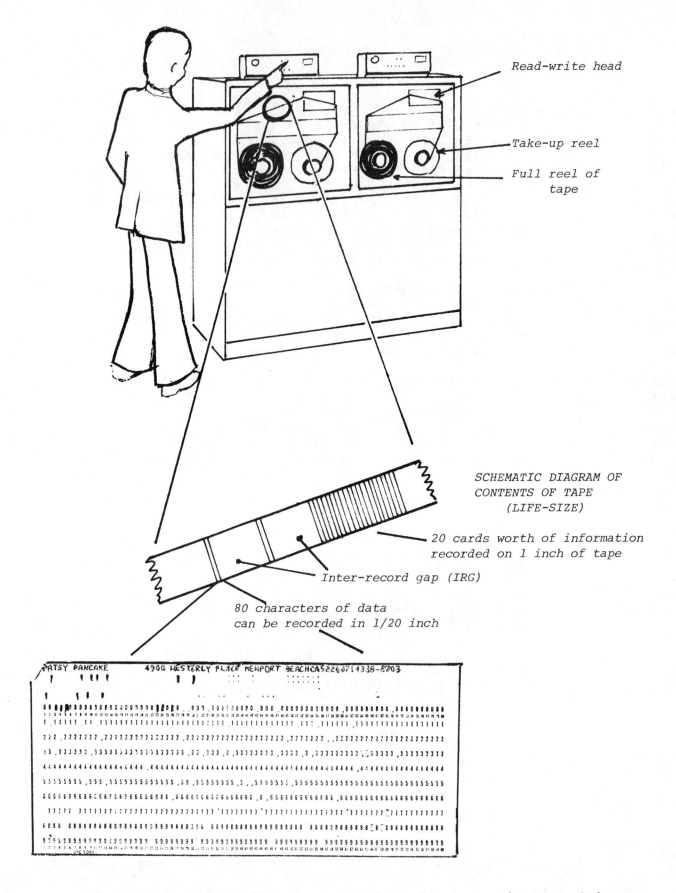

Figure 6.5  Schematic representation of a magnetic tape drive

# CHAPTER 7:   GETTING DATA IN AND OUT OF THE COMPUTER

Up until now we have done some quite complex processing of data, all stored on punched cards.  As you will realize, cards are very convenient for low volumes of data of the kind you have been using, but once you start to deal with more than a few hundred records they begin to get heavy, they wear and cause reading problems when used a lot, and they may get out of order. Have you dropped a card deck yet, and had to put it back in sequence?  It happens.


## 7.1    MAGNETIC TAPE

For large volumes of data, magnetic tape is often used. This is a larger, more precision-engineered version of the tape used in a tape recorder, with the recording consisting of magnetized spots corresponding to the holes in a card.   The picture opposite shows a modern tape drive, with a reel of computer tape mounted on it.  The tape can typically hold 1,600 characters per inch, that is to say 20 punched cards can be recorded on one inch of magnetic tape.

Q.    If a reel of tape is 2,400 feet long, how many
        punched cards could in principle be recorded on
        one reel?

A.    2,400 feet X 12 inches X 20 cards per inch
            = 576,000 cards.

Not only can magnetic tape store information much more compactly than punched cards, but tape can also be read by the computer much more quickly.


The inset diagram opposite shows a magnified version of the contents of a short piece of tape.  It is standard for the tape to have a gap of 3/4 inch between areas on which data is recorded; this is called the inter-record gap (IRG).  You can see that if you record cards one by one on tape, and each card takes up only 1/20th of an inch, you will waste a lot of tape. For this reason it is usual to write 5 or 10 or 20 or more records on tape together as a block, as shown in the insert.


As well as being blocked, a tape file has a coded label written by the computer as the first and last record on the tape.  If you want, you can specify your own format for the label, but it is more common to use the format provided as standard by the operating system.

Here is a sample FD for a file to be written on tape:

```
FD  TAPE-FILE
    LABEL RECORDS ARE STANDARD
    BLOCK CONTAINS 10 RECORDS.
01  NAME-AND-ADDRESS              PIC X(80).
```

Q.   How many characters will there be in each block
     on this tape?

A.   800:  80 per record, 10 records per block.


## 7.1.1    FILE-CONTROL Paragraph for Tape Files


The SELECT statements for tape files are written in a
way similar to the card and print files with which you are
already familiar.  The system-name can take a wide variety of
forms depending on the operating system.  Find out which form
is appropriate for your installation.

For example, the SELECT statement for a tape file might
read:

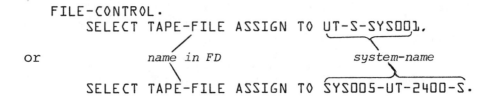

```
    FILE-CONTROL.
        SELECT TAPE-FILE ASSIGN TO UT-S-SYS001.

or              name in FD              system-name

        SELECT TAPE-FILE ASSIGN TO SYS005-UT-2400-S.
```


## 7.1.2    OPEN and CLOSE for Tape Files


When an OPEN is executed for a tape file, the computer
system checks to see that the correct tape with a correct
label is mounted on the correct tape drive ready for use, and
positions the first block of records to be read.  You don't
have to worry about separating each block into its component
records; the computer system will do that for you and will
present you with a record in the input buffer, as specified
in your FD, every time you issue a READ statement.  You must
open a tape file as either INPUT or OUTPUT depending on whether
you want to read from it or write to it.

When you write CLOSE for a tape file, the system will write the correct label on the tape, if necessary, so that it can be used again, and rewind the tape to the beginning, so that the computer operator can take the reel off the tape drive, and put it away until the next time it is needed.

### 7.1.3  *READ and WRITE for Tape Files*

You code the READ and WRITE statements much as you coded for a card file.  A tape file has a special end-of-file record which is automatically inserted by the system.  When this is read, the AT END condition exists, and can be used to set a flag as we have done in previous chapters.

Once you have written the BLOCK CONTAINS clause in the FD, you do not have to worry about separating records from blocks on a READ or combining them into blocks on a WRITE; that is all handled by the computer system.

### 7.1.4  *Creating a Tape File*

We want to store all the data about those mail-order customers for whom we have approved a credit limit.  To do this, we want to build a Customer Master File on tape, so that we do not have to keep on reading punched cards.

You now have to design and code a program, to be called CREATEMF, which will read pairs of cards as in CREDCALC, make the same checks on the cards, calculate discretionary income and credit limit, and write a record onto tape for each accepted applicant, printing out error messages for each rejected applicant, and rejecting their cards.  When all the good applicants have been processed, we want to rewind the tape, and then check that we have actually written our master file on tape by reading the records on the tape and printing out the contents of the file, one record to a line.

This means that when all the cards have been processed, you will need to CLOSE the tape file, and OPEN it again as an INPUT file.  Remember that the CLOSE statement will automatically rewind the tape.

The tape master file should have the following record format:

| Field | Length | Note |
|---|---|---|
| Account number | 6 | |
| Name | 20 | |
| Street | 20 | |
| City | 13 | |
| State | 2 | |
| Zip code | 5 | |
| Phone | 10 | - ten digits, no hyphen |
| Sex | 1 | |
| Marital status | 1 | |
| Number of dependents | 2 | |
| Income in hundreds | 3 | |
| Years in present job | 2 | |
| Owner or renter | 1 | |
| Mortgage or rental | 3 | |
| Other monthly payments | 3 | |
| Discretionary income | 4 | |
| Credit limit | 4 | |
| Current balance owing | 8 | - this field will be used later |
| Spare | 20 | |
| | 128 | |

We have added 20 characters to set the size of the record at 128 characters, because we may want to add some additional fields later, and because many computers handle blocking more effectively when the lengths of the records are a power of 2 characters: 64, 128, 256, and so on. Though we do not have many records in our test data, we want to be able to open accounts for up to 100,000 applicants; so we will use a block size of 10 records, to give a reasonably efficient use of the tape.

Given this information, draw a program graph and structure chart for CREATEMF, showing what functions you will need performed, and compare them with the model opposite. Notice that in this case we are using a slightly different convention for naming modules, in which 21 performs 211, 212, etc.; 22 would perform 221, 222, 223, etc; and 211 would perform 2111, 2112, and so on. While this is somewhat more trouble to code than the letter-plus-digit system we used in SAMPLE-4 and CREDCALC, it is a helpful technique in large programs, because you can see at a glance that, say, 3242 is performed from 324 (though remember it may be performed from other places as well).

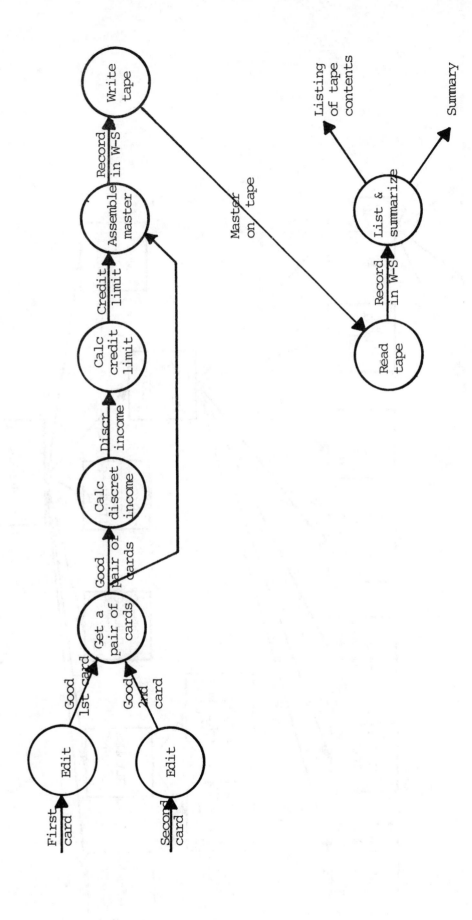

Figure 7.1   Program graph for tape master file creation

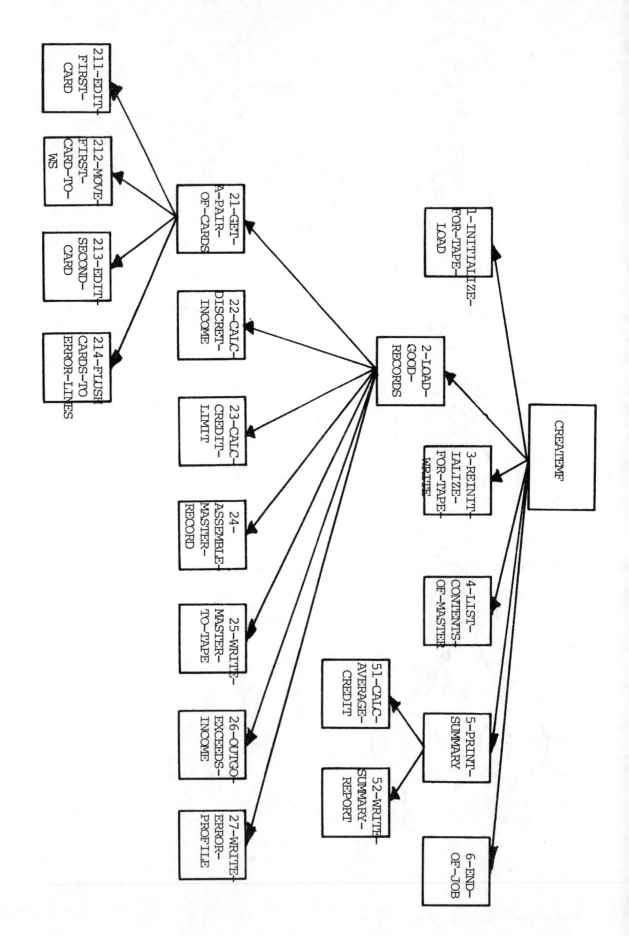

Figure 7.2  Structure chart for CREATEMF

Assume that the data structures and all the procedures of
CREDCALC are cataloged for you in the Source Statement Library
with the library names as set out below.

```
FD APPLICATION-CARDS cataloged as FDCARDS
HEADER-WS                      "   HEADRWS
APPLICATION-DATA               "   CARDSWS
DISCR-INCOME-CALC-FIELDS       "   DISIFLDS
CRED-LIMIT-CALC-FIELDS         "   CREDFLDS
LINE-OF-ASTERISKS              "   LINASTSK
SIDE-DELIMITER                 "   SIDELIMT
SUMMARY-LINE                   "   SUMARYLN
CARD-ERROR-LINE1               "   ERRLINE1
CARD-ERROR-LINE2               "   ERRLINE2
GET-A-PAIR-OF-CARDS            "   GETPRCDS
CALC-DISCRETNRY-INCOME         "   DISCINCM
CALC-CREDIT-LIMIT              "   CALCREDT
OUTGO-EXCEEDS-INCOME           "   OUTEXCDI
WRITE-ERROR-PROFILE            "   WRTERRPR
CALC-AVERAGE-CREDIT            "   CALAVGEC
WRITE-SUMMARY-REPORT           "   WRITSMRY
EDIT-FIRST-CARD                "   EDT1STCD
MOVE-FIRST-CARD-TO-WS          "   MOV1STCD
EDIT-SECOND-CARD               "   EDT2NDCD
FLUSH-CARDS-TO-ERROR-LINES     "   FLUSHCDS
```

Use these library entries to code CREATEMF; the model
solution on the following pages gives the 80:80 listing before
the COPY statements are expanded, followed by the completely
compiled listing.

```
CBL LIB
      IDENTIFICATION DIVISION.
      PROGRAM-ID. CREATEMF.

      ENVIRONMENT DIVISION.
      INPUT-OUTPUT SECTION.
      FILE-CONTROL. COPY FILECONT.
          SELECT CREDIT-MASTER-FILE       ASSIGN TO SYS005-UT-2400-S.

      DATA DIVISION.
      FILE SECTION.

      FD  APPLICATION-CARDS-FILE    COPY FCCARDS.

      FD  PROFILE-LISTING
              LABEL RECORDS ARE OMITTED.
      01  PRINT-LINE-OUT                    PIC X(132).

      FD  CREDIT-MASTER-FILE
          LABEL RECORDS ARE STANDARD
          BLOCK CONTAINS 10 RECORDS.
      01  CREDIT-MASTER-RECORD.
          05  ACCT-NUM-MAS                  PIC 9(6).
          05  NAME-AND-ADDRESS-MAS.
              10  NAME-MAS                  PIC X(20).
              10  STREET-MAS                PIC X(20).
              10  CITY-MAS                  PIC X(13).
              10  STATE-MAS                 PIC XX.
              10  ZIP-MAS                   PIC 9(5).
          05  PHONE-MAS.
              10  AREA-CODE-MAS             PIC 9(3).
              10  NUMBR-MAS                 PIC 9(7).
          05  CREDIT-INFO-MAS.
              10  SEX-MAS                   PIC X.
              10  MARITAL-STATUS-MAS        PIC X.
              10  NUMBER-DEPENS-MAS         PIC 99.
              10  INCOME-HUNDREDS-MAS       PIC 9(3).
              10  YEARS-EMPLOYED-MAS        PIC 99.
              10  OWN-OR-RENT-MAS           PIC X.
              10  MORTGAGE-OR-RENTAL-MAS    PIC 9(3).
              10  OTHER-PAYMENTS-MAS        PIC 9(3).
          05  ACCOUNT-INFO-MAS.
              10  DISCR-INCOME-MAS          PIC S9(3).
              10  CREDIT-LIMIT-MAS          PIC 9(4).
              10  CURRENT-BALANCE-OWING     PIC S9(6)V99.
          05  SPARE-CHARACTERS              PIC X(20).
```

Figure 7.3    CREATEMF, 80:80 listing, page 1 of 5

```
WORKING-STORAGE SECTION.

01   COMMON-WS.
     05   CARDS-LEFT                      PIC X(3).
     05   MASTER-RECORDS-LEFT             PIC X(3).
     05   FIRST-CARD                      PIC X(4).
     05   SECOND-CARD                     PIC X(4).
     05   ACCT-NUM-MATCH                  PIC X(4).
     05   PAIR-VALIDITY                   PIC X(4).
     05   APPLICATIONS-ACCEPTED-ACCUM  PIC 9(4).
     05   APPLICATIONS-REJECTED-ACCUM  PIC 9(4).

01   HEADER-WS3.
     05   FILLER                          PIC X(51)   VALUE SPACES.
     05   TITLE                           PIC X(30)
               VALUE 'CONTENTS OF CREDIT MASTER FILE'.
     05   FILLER                          PIC X(51)   VALUE SPACES.

01   APPLICATION-DATA-WS21 COPY CARDSWS.

01   DISCR-INCOME-CALC-FIELDS-WS22 COPY DISIFLDS.

01   CRED-LIMIT-CALC-FIELDS-WS23 COPY CREDFLDS.

01   ASSEMBLE-MASTER-WS24.
     05   TEL-NUMBR-WITH-HYPHEN-WS24.
          10   EXCHANGE-IN                PIC 9(3).
          10   FILLER                     PIC X.
          10   FOUR-DIGIT-NUMBR-IN        PIC 9(4).
     05   TEL-NUMBR-WITHOUT-HYPHEN-WS24.
          10   EXCHANGE                   PIC 9(3).
          10   FOUR-DIGIT-NUMBR           PIC 9(4).


01   LINE-OF-ASTERISKS-WS52 COPY LINASTSK.

01   SIDE-DELIMITER-WS52 COPY SIDELIMT.

01   SUMMARY-LINE-WS52 COPY SUMARYLN.

01   CARD-ERROR-LINE1-WS214 COPY ERRLINE1.

01   CARD-ERROR-LINE2-WS214 COPY ERRLINE2.
```

Figure 7.3 continued.   CREATEMF, 80:80 listing, page 2 of 5

```
PROCEDURE DIVISION.
    PERFORM 1-INITIALIZE-FOR-TAPE-LOAD.
    PERFORM 2-LOAD-GOOD-RECORDS-TO-MASTER
       UNTIL CARDS-LEFT IS EQUAL TO 'NO '.
    PERFORM 3-REINITIALIZE-FOR-TAPE-WRITE.
    PERFORM 4-LIST-CONTENTS-OF-MASTER
       UNTIL MASTER-RECORDS-LEFT = 'NO '.
    PERFORM 5-PRINT-SUMMARY.
    PERFORM 6-END-OF-JOB.
    STOP RUN.




1-INITIALIZE-FOR-TAPE-LOAD.
    OPEN INPUT APPLICATION-CARDS-FILE
         OUTPUT PROFILE-LISTING
                CREDIT-MASTER-FILE.
    MOVE SPACES TO FIRST-CARD.
    MOVE SPACES TO SECOND-CARD.
    MOVE SPACES TO PAIR-VALIDITY.
    MOVE ZEROES TO APPLICATIONS-ACCEPTED-ACCUM.
    MOVE ZEROES TO APPLICATIONS-REJECTED-ACCUM.
    MOVE ZEROES TO ANNUAL-INCOME-WS.
    MOVE ZEROES TO ANNUAL-TAX-WS.
    MOVE ZEROES TO MONTHLY-NET-INCOME-WS.
    MOVE ZEROES TO MONTHLY-PAYMENTS-WS.
    MOVE ZEROES TO DISCR-INCOME-WS.
    MOVE ZEROES TO CREDIT-FACTOR.
    MOVE ZEROES TO CREDIT-LIMIT-WS.
    MOVE ZEROES TO TOTAL-CREDIT-GIVEN-WS.
    MOVE ZEROES TO TOTAL-CREDIT-GIVEN.
    MOVE ZEROES TO AVERAGE-CREDIT.
    MOVE ZEROES TO APPLICATIONS-ACCEPTED.
    MOVE ZEROES TO APPLICATIONS-REJECTED.
    MOVE 'YES' TO CARDS-LEFT.
    READ APPLICATION-CARDS-FILE
        AT END MOVE 'NO ' TO CARDS-LEFT.
* FIRST CARD IS NOW IN BUFFER
```

Figure 7.3 continued.   CREATEMF, 80:80 listing, page 3 of 5

```
2-LOAD-GOOD-RECORDS-TO-MASTER.
    PERFORM 21-GET-A-PAIR-OF-CARDS.
    IF PAIR-VALIDITY = 'GOOD'
        PERFORM 22-CALC-DISCRETNRY-INCOME
        IF DISCR-INCOME-WS IS POSITIVE
            PERFORM 23-CALC-CREDIT-LIMIT
            PERFORM 24-ASSEMBLE-MASTER-RECORD
            PERFORM 25-WRITE-MASTER-TO-TAPE
        ELSE
            PERFORM 26-OUTGO-EXCEEDS-INCOME
    ELSE
        PERFORM 27-WRITE-ERROR-PROFILE.

3-REINITIALIZE-FOR-TAPE-WRITE.
    CLOSE CREDIT-MASTER-FILE.
    OPEN INPUT CREDIT-MASTER-FILE.
    WRITE PRINT-LINE-OUT FROM HEADER-WS3
                        AFTER ADVANCING 10 LINES.
    MOVE 'YES' TO MASTER-RECORDS-LEFT.
    READ CREDIT-MASTER-FILE
      AT END MOVE 'NO ' TO MASTER-RECORDS-LEFT.

4-LIST-CONTENTS-OF-MASTER.
    MOVE SPACES TO PRINT-LINE-OUT.
    WRITE PRINT-LINE-OUT FROM CREDIT-MASTER-RECORD
                AFTER ADVANCING 2 LINES.
    READ CREDIT-MASTER-FILE
      AT END MOVE 'NO ' TO MASTER-RECORDS-LEFT.

5-PRINT-SUMMARY.
    PERFORM 51-CALC-AVERAGE-CREDIT.
    PERFORM 52-WRITE-SUMMARY-REPORT.

6-END-OF-JOB.
    CLOSE APPLICATION-CARDS-FILE
            PROFILE-LISTING
            CREDIT-MASTER-FILE.
```

Figure 7.3 continued.  CREATEMF, 80:80 listing, page 4 of 5

```
21-GET-A-PAIR-OF-CARDS. COPY GETPRCDS REPLACING
        C1-EDIT-FIRST-CARD           BY   211-EDIT-FIRST-CARD
        C2-MOVE-FIRST-CARD-TO-WS     BY   212-MOVE-FIRST-CARD-TO-WS
        C3-EDIT-SECOND-CARD          BY   213-EDIT-SECOND-CARD
        C4-FLUSH-CARDS-TO-ERROR-LINES
                                     BY
        214-FLUSH-CARDS-TO-ERROR-LINES.

22-CALC-DISCRETNRY-INCOME. COPY DISCINCM.

23-CALC-CREDIT-LIMIT. COPY CALCREDT.

24-ASSEMBLE-MASTER-RECORD.
    MOVE ACCT-NUM-WS TO ACCT-NUM-MAS.
    MOVE NAME-AND-ADDRESS-WS TO NAME-AND-ADDRESS-MAS.
    MOVE AREA-CODE-WS TO AREA-CODE-MAS.
    PERFORM 241-REMOVE-HYPHEN-FROM-TEL-NUM.
    MOVE CREDIT-INFO-WS TO CREDIT-INFO-MAS.
    MOVE DISCR-INCOME-WS TO DISCR-INCOME-MAS.
    MOVE CREDIT-LIMIT-WS TO CREDIT-LIMIT-MAS.
    MOVE ZEROS TO CURRENT-BALANCE-OWING.
    MOVE SPACES TO SPARE-CHARACTERS.

25-WRITE-MASTER-TO-TAPE.
    WRITE CREDIT-MASTER-RECORD.
    ADD 1 TO APPLICATIONS-ACCEPTED-ACCUM.

26-OUTGO-EXCEEDS-INCOME. COPY OUTEXCDI REPLACING
        B7-WRITE-ERROR-PROFILE  BY   27-WRITE-ERROR-PROFILE.

27-WRITE-ERROR-PROFILE. COPY WRTERRPR REPLACING
        CARD-ERROR-LINE1-WSC4    BY   CARD-ERROR-LINE1-WS214
        CARD-ERROR-LINE2-WSC4    BY   CARD-ERROR-LINE2-WS214.

51-CALC-AVERAGE-CREDIT. COPY CALAVGEC.

52-WRITE-SUMMARY-REPORT. COPY WRITSMRY REPLACING
        LINE-OF-ASTERISKS-WSB9 BY LINE-OF-ASTERISKS-WS52
        SIDE-DELIMITER-WSB9 BY SIDE-DELIMITER-WS52
        SUMMARY-LINE-WSB9 BY SUMMARY-LINE-WS52.

211-EDIT-FIRST-CARD. COPY EDT1STCD.

212-MOVE-FIRST-CARD-TO-WS. COPY MOV1STCD.

213-EDIT-SECOND-CARD. COPY EDT2NDCD.

214-FLUSH-CARDS-TO-ERROR-LINES. COPY FLUSHCDS.

241-REMOVE-HYPHEN-FROM-TEL-NUM.
        MOVE NUMBR-WS TO TEL-NUMBR-WITH-HYPHEN-WS24.
        MOVE EXCHANGE-IN TO EXCHANGE.
        MOVE FOUR-DIGIT-NUMBR-IN TO FOUR-DIGIT-NUMBR.
        MOVE TEL-NUMBR-WITHOUT-HYPHEN-WS24 TO NUMBR-MAS.
```

Figure 7.3 continued.  CREATEMF, 80:80 listing, page 5 of 5

```
CBL LIB
00001              IDENTIFICATION DIVISION.
00002              PROGRAM-ID. CREATEMF.
00003
00004              ENVIRONMENT DIVISION.
00005              INPUT-OUTPUT SECTION.
00006              FILE-CONTROL. COPY FILECONT.
00007 C                SELECT APPLICATION-CARDS-FILE ASSIGN TO SYS031-UR-2540R-S.
00008 C                SELECT PROFILE-LISTING        ASSIGN TO SYS033-UR-1403-S.
00009                  SELECT CREDIT-MASTER-FILE     ASSIGN TO SYS005-UT-2400-S.
00010
00011              DATA DIVISION.
00012              FILE SECTION.
00013
00014              FD  APPLICATION-CARDS-FILE   COPY FDCARDS.
00015 C                   LABEL RECORDS ARE OMITTED
00016 C                   DATA RECORDS ARE NAME-ADDRESS-AND-PHONE-IN
00017 C                                     CREDIT-INFORMATION-IN.
00018 C              01  NAME-ADDRESS-AND-PHONE-IN.
00019 C                  05  NAME-IN                      PIC X(20).
00020 C                  05  ADDRESS-IN                   PIC X(40).
00021 C                  05  PHONE-IN                     PIC X(11).
00022 C                  05  FILLER                       PIC X(3).
00023 C                  05  ACCT-NUM-IN1                 PIC 9(5).
00024 C              01  CREDIT-INFORMATION-IN.
00025 C                  05  CARD-TYPE-IN                 PIC X.
00026 C                  05  ACCT-NUM-IN2                 PIC 9(5).
00027 C                  05  FILLER                       PIC X.
00028 C                  05  CREDIT-INFO-IN               PIC X(22).
00029 C                  05  FILLER                       PIC X(50).
00030
00031              FD  PROFILE-LISTING
00032                     LABEL RECORDS ARE OMITTED.
00033              01  PRINT-LINE-OUT                      PIC X(132).
00034
```

Figure 7.4    CREATEMF, full compilation, page 1 of 10

```
00035          FD   CREDIT-MASTER-FILE
00036               LABEL RECORDS ARE STANDARD
00037               BLOCK CONTAINS 10 RECORDS.
00038          01   CREDIT-MASTER-RECORD.
00039               05   ACCT-NUM-MAS                    PIC 9(6).
00040               05   NAME-AND-ADDRESS-MAS.
00041                    10   NAME-MAS                   PIC X(20).
00042                    10   STREET-MAS                 PIC X(20).
00043                    10   CITY-MAS                   PIC X(13).
00044                    10   STATE-MAS                  PIC XX.
00045                    10   ZIP-MAS                    PIC 9(5).
00046               05   PHONE-MAS.
00047                    10   AREA-CODE-MAS              PIC 9(3).
00048                    10   NUMBR-MAS                  PIC 9(7).
00049               05   CREDIT-INFO-MAS.
00050                    10   SEX-MAS                    PIC X.
00051                    10   MARITAL-STATUS-MAS         PIC X.
00052                    10   NUMBER-DEPENS-MAS          PIC 99.
00053                    10   INCOME-HUNDREDS-MAS        PIC 9(3).
00054                    10   YEARS-EMPLOYED-MAS         PIC 99.
00055                    10   OWN-OR-RENT-MAS            PIC X.
00056                    10   MORTGAGE-OR-RENTAL-MAS     PIC 9(3).
00057                    10   OTHER-PAYMENTS-MAS         PIC 9(3).
00058               05   ACCOUNT-INFO-MAS.
00059                    10   DISCR-INCOME-MAS           PIC S9(3).
00060                    10   CREDIT-LIMIT-MAS           PIC 9(4).
00061                    10   CURRENT-BALANCE-OWING      PIC S9(5)V99.
00062               05   SPARE-CHARACTERS               PIC X(20).
```

Figure 7.4 continued.  CREATEMF, full compilation, page 2 of 10

```
00064              WORKING-STORAGE SECTION.
00065
00066         01   COMMON-WS.
00067              05   CARDS-LEFT                    PIC X(3).
00068              05   MASTER-RECORDS-LEFT           PIC X(3).
00069              05   FIRST-CARD                    PIC X(4).
00070              05   SECOND-CARD                   PIC X(4).
00071              05   ACCT-NUM-MATCH                PIC X(4).
00072              05   PAIR-VALIDITY                 PIC X(4),
00073              05   APPLICATIONS-ACCEPTED-ACCUM   PIC 9(4),
00074              05   APPLICATIONS-REJECTED-ACCUM   PIC 9(4),
00075
00076         01   HEADER-WS3.
00077              05   FILLER                        PIC X(51)    VALUE SPACES.
00078              05   TITLE                         PIC X(30)
00079                        VALUE 'CONTENTS OF CREDIT MASTER FILE'.
00080              05   FILLER                        PIC X(51)    VALUE SPACES.
00081
00082         01   CREDIT-MASTER-PRINT-LINE-WS4,
00083              05   FILLER                        PIC X(4)     VALUE SPACES.
00084              05   CREDIT-MASTER-OUT             PIC X(128),
00085
00086         01   APPLICATION-DATA-WS21 COPY CARDSWS,
00087 C       01   APPLICATION-DATA-WS21.
00088 C            05   NAME-AND-ADDRESS-WS.
00089 C                 10   NAME-WS                  PIC X(20),
00090 C                 10   ADDRESS-WS,
00091 C                      15   STREET-WS           PIC X(20).
00092 C                      15   CITY-WS             PIC X(13),
00093 C                      15   STATE-WS            PIC XX,
00094 C                      15   ZIP-WS              PIC X(5).
00095 C            05   PHONE-WS.
00096 C                 10   AREA-CODE-WS             PIC 9(3).
00097 C                 10   NUMBR-WS                 PIC X(8).
00098 C            05   FILLER                        PIC X(3).
00099 C            05   ACCT-NUM-WS                   PIC 9(5).
00100 C            05   CREDIT-INFO-WS.
00101 C                 10   SEX-WS                   PIC X,
00102 C                      88   MALE      VALUE 'M',
00103 C                      88   FEMALE    VALUE 'F',
00104 C                 10   FILLER                   PIC X.
00105 C                 10   MARITAL-STATUS-WS        PIC X.
00106 C                      88   SINGLE    VALUE 'S',
00107 C                      88   MARRIED   VALUE 'M',
00108 C                      88   DIVORCED  VALUE 'D',
00109 C                      88   WIDOWED   VALUE 'W',
00110 C                 10   FILLER                   PIC X.
00111 C                 10   NUMBER-DEPENS-WS         PIC 9.
00112 C                 10   FILLER                   PIC X.
00113 C                 10   INCOME-HUNDREDS-WS       PIC 9(3).
00114 C                 10   FILLER                   PIC X.
00115 C                 10   YEARS-EMPLOYED-WS        PIC 99,
00116 C                 10   FILLER                   PIC X,
00117 C                 10   OWN-OR-RENT-WS           PIC X,
00118 C                      88   OWNED     VALUE 'O',
00119 C                      88   RENTED    VALUE 'R',
00120 C                 10   FILLER                   PIC X.
00121 C                 10   MORTGAGE-OR-RENTAL-WS    PIC 9(3),
00122 C                 10   FILLER                   PIC X.
00123 C                 10   OTHER-PAYMENTS-WS        PIC 9(3),
```

Figure 7.4  continued. CREATEMF, full compilation, page 3 of 10

```
00124
00125            01   DISCR-INCOME-CALC-FIELDS-WS22 COPY DISIFLDS.
00126 C          01   DISCR-INCOME-CALC-FIELDS-WS22.
00127 C               05   ANNUAL-INCOME-WS              PIC 9(5).
00128 C               05   ANNUAL-TAX-WS                 PIC 9(5).
00129 C               05   TAX-RATE-WS                   PIC 9V99    VALUE 0.25.
00130 C               05   MONTHS-IN-YEAR                PIC 99      VALUE 12.
00131 C               05   MONTHLY-NET-INCOME-WS         PIC 9(4).
00132 C               05   MONTHLY-PAYMENTS-WS           PIC 9(4).
00133 C               05   DISCR-INCOME-WS               PIC S9(3).
00135            01   CRED-LIMIT-CALC-FIELDS-WS23 COPY CREDFLDS.
00136 C          01   CRED-LIMIT-CALC-FIELDS-WS23.
00137 C               05   CREDIT-FACTOR                 PIC 9.
00138 C               05   FACTOR1                       PIC 9       VALUE 1.
00139 C               05   FACTOR2                       PIC 9       VALUE 2.
00140 C               05   FACTOR3                       PIC 9       VALUE 3.
00141 C               05   FACTOR4                       PIC 9.      VALUE 4.
00142 C               05   FACTOR5                       PIC 9       VALUE 5.
00143 C               05   CREDIT-LIMIT-WS               PIC 9(4).
00144 C               05   UPPER-LIMIT-WS                PIC 9(4)    VALUE 2500.
00145 C               05   TOTAL-CREDIT-GIVEN-WS         PIC 9(7).
00146
00147            01   ASSEMBLE-MASTER-WS24.
00148                 05   TEL-NUMBR-WITH-HYPHEN-WS24.
00149                      10   EXCHANGE-IN               PIC 9(3).
00150                      10   FILLER                    PIC X.
00151                      10   FOUR-DIGIT-NUMBR-IN       PIC 9(4).
00152                 05   TEL-NUMBR-WITHOUT-HYPHEN-WS24.
00153                      10   EXCHANGE                  PIC 9(3).
00154                      10   FOUR-DIGIT-NUMBR          PIC 9(4).
00155
00156
00157            01   LINE-OF-ASTERISKS-WS52 COPY LINASTSK.
00158 C          01   LINE-OF-ASTERISKS-WS52.
00159 C               05   FILLER                        PIC X(6)    VALUE '      *'.
00160 C               05   FILLER                        PIC X(120)
00161 C                    VALUE '********************************************************************
00162 C          -   '********************************************************************
00163 C          -   '**********'.
00164 C               05   FILLER                        PIC X(5)    VALUE '*    '.
00165
00166            01   SIDE-DELIMITER-WS52 COPY SIDELIMT.
00167 C          01   SIDE-DELIMITER-WS52.
00168 C               05   FILLER                        PIC X(5)    VALUE '    *'.
00169 C               05   FILLER                        PIC X(120)  VALUE SPACES.
00170 C               05   FILLER                        PIC X(5)    VALUE '*    '.
00171
```

Figure 7.4 continued.  CREATEMF, full compilation, page 4 of 10

```
00172              01    SUMMARY-LINE-WS52 COPY SUMARYLN,
00173 C            01    SUMMARY-LINE-WS52,
00174 C               05    FILLER                      PIC X(5)      VALUE '       *',
00175 C               05    FILLER                      PIC X(24)
00176 C                           VALUE '    TOTAL CREDIT GIVEN: $',
00177 C               05    TOTAL-CREDIT-GIVEN          PIC 9(7),
00178 C               05    FILLER                      PIC X(27)
00179 C                           VALUE '      AVERAGE CREDIT GIVEN: $',
00180 C               05    AVERAGE-CREDIT              PIC 9(6),
00181 C               05    FILLER                      PIC X(4)      VALUE ' ON ',
00182 C               05    APPLICATIONS-ACCEPTED       PIC 9(4),
00183 C               05    FILLER                      PIC X(24)
00184 C                           VALUE ' ACCEPTED APPLICATIONS. ',
00185 C               05    FILLER                      PIC X(20)
00186 C                           VALUE '    NUMBER REJECTED ',
00187 C               05    APPLICATIONS-REJECTED       PIC 9(3),
00188 C               05    FILLER                      PIC X(10)
00189 C                           VALUE ' *           ',
00190
00191              01    CARD-ERROR-LINE1-WS214 COPY ERRLINE1,
00192 C            01    CARD-ERROR-LINE1-WS214,
00193 C               05    FILLER                      PIC X(5)      VALUE SPACES.
00194 C               05    FILLER                      PIC X(12)
00195 C                           VALUE 'FIRST CARD ',
00196 C               05    FIRST-CARD-ERR1             PIC X(4),
00197 C               05    FILLER                      PIC XX        VALUE SPACES,
00198 C               05    NAME-ERR1                   PIC X(20),
00199 C               05    ADDRESS-ERR1                PIC X(40),
00200 C               05    PHONE-ERR1                  PIC X(11),
00201 C               05    FILLER                      PIC X(3)      VALUE SPACES.
00202 C               05    ACCT-NUM-ERR1               PIC 9(5),
00203
00204              01    CARD-ERROR-LINE2-WS214 COPY ERRLINE2,
00205 C            01    CARD-ERROR-LINE2-WS214,
00206 C               05    FILLER                      PIC X(5)      VALUE SPACES.
00207 C               05    FILLER                      PIC X(12)
00208 C                           VALUE 'SECOND CARD ',
00209 C               05    SECOND-CARD-ERR2            PIC X(4),
00210 C               05    FILLER                      PIC X(2)      VALUE SPACES.
00211 C               05    CREDIT-INFO-ERR2            PIC X(80),
00212 C               05    MESSAGE-ERR-LINE-2          PIC X(29)     VALUE SPACES,
00213
```

Figure 7.4 continued.  CREATEMF, full compilation, page 5 of 10

```
00214          PROCEDURE DIVISION.
00215              PERFORM 1-INITIALIZE-FOR-TAPE-LOAD.
00216              PERFORM 2-LOAD-GOOD-RECORDS-TO-MASTER
00217                  UNTIL CARDS-LEFT IS EQUAL TO 'NO ',
00218              PERFORM 3-REINITIALIZE-FOR-TAPE-WRITE,
00219              PERFORM 4-LIST-CONTENTS-OF-MASTER
00220                  UNTIL MASTER-RECORDS-LEFT = 'NO ',
00221              PERFORM 5-PRINT-SUMMARY.
00222              PERFORM 6-END-OF-JOB.
00223              STOP RUN.
00224
00225          1-INITIALIZE-FOR-TAPE-LOAD.
00226              OPEN INPUT APPLICATION-CARDS-FILE
00227                   OUTPUT PROFILE-LISTING
00228                          CREDIT-MASTER-FILE.
00229              MOVE SPACES TO FIRST-CARD,
00230              MOVE SPACES TO SECOND-CARD,
00231              MOVE SPACES TO PAIR-VALIDITY,
00232              MOVE ZEROES TO APPLICATIONS-ACCEPTED-ACCUM,
00233              MOVE ZEROES TO APPLICATIONS-REJECTED-ACCUM,
00234              MOVE ZEROES TO ANNUAL-INCOME-WS,
00235              MOVE ZEROES TO ANNUAL-TAX-WS,
00236              MOVE ZEROES TO MONTHLY-NET-INCOME-WS,
00237              MOVE ZEROES TO MONTHLY-PAYMENTS-WS,
00238              MOVE ZEROES TO DISCR-INCOME-WS,
00239              MOVE ZEROES TO CREDIT-FACTOR,
00240              MOVE ZEROES TO CREDIT-LIMIT-WS,
00241              MOVE ZEROES TO TOTAL-CREDIT-GIVEN-WS,
00242              MOVE ZEROES TO TOTAL-CREDIT-GIVEN,
00243              MOVE ZEROES TO AVERAGE-CREDIT,
00244              MOVE ZEROES TO APPLICATIONS-ACCEPTED,
00245              MOVE ZEROES TO APPLICATIONS-REJECTED.
00246              MOVE 'YES' TO CARDS-LEFT.
00247              READ APPLICATION-CARDS-FILE
00248                  AT END MOVE 'NO ' TO CARDS-LEFT.
00249          * FIRST CARD IS NOW IN BUFFER
00250
00251          2-LOAD-GOOD-RECORDS-TO-MASTER.
00252              PERFORM 21-GET-A-PAIR-OF-CARDS,
00253              IF PAIR-VALIDITY = 'GOOD'
00254                  PERFORM 22-CALC-DISCRETNRY-INCOME
00255                  IF DISCR-INCOME-WS IS POSITIVE
00256                      PERFORM 23-CALC-CREDIT-LIMIT
00257                      PERFORM 24-ASSEMBLE-MASTER-RECORD
00258                      PERFORM 25-WRITE-MASTER-TO-TAPE
00259              ELSE
00260                      PERFORM 26-OUTGO-EXCEEDS-INCOME
00261              ELSE
00262                  PERFORM 27-WRITE-ERROR-PROFILE,
00263
00264          3-REINITIALIZE-FOR-TAPE-WRITE.
00265              CLOSE CREDIT-MASTER-FILE,
00266              OPEN INPUT CREDIT-MASTER-FILE,
00267              WRITE PRINT-LINE-OUT FROM HEADER-WS3
00268                                 AFTER ADVANCING 10 LINES,
00269              MOVE 'YES' TO MASTER-RECORDS-LEFT.
00270              READ CREDIT-MASTER-FILE
00271                  AT END MOVE 'NO ' TO MASTER-RECORDS-LEFT.
```

Figure 7.4 continued.  CREATEMF, full compilation, page 6 of 10

```
00272
00273              4-LIST-CONTENTS-OF-MASTER.
00274                  MOVE SPACES TO CREDIT-MASTER-PRINT-LINE-WS4.
00275                  MOVE CREDIT-MASTER-RECORD TO CREDIT-MASTER-OUT.
00276                  WRITE PRINT-LINE-OUT FROM CREDIT-MASTER-PRINT-LINE-WS4
00277                           AFTER ADVANCING 2 LINES.
00278                  READ CREDIT-MASTER-FILE
00279                    AT END MOVE 'NO ' TO MASTER-RECORDS-LEFT.
00280
00281              5-PRINT-SUMMARY.
00282                  PERFORM 51-CALC-AVERAGE-CREDIT.
00283                  PERFORM 52-WRITE-SUMMARY-REPORT.
00284
00285              6-END-OF-JOB.
00286                  CLOSE APPLICATION-CARDS-FILE
00287                          PROFILE-LISTING
00288                          CREDIT-MASTER-FILE.

00290              21-GET-A-PAIR-OF-CARDS. COPY GETPRCDS REPLACING
00291                      C1-EDIT-FIRST-CARD        BY   211-EDIT-FIRST-CARD
00292                      C2-MOVE-FIRST-CARD-TO-WS  BY   212-MOVE-FIRST-CARD-TO-WS
00293                      C3-EDIT-SECOND-CARD       BY   213-EDIT-SECOND-CARD
00294                      C4-FLUSH-CARDS-TO-ERROR-LINES
00295                                               BY
00296                          214-FLUSH-CARDS-TO-ERROR-LINES.
00297 C            PERFORM 211-EDIT-FIRST-CARD.
00298 C            PERFORM 212-MOVE-FIRST-CARD-TO-WS.
00299 C            READ APPLICATION-CARDS-FILE
00300 C              AT END MOVE 'NO ' TO CARDS-LEFT.
00301 C     * SECOND CARD OF PAIR IS NOW IN BUFFER
00302 C            PERFORM 213-EDIT-SECOND-CARD.
00303 C            IF    (FIRST-CARD = 'GOOD')
00304 C              AND (SECOND-CARD = 'GOOD')
00305 C              AND (ACCT-NUM-MATCH = 'GOOD')
00306 C                  MOVE 'GOOD' TO PAIR-VALIDITY
00307 C                  MOVE CREDIT-INFO-IN TO CREDIT-INFO-WS
00308 C            ELSE
00309 C                MOVE 'BAD ' TO PAIR-VALIDITY
00310 C                PERFORM 214-FLUSH-CARDS-TO-ERROR-LINES.
00311 C            READ APPLICATION-CARDS-FILE
00312 C              AT END MOVE 'NO ' TO CARDS-LEFT.
00313 C     * FIRST CARD OF NEXT PAIR IS NOW IN BUFFER
00314
00315              22-CALC-DISCRETNRY-INCOME. COPY DISCINCM.
00316 C            COMPUTE ANNUAL-INCOME-WS = INCOME-HUNDREDS-WS * 100.
00317 C            COMPUTE ANNUAL-TAX-WS    = ANNUAL-INCOME-WS * TAX-RATE-WS.
00318 C            COMPUTE MONTHLY-NET-INCOME-WS ROUNDED
00319 C               = (ANNUAL-INCOME-WS - ANNUAL-TAX-WS) / MONTHS-IN-YEAR.
00320 C            COMPUTE MONTHLY-PAYMENTS-WS = MORTGAGE-OR-RENTAL-WS
00321 C                                     + OTHER-PAYMENTS-WS.
00322 C            COMPUTE DISCR-INCOME-WS = MONTHLY-NET-INCOME-WS
00323 C                                   - MONTHLY-PAYMENTS-WS
00324 C             ON SIZE ERROR MOVE 999 TO DISCR-INCOME-WS.
00325 C     *   DISCRETIONARY INCOMES OVER $999 PER MONTH ARE SET AT $999
```

Figure 7.4 continued.  CREATEMF, full compilation, page 7 of 10

```
00327                    23-CALC-CREDIT-LIMIT. COPY CALCREDT.
00328 C      *      MARRIED?           Y Y Y Y N N N N      THIS DECISION TABLE
00329 C      *      OWNED?             Y Y N N Y Y N N      SETS OUT COMPANY POLICY
00330 C      *      2 OR MORE YEARS? Y N Y N Y N Y N        FOR DETERMINING CREDIT
00331 C      *      ------------------------------------    LIMIT FROM DISCRETIONARY
00332 C      *      CREDIT   FACTOR1              X X       INCOME. FACTOR1 ETC ARE
00333 C      *      LIMIT IS        2       X  X            SET UP IN WS33.
00334 C      *      MULTIPLE        3            X
00335 C      *      OF DISCR        4     X X
00336 C      *      INCOME.         5  X
00337 C             IF MARRIED
00338 C                 IF OWNED
00339 C                     IF YEARS-EMPLOYED-WS NOT LESS THAN 02
00340 C                         MOVE FACTOR5 TO CREDIT-FACTOR
00341 C                     ELSE
00342 C                         MOVE FACTOR4 TO CREDIT-FACTOR
00343 C                 ELSE
00344 C                     IF YEARS-EMPLOYED-WS NOT LESS THAN 02
00345 C                         MOVE FACTOR4 TO CREDIT-FACTOR
00346 C                     ELSE
00347 C                         MOVE FACTOR2 TO CREDIT-FACTOR
00348 C             ELSE
00349 C                 IF OWNED
00350 C                     IF YEARS-EMPLOYED-WS NOT LESS THAN 02
00351 C                         MOVE FACTOR3 TO CREDIT-FACTOR
00352 C                     ELSE
00353 C                         MOVE FACTOR2 TO CREDIT-FACTOR
00354 C                 ELSE
00355 C                     MOVE FACTOR1 TO CREDIT-FACTOR.
00356 C             COMPUTE CREDIT-LIMIT-WS = DISCR-INCOME-WS * CREDIT-FACTOR.
00357 C             IF CREDIT-LIMIT-WS IS GREATER THAN UPPER-LIMIT-WS
00358 C                 MOVE UPPER-LIMIT-WS TO CREDIT-LIMIT-WS.
00359 C             ADD CREDIT-LIMIT-WS TO TOTAL-CREDIT-GIVEN-WS.

00361             24-ASSEMBLE-MASTER-RECORD.
00362                 MOVE ACCT-NUM-WS TO ACCT-NUM-MAS.
00363                 MOVE NAME-AND-ADDRESS-WS TO NAME-AND-ADDRESS-MAS.
00364                 MOVE AREA-CODE-WS TO AREA-CODE-MAS.
00365                 PERFORM 241-REMOVE-HYPHEN-FROM-TEL-NUM.
00366                 MOVE SEX-WS               TO SEX-MAS.
00367                 MOVE MARITAL-STATUS-WS    TO MARITAL-STATUS-MAS.
00368                 MOVE NUMBER-DEPENS-WS     TO NUMBER-DEPENS-MAS.
00369                 MOVE INCOME-HUNDREDS-WS   TO INCOME-HUNDREDS-MAS
00370                 MOVE YEARS-EMPLOYED-WS    TO YEARS-EMPLOYED-MAS.
00371                 MOVE OWN-OR-RENT-WS       TO OWN-OR-RENT-MAS.
00372                 MOVE MORTGAGE-OR-RENTAL-WS TO MORTGAGE-OR-RENTAL-MAS.
00373                 MOVE OTHER-PAYMENTS-WS     TO OTHER-PAYMENTS-MAS.
00374                 MOVE DISCR-INCOME-WS TO DISCR-INCOME-MAS.
00375                 MOVE CREDIT-LIMIT-WS TO CREDIT-LIMIT-MAS.
00376                 MOVE ZEROS TO CURRENT-BALANCE-OWING.
00377                 MOVE SPACES TO SPARE-CHARACTERS.
00378
```

Figure 7.4 continued.  CREATEMF, full compilation, page 8 of 10

```
00379              25-WRITE-MASTER-TO-TAPE.
00380                  WRITE CREDIT-MASTER-RECORD,
00381                  ADD 1 TO APPLICATIONS-ACCEPTED-ACCUM,
00382
00383              26-OUTGO-EXCEEDS-INCOME. COPY OUTEXCDI REPLACING
00384                      B7-WRITE-ERROR-PROFILE  BY  27-WRITE-ERROR-PROFILE,
00385 C            MOVE SPACES TO FIRST-CARD-ERR1.
00386 C            MOVE NAME-WS TO NAME-ERR1.
00387 C            MOVE ADDRESS-WS TO ADDRESS-ERR1,
00388 C            MOVE PHONE-WS TO PHONE-ERR1,
00389 C            MOVE ACCT-NUM-WS TO ACCT-NUM-ERR1,
00390 C            MOVE SPACES TO SECOND-CARD-ERR2,
00391 C            MOVE CREDIT-INFO-WS TO CREDIT-INFO-ERR2,
00392 C            MOVE 'OUTGO EXCEEDS INCOME: REJECT' TO MESSAGE-ERR-LINE-2,
00393 C            PERFORM 27-WRITE-ERROR-PROFILE.
00394
00395              27-WRITE-ERROR-PROFILE. COPY WRTERROR REPLACING
00396                      CARD-ERROR-LINE1-WSC4    BY    CARD-ERROR-LINE1-WS214
00397                      CARD-ERROR-LINE2-WSC4    BY    CARD-ERROR-LINE2-WS214,
00398 C            MOVE SPACES TO PRINT-LINE-OUT,
00399 C            WRITE PRINT-LINE-OUT FROM CARD-ERROR-LINE1-WS214
00400 C                                 AFTER ADVANCING 4 LINES,
00401 C            WRITE PRINT-LINE-OUT FROM CARD-ERROR-LINE2-WS214
00402 C                                 AFTER ADVANCING 1 LINES,
00403 C            ADD 1 TO APPLICATIONS-REJECTED-ACCUM,
00404
00405              51-CALC-AVERAGE-CREDIT. COPY CALAVGEC,
00406 C            MOVE TOTAL-CREDIT-GIVEN-WS TO TOTAL-CREDIT-GIVEN,
00407 C            IF TOTAL-CREDIT-GIVEN = 0
00408 C                MOVE ZEROES TO AVERAGE-CREDIT
00409 C            ELSE
00410 C                DIVIDE APPLICATIONS-ACCEPTED-ACCUM
00411 C                    INTO TOTAL-CREDIT-GIVEN
00412 C                    GIVING AVERAGE-CREDIT   ROUNDED,
00413
00414              52-WRITE-SUMMARY-REPORT. COPY WRITSMRY REPLACING
00415                      LINE-OF-ASTERISKS-WSB9 BY LINE-OF-ASTERISKS-WS52
00416                      SIDE-DELIMITER-WSB9 BY SIDE-DELIMITER-WS52
00417                      SUMMARY-LINE-WSB9 BY SUMMARY-LINE-WS52,
00418 C            MOVE APPLICATIONS-ACCEPTED-ACCUM TO APPLICATIONS-ACCEPTED,
00419 C            MOVE APPLICATIONS-REJECTED-ACCUM TO APPLICATIONS-REJECTED,
00420 C            WRITE PRINT-LINE-OUT FROM LINE-OF-ASTERISKS-WS52
00421 C                                 AFTER ADVANCING 6 LINES,
00422 C            WRITE PRINT-LINE-OUT FROM SIDE-DELIMITER-WS52
00423 C                                 AFTER ADVANCING 1 LINES,
00424 C            WRITE PRINT-LINE-OUT FROM SUMMARY-LINE-WS52
00425 C                                 AFTER ADVANCING 1 LINES,
00426 C            WRITE PRINT-LINE-OUT FROM SIDE-DELIMITER-WS52
00427 C                                 AFTER ADVANCING 1 LINES,
00428 C            WRITE PRINT-LINE-OUT FROM LINE-OF-ASTERISKS-WS52
00429 C                                 AFTER ADVANCING 1 LINES.
00430
```

Figure 7.4 continued.  CREATEMF, full compilation, page 9 of 10

```
00431          211-EDIT-FIRST-CARD.  COPY EDT1STCD,
00432  C           MOVE 'GOOD' TO FIRST-CARD.
00433  C           IF NAME-IN IS EQUAL TO SPACES
00434  C               MOVE '*** NAME MISSING ***' TO NAME-IN
00435  C               MOVE 'BAD ' TO FIRST-CARD.
00436  C           IF ADDRESS-IN IS EQUAL TO SPACES
00437  C               MOVE '**** ADDRESS MISSING ****' TO ADDRESS-IN
00438  C               MOVE 'BAD ' TO FIRST-CARD.
00439  C           IF PHONE-IN IS EQUAL TO SPACES
00440  C               MOVE 'NO PHONE **' TO PHONE-IN
00441  C               MOVE 'BAD ' TO FIRST-CARD.

00443          212-MOVE-FIRST-CARD-TO-WS.  COPY MOV1STCD.
00444  C           MOVE NAME-IN TO NAME-WS.
00445  C           MOVE ADDRESS-IN TO ADDRESS-WS.
00446  C           MOVE PHONE-IN TO PHONE-WS.
00447  C           MOVE ACCT-NUM-IN1 TO ACCT-NUM-WS.
00448

00449          213-EDIT-SECOND-CARD.  COPY EDT2NDCD,
00450  C           MOVE 'GOOD' TO SECOND-CARD.
00451  C           MOVE 'GOOD' TO ACCT-NUM-MATCH.
00452  C           IF CARD-TYPE-IN IS NOT EQUAL TO 'C'
00453  C               MOVE 'BAD ' TO SECOND-CARD,
00454  C           IF ACCT-NUM-IN2 IS NOT EQUAL TO ACCT-NUM-WS
00455  C               MOVE 'BAD' TO ACCT-NUM-MATCH,
00456

00457          214-FLUSH-CARDS-TO-ERROR-LINES,  COPY FLUSHCDS,
00458  C           MOVE FIRST-CARD TO FIRST-CARD-ERR1,
00459  C           MOVE NAME-WS TO NAME-ERR1.
00460  C           MOVE ADDRESS-WS TO ADDRESS-ERR1.
00461  C           MOVE PHONE-WS TO PHONE-ERR1,
00462  C           MOVE ACCT-NUM-WS TO ACCT-NUM-ERR1,
00463  C           MOVE SECOND-CARD TO SECOND-CARD-ERR2.
00464  C           MOVE CREDIT-INFO-WS TO CREDIT-INFO-ERR2.
00465  C           IF ACCT-NUM-MATCH = 'BAD '
00466  C               MOVE 'ACCOUNT NUMBERS DO NOT MATCH'
00467  C                                   TO MESSAGE-ERR-LINE-2
00468  C           ELSE
00469  C               MOVE SPACES TO MESSAGE-ERR-LINE-2.
00470

00471          241-REMOVE-HYPHEN-FROM-TEL-NUM,
00472              MOVE NUMBR-WS TO TEL-NUMBR-WITH-HYPHEN-WS24,
00473              MOVE EXCHANGE-IN TO EXCHANGE.
00474              MOVE FOUR-DIGIT-NUMBR-IN TO FOUR-DIGIT-NUMBR,
00475              MOVE TEL-NUMBR-WITHOUT-HYPHEN-WS24 TO NUMBR-WS,
```

Figure 7.4 continued.  CREATEMF, full compilation, page 10 of 10

Now that we have created a tape master file and rid ourselves of the large decks of cards and the problems of handling
them, we have to consider how we update the tape file.  Remember
with the card decks, how easy it was to change a record by merely
repunching the cards and replacing them in the original decks?

Q.    What types of changes have you made to your card
      decks?

A.    Changes or updates to fields on existing cards,
      adding new cards, and removing cards.

Maintaining tape files also requires changing fields and adding
or deleting records as people relocate, open new accounts, or
close accounts.


The tapes we create are normally read and written in only
one sequence -- either in a forward direction or a backward
direction.  It is usually impractical to skip forward from the
beginning of the tape to the first record that we wish to deal
with, and then backwards toward the beginning of the tape to
deal with the next record, and then forward again.  Instead, we
read each record one after the other and deal with any required
changes as the records are read; in most cases, only a small
fraction of the tape records will require processing.

Q.    What would happen if we tried to add a new
      record in the middle of a tape file?

A.    We would over-write the next record and
      therefore lose one original record.

Each time we need to update a tape file, we will need to
create a new copy of the tape file which will contain all the
new additions, changes, and deletions.  These updates have to
be made in such a way as to maintain the original sequence of
the file.

Q.    What would be the sequence of the new customer
      file if we add a new customer with an account
      number of 012345 to an existing tape file whose
      account number sequence was:

                     010101
                     020202
                     030303

                       etc.

- 175 -

A.    The new customer file would now look like this:

```
010101
012345
020202
030303
```

etc.

Each time we update a tape file, we must remember to copy all the existing records which have not been changed, together with all the changes and additions.  Since we are creating a new copy, we delete a record by not copying it.  Let us look at how we would program all the updates for a tape file one at a time.  In all tape-file changes, the file of the changes must be in the same sequence as the tape file.

Changes to a Record

Assuming that we only have changes to existing records:

```
READ old-tape-record
READ change-record
While there are more old-tape-records or change-records
    IF the change applies to this old-tape-record
        While there are more old-tape-record fields
            IF field is to be changed
                MOVE update-field to new-tape-field
            ELSE
                MOVE old-tape-field to new-tape-field
        WRITE new-tape-record
        READ next-change-record
        READ next-old-tape-record
    ELSE
        WRITE new-tape-record from old-tape-record
        READ next-old-tape-record.
```

Additions

Assuming that we only have additions to the tape, we still have to find the correct sequential position for the record addition in the new tape file.  We will need to find the first old-tape record which will follow the new addition in order to be certain that the new record is added in the correct position, as follows:

```
READ old-tape-record
READ record-addition
While there are more tape-records or additions
    IF the old-tape-record-number is higher than the
                                record-addition-number
        WRITE new-tape-record from record-addition
        READ next-record-addition
    ELSE
        WRITE new-tape-record from old-tape-record
        READ next-old-tape-record.
```

## Deletions

Assuming that we only have deletions to the file:

```
READ delete-record
READ old-tape-record
While there are more old-tape-records or delete-records
    IF delete applies to this old-tape-record
        READ next-old-tape-record
        READ next-delete-record
    ELSE
        WRITE new-tape-record from old-tape-record
        READ  next-old-tape-record.
```

In all the pseudocode examples for updating a tape file, we have assumed that only one type of update is expected. In most of the file maintenance work that you will do, you will normally be expected to make additions, changes, and deletions on the file with the same program.

Q.   Assuming that you have read the first old-tape record and the first update record, what action would you take?

A.   a.   If the update record did not apply to that tape record, then WRITE the new tape record from the old tape record.

b.   If the update did apply to that tape record, the tape record would be updated depending on the type of update:  change or delete

If the update was a delete, then no new tape record would be written.

If the update was a change to existing fields, the new fields would be updated and then the new tape record written from the updated record.

c.   If the update was an addition to the file which had a record number less than the first old-tape record, then the first new-tape record would be written from the addition record and the second new-tape record written from the old tape record.

Since the contents of the new tape file records must be determined each time we read a record from the update file and the old tape file, we need a simple means of determining the possible types of updates. We use the record number sequence on both the files to determine whether the update is a change or deletion, an addition, or no update is required, as follows:

Old-tape-record-number is equal to update-record-number:  change
                                                          or delete

    "          less than          "           no change

    "          greater than       "           add new
                                              record

In pseudocode, we can express the logic of all possible updates resulting from the first record on each file, as follows:

    READ first-update-record
    READ first-old-tape-record

    IF old-tape-record-number less than update-record-number
        WRITE new-tape-record from old-tape-record

    ELSE IF old-tape-record-number equal to update-record-number
        PERFORM CHANGE-OR-DELETE-ROUTINE

    ELSE old-tape-record-number is greater than update-record-number
        WRITE new-tape-record from update-record.

The above pseudocode processes the first record from each of the files.

    Q.    Modify the pseudocode to process all the records
          on both the update file and the old tape file.
          Whenever the old tape records are modified, or
          additions made, PERFORM a routine at the time of
          the change which will print out the update. For
          the sake of simplicity, assume that both the up-
          date file and the old tape file reach end-of-file (eof)
          at the same time; we will look at how we deal with
          other end-of-file situations once we have the basic
          logic correct.

```
A.    READ first-update-record
      READ first-old-tape-record

      PERFORM UPDATE-TAPE
        UNTIL eof on both files.

      UPDATE-TAPE.

          IF old-tape-record-number less than update-record-number
              WRITE new-tape-record from old-tape-record
              READ next-old-tape-record

          ELSE IF old-tape-record-number is equal to update-record-number
              PERFORM CHANGE-OR-DELETE-ROUTINE
              READ next-update-record
              READ next-old-tape-record

          ELSE
              PERFORM ADD-NEW-RECORD
              READ next-update-record.

      CHANGE-OR-DELETE-ROUTINE.

          IF change
              While there are more old-tape-fields
                  IF field is to be changed
                      MOVE update-field to new-tape-field
                  ELSE
                      MOVE old-tape-field to new-tape-field
              WRITE new-tape-record from merged field
              PERFORM PRINT-CHANGE
              READ next-update-record
              READ next-old-tape-record

          ELSE IF deletion
              Double-check that this is a deletion - it is much
              more difficult to recover from an accidentally
              deleted record than to double-check in the first
              place.

              PERFORM PRINT-CHANGE
              READ next-update-record
              READ next-old-tape-record

          ELSE
              PERFORM UPDATE-NOT-CHANGE-OR-DELETE.

      ADD-NEW-RECORD.

          Check that all mandatory fields are present, and do
          any calculations that may be necessary.

          MOVE update-fields to new-tape-fields
          WRITE new-tape-record
          PERFORM PRINT-CHANGE
          READ next-update-record.
```

Now that we have the pseudocode for the basic logic, we must consider the case when both files do not reach end-of-file at the same time; it would be very unusual if they did in a normal updating program.

Q.  What processing would be required if the update file reached end-of-file and the old tape file had not?

A.  We would want to copy over the remaining old tape records onto the new tape file.

Q.  What processing would be required if the old tape file reached end-of-file but there were still more update records?

A.  All the update records would be additions at the end of the master file, so we would want to add the update records to the new tape file.

This situation is best dealt with by performing normal processing until either there are no more old tape records OR there are no more update records, then testing to see which condition has caused processing to halt and reacting accordingly. The pseudocode of the highest level module is this:

```
PERFORM UPDATE-MASTER
   UNTIL no-more-old-tape-records
      OR no-more-updates.

IF no-more-updates
    PERFORM copy-remaining-old-tape-records
       UNTIL no-more-old-tape-records

ELSE
    PERFORM add-remaining-updates
       UNTIL no-more-updates.
```

    Now that we have the pseudocode for a tape maintenance
program, we can prepare to write a program, MAINTMFS, which has
the following specifications:

Customer master file:  The customer master file which we will
update is the same file which we created with the program
CREATEMF.

Updates to the tape file will be submitted on pairs of cards
as in SAMPLE-4.  Any updates to the file should be printed so
that we can check that the right updates were made.

Additions to the master file will be contained on the pair of
cards.  These pairs of cards should be edited in the same
manner as in CREDCALC.

Changes to existing customer records will be indicated by the
letters "CH" in cc 73 and 74 of the first card.  All changes
will contain the name, address, and phone number in the first
three fields on the first card.  Any changes to the credit
information on the second card must be punched together with
the unchanged credit information.  You can assume that all the
credit information on the second card will be correct, although
you should check that the second card is with the correct first
card, as in CREDCALC.

Deletions to the existing customer master file will be indicated
by the letters "DE" in cc 73 and 74 of the first card.  The
name, address, and phone number will be on the first card.  This
will allow cross-checking of the information if we find that any
records are being deleted by mistake.  For now, just check
that they exist in the first card.  There will be no credit
information in the second card, just a "C" in cc 1 and the account
number in cc 2 - 7.  If there is any credit information in the
second card, do not delete the original customer record.


    As a check on the program's logic, as a sound business
practice, we want to create a log of all changes made to the
master file.  So, when you have made an addition, print out
the contents of the update cards and the new tape record with
a message saying that the record has been added.  Likewise,
when you delete a record, print out the card contents and the
record that you deleted, with an appropriate message.  If you
change a record, print out the record before the change, the
card contents, and the record after the change.

When all the updates have been processed, rewind the tape and list the contents of the new master file. This will serve as an additional check that the updates have been made correctly.

Before you design and code MAINTMFS, specify the test data that you are going to use as updates, and what the contents of the master file should be as a result of these updates.

A solution for MAINTMFS appears on the following pages.

```
CBL LIB
00001          IDENTIFICATION DIVISION.
00002          PROGRAM-ID. MAINTMFS.
00003
00004          ENVIRONMENT DIVISION.
00005          INPUT-OUTPUT SECTION.
00006          FILE-CONTROL.
00007              SELECT APPLICATION-CARDS-FILE ASSIGN TO SYS031-UR-2540R-S,
00008              SELECT UPDATE-LISTING         ASSIGN TO SYS033-UR-1403-S.
00009              SELECT CREDIT-MASTER-OLD-FILE ASSIGN TO SYS005-UT-2400-S.
00010              SELECT CREDIT-MASTER-NEW-FILE ASSIGN TO SYS005-UT-2400-S.
00011
00012          DATA DIVISION,
00013          FILE SECTION.
00014
00015          FD  APPLICATION-CARDS-FILE
00016              LABEL RECORDS ARE OMITTED
00017              DATA RECORDS ARE NAME-ADDRESS-AND-PHONE-IN
00018                            CREDIT-INFORMATION-IN,
00019          01  NAME-ADDRESS-AND-PHONE-IN.
00020              05  NAME-AND-ADDRESS-IN.
00021                  10  NAME-IN                PIC X(20),
00022                  10  ADDRESS-IN.
00023                      15  STREET-IN          PIC X(20),
00024                      15  CITY-IN            PIC X(13),
00025                      15  STATE-IN           PIC XX,
00026                      15  ZIP-IN             PIC X(5).
00027              05  PHONE-IN                   PIC X(11),
00028              05  FILLER                     PIC X,
00029              05  CHANGE-CODE-IN             PIC XX,
00030              05  ACCT-NUM-IN1               PIC 9(6),
00031          01  CREDIT-INFORMATION-IN,
00032              05  CARD-TYPE-IN               PIC X,
00033              05  ACCT-NUM-IN2               PIC 9(5),
00034              05  FILLER                     PIC X,
00035              05  CREDIT-INFO-IN             PIC X(22),
00036              05  FILLER                     PIC X(50),
00037
00038          FD  UPDATE-LISTING
00039              LABEL RECORDS ARE OMITTED.
00040          01  PRINT-LINE-OUT                 PIC X(132),
00041
```

Figure 7.5    MAINTMFS, full compilation, page 1 of 11

```
00042          FD  CREDIT-MASTER-OLD-FILE
00043              LABEL RECORDS ARE STANDARD
00044              BLOCK CONTAINS 10 RECORDS.
00045          01  CREDIT-MASTER-OLD-RECORD.
00046              05  ACCT-NUM-MAS-OLD              PIC 9(6).
00047              05  NAME-AND-ADDRESS-MAS-OLD.
00048                  10  NAME-MAS-OLD             PIC X(20).
00049                  10  STREET-MAS-OLD           PIC X(20).
00050                  10  CITY-MAS-OLD             PIC X(13).
00051                  10  STATE-MAS-OLD            PIC XX.
00052                  10  ZIP-MAS-OLD              PIC 9(5).
00053              05  PHONE-MAS-OLD.
00054                  10  AREA-CODE-MAS-OLD        PIC 9(3).
00055                  10  NUMBR-MAS-OLD            PIC 9(7).
00056              05  CREDIT-INFO-MAS-OLD.
00057                  10  SEX-MAS-OLD              PIC X.
00058                  10  MARITAL-STATUS-MAS-OLD   PIC X.
00059                  10  NUMBER-DEPENS-MAS-OLD    PIC 99.
00060                  10  INCOME-HUNDREDS-MAS-OLD  PIC 9(3).
00061                  10  YEARS-EMPLOYED-MAS-OLD   PIC 99.
00062                  10  OWN-OR-RENT-MAS-OLD      PIC X.
00063                  10  MORTGAGE-OR-RENTAL-MAS-OLD   PIC 9(3).
00064                  10  OTHER-PAYMENTS-MAS-OLD   PIC 9(3)
00065              05  ACCOUNT-INFO-MAS-OLD.
00066                  10  DISCR-INCOME-MAS-OLD     PIC S9(3).
00067                  10  CREDIT-LIMIT-MAS-OLD     PIC 9(4).
00068                  10  CURRENT-BALANCE-OWING-OLD    PIC S9(6)V99.
00069              05  SPARE-CHARACTERS-OLD         PIC X(20).
00070
00071          FD  CREDIT-MASTER-NEW-FILE
00072              LABEL RECORDS ARE STANDARD
00073              BLOCK CONTAINS 10 RECORDS.
00074          01  CREDIT-MASTER-NEW-RECORD.
00075              05  ACCT-NUM-MAS-NEW             PIC 9(6).
00076              05  NAME-AND-ADDRESS-MAS-NEW.
00077                  10  NAME-MAS-NEW             PIC X(20).
00078                  10  STREET-MAS-NEW           PIC X(20).
00079                  10  CITY-MAS-NEW             PIC X(13).
00080                  10  STATE-MAS-NEW            PIC XX.
00081                  10  ZIP-MAS-NEW              PIC 9(5).
00082              05  PHONE-MAS-NEW.
00083                  10  AREA-CODE-MAS-NEW        PIC 9(3).
00084                  10  NUMBR-MAS-NEW            PIC 9(7).
00085              05  CREDIT-INFO-MAS-NEW.
00086                  10  SEX-MAS-NEW              PIC X.
00087                  10  MARITAL-STATUS-MAS-NEW   PIC X.
00088                  10  NUMBER-DEPENS-MAS-NEW    PIC 99.
00089                  10  INCOME-HUNDREDS-MAS-NEW  PIC 9(3).
00090                  10  YEARS-EMPLOYED-MAS-NEW   PIC 99.
00091                  10  OWN-OR-RENT-MAS-NEW      PIC X.
00092                  10  MORTGAGE-OR-RENTAL-MAS-NEW   PIC 9(3).
00093                  10  OTHER-PAYMENTS-MAS-NEW   PIC 9(3).
00094              05  ACCOUNT-INFO-MAS-NEW.
00095                  10  DISCR-INCOME-MAS-NEW     PIC S9(3).
00096                  10  CREDIT-LIMIT-MAS-NEW     PIC 9(4).
00097                  10  CURRENT-BALANCE-OWING-NEW    PIC S9(6)V99.
00098              05  SPARE-CHARACTERS-NEW         PIC X(20).
00099
00100
```

Figure 7.5 continued.  MAINTMFS, full compilation, page 2 of 11  – 184

```
00101          WORKING-STORAGE SECTION.
00102
00103          01    COMMON-WS.
00104                05    CARDS-LEFT                    PIC X(3)
00105                05    OLD-MASTER-RECORDS-LEFT       PIC X(3),
00106                05    NEW-MASTER-RECORDS-LEFT       PIC X(3),
00107                05    FIRST-CARD                    PIC X(4),
00108                05    SECOND-CARD                   PIC X(4),
00109                05    ACCT-NUM-MATCH                PIC X(4),
00110                05    PAIR-VALIDITY                 PIC X(4),
00111
00112          01    LOG-HEADER-WSA1.
00113                05    FILLER                        PIC X(47)   VALUE SPACES.
00114                05    FILLER                        PIC X(38)
00115                      VALUE 'LOG OF ADDITIONS DELETIONS AND CHANGES',
00116                05    FILLER                        PIC X(47)   VALUE SPACES.
00117
00118          01    HEADER-WSA5.
00119                05    FILLER                        PIC X(51)   VALUE SPACES.
00120                05    TITLE                         PIC X(30)
00121                      VALUE 'CONTENTS OF CREDIT MASTER FILE',
00122                05    FILLER                        PIC X(51)   VALUE SPACES.
00124          01    APPLICATION-DATA-WSB2.
00125                05    NAME-AND-ADDRESS-WS.
00126                      10    NAME-WS                 PIC X(20),
00127                      10    ADDRESS-WS.
00128                            15    STREET-WS         PIC X(20),
00129                            15    CITY-WS           PIC X(13).
00130                            15    STATE-WS          PIC XX,
00131                            15    ZIP-WS            PIC X(5),
00132                05    PHONE-WS.
00133                      10    AREA-CODE-WS            PIC 9(3),
00134                      10    NUMBR-WS                PIC X(8).
00135                05    FILLER                        PIC X          VALUE SPACE,
00136                05    CHANGE-CODE-WS                PIC XX,
00137                05    ACCT-NUM-WS                   PIC 9(6),
00138                05    CREDIT-INFO-WS.
00139                      10    SEX-WS                  PIC X,
00140                            88    MALE      VALUE 'M',
00141                            88    FEMALE    VALUE 'F',
00142                      10    FILLER                  PIC X.
00143                      10    MARITAL-STATUS-WS       PIC X.
00144                            88    SINGLE    VALUE 'S',
00145                            88    MARRIED   VALUE 'M',
00146                            88    DIVORCED  VALUE 'D',
00147                            88    WIDOWED   VALUE 'W',
00148                      10    FILLER                  PIC X.
00149                      10    NUMBER-DEPENS-WS        PIC 9.
00150                      10    FILLER                  PIC X,
00151                      10    INCOME-HUNDREDS-WS      PIC 9(3),
00152                      10    FILLER                  PIC X.
00153                      10    YEARS-EMPLOYED-WS       PIC 99,
00154                      10    FILLER                  PIC X.
00155                      10    OWN-OR-RENT-WS          PIC X,
00156                            88    OWNED     VALUE 'O',
00157                            88    RENTED    VALUE 'R',
00158                      10    FILLER                  PIC X.
00159                      10    MORTGAGE-OR-RENTAL-WS   PIC 9(3),
00160                      10    FILLER                  PIC X,
00161                      10    OTHER-PAYMENTS-WS       PIC 9(3),
```

Figure 7.5  continued.  MAINTMFS, full compilation, page 3 of 11

- 185 -

```
00162
00163            01    UPDATE-MESSAGE-AREA-WSB2.
00164                  05   UPDATE-MESSAGE-AREA            PIC X(15).
00165
00166            01    CREDIT-MASTER-PRINT-LINE.
00167                  05   FILLER                         PIC X(4)      VALUE SPACES.
00168                  05   CREDIT-MASTER-OUT              PIC X(128).
00169
00170            01    UPDATE-RECORD-PRINT-LINE.
00171                  05   FILLER                         PIC X(4)      VALUE SPACES.
00172                  05   APPLICATION-DATA-OUT           PIC X(102).
00173                  05   FILLER                         PIC X(4)      VALUE SPACES.
00174                  05   MESSAGE-AREA-OUT               PIC X(15).
00175
00176            01    DISCR-INCOME-CALC-FIELDS-WSC8   COPY DISIFLDS.
00177 C          01    DISCR-INCOME-CALC-FIELDS-WSC8.
00178 C                05   ANNUAL-INCOME-WS              PIC 9(5).
00179 C                05   ANNUAL-TAX-WS                 PIC 9(5).
00180 C                05   TAX-RATE-WS                   PIC 9V99      VALUE 0.25.
00181 C                05   MONTHS-IN-YEAR                PIC 99        VALUE 12.
00182 C                05   MONTHLY-NET-INCOME-WS         PIC 9(4).
00183 C                05   MONTHLY-PAYMENTS-WS           PIC 9(4).
00184 C                05   DISCR-INCOME-WS               PIC S9(3).
00185
00186            01    CRED-LIMIT-CALC-FIELDS-WSC9 COPY CREDFLDS.
00187 C          01    CRED-LIMIT-CALC-FIELDS-WSC9.
00188 C                05   CREDIT-FACTOR                 PIC 9.
00189 C                05   FACTOR1                       PIC 9         VALUE 1.
00190 C                05   FACTOR2                       PIC 9         VALUE 2.
00191 C                05   FACTOR3                       PIC 9         VALUE 3.
00192 C                05   FACTOR4                       PIC 9         VALUE 4.
00193 C                05   FACTOR5                       PIC 9         VALUE 5.
00194 C                05   CREDIT-LIMIT-WS               PIC 9(4).
00195 C                05   UPPER-LIMIT-WS                PIC 9(4)      VALUE 2500.
00196 C                05   TOTAL-CREDIT-GIVEN-WS         PIC 9(7).
```

Figure 7.5 continued.  MAINTMFS, full compilation, page 4 of 11

```
00198          01   ASSEMBLE-TEL-NUM-WSD1.
00199               05   TEL-NUMBR-WITH-HYPHEN.
00200                    10   EXCHANGE-IN              PIC 9(3),
00201                    10   FILLER                   PIC X.
00202                    10   FOUR-DIGIT-NUMBR-IN      PIC 9(4),
00203               05   TEL-NUMBR-WITHOUT-HYPHEN.
00204                    10   EXCHANGE                 PIC 9(3),
00205                    10   FOUR-DIGIT-NUMBR         PIC 9(4),
00206
00207          01   CARD-ERROR-LINE1-WS     COPY ERRLINE1,
00208 C        01   CARD-ERROR-LINE1-WS.
00209 C             05   FILLER                         PIC X(5)      VALUE SPACES,
00210 C             05   FILLER                         PIC X(12)
00211 C                                           VALUE 'FIRST CARD  ',
00212 C             05   FIRST-CARD-ERR1                PIC X(4).
00213 C             05   FILLER                         PIC XX        VALUE SPACES,
00214 C             05   NAME-ERR1                      PIC X(20),
00215 C             05   ADDRESS-ERR1                   PIC X(40),
00216 C             05   PHONE-ERR1                     PIC X(11),
00217 C             05   FILLER                         PIC X(3)      VALUE SPACES,
00218 C             05   ACCT-NUM-ERR1                  PIC 9(5),
00219
00220          01   CARD-ERROR-LINE2-WS     COPY ERRLINE2,
00221 C        01   CARD-ERROR-LINE2-WS.
00222 C             05   FILLER                         PIC X(5)      VALUE SPACES,
00223 C             05   FILLER                         PIC X(12)
00224 C                                           VALUE 'SECOND CARD ',
00225 C             05   SECOND-CARD-ERR2               PIC X(4).
00226 C             05   FILLER                         PIC X(2)      VALUE SPACES,
00227 C             05   CREDIT-INFO-ERR2               PIC X(80),
00228 C             05   MESSAGE-ERR-LINE-2             PIC X(29)     VALUE SPACES,
00229
```

Figure 7.5 continued.  MAINTMFS, full compilation, page 5 of 11

```
00231          PROCEDURE DIVISION.
00232
00233
00234              PERFORM A1-INITIALIZE.
00235              PERFORM A2-UPDATE-MASTER
00236                UNTIL OLD-MASTER-RECORDS-LEFT = 'NO '
00237                  OR CARDS-LEFT = 'NO '.
00238              IF CARDS-LEFT = 'NO '
00239      *                                   THERE ARE MORE OLD MASTER RECS
00240                  PERFORM A3-COPY-REMAINING-OLD-MASTER
00241                     UNTIL OLD-MASTER-RECORDS-LEFT = 'NO '
00242              ELSE
00243      *                                   THERE ARE MORE CARDS, SO
00244                  PERFORM A4-ADD-REMAINING-CARDS
00245                     UNTIL CARDS-LEFT = 'NO '.
00246              PERFORM A5-REINITIALIZE-FOR-TAPE-WRITE.
00247              PERFORM A6-LIST-CONTENTS-OF-MASTER
00248                UNTIL NEW-MASTER-RECORDS-LEFT = 'NO '.
00249              PERFORM A7-END-OF-JOB.
00250              STOP RUN.
00251
00252          A1-INITIALIZE.
00253              OPEN INPUT   APPLICATION-CARDS-FILE
00254                           CREDIT-MASTER-OLD-FILE
00255                   OUTPUT CREDIT-MASTER-NEW-FILE
00256                           UPDATE-LISTING.
00257              MOVE SPACES TO FIRST-CARD.
00258              MOVE SPACES TO SECOND-CARD.
00259              MOVE SPACES TO ACCT-NUM-MATCH.
00260              MOVE SPACES TO PAIR-VALIDITY.
00261              MOVE ZEROES TO ANNUAL-INCOME-WS.
00262              MOVE ZEROES TO ANNUAL-TAX-WS.
00263              MOVE ZEROES TO MONTHLY-NET-INCOME-WS.
00264              MOVE ZEROES TO MONTHLY-PAYMENTS-WS.
00265              MOVE ZEROES TO DISCR-INCOME-WS.
00266              MOVE ZEROES TO CREDIT-FACTOR.
00267              MOVE ZEROES TO CREDIT-LIMIT-WS.
00268              MOVE ZEROES TO TOTAL-CREDIT-GIVEN-WS.
00269              MOVE 'YES' TO CARDS-LEFT.
00270              MOVE 'YES' TO OLD-MASTER-RECORDS-LEFT.
00271              READ APPLICATION-CARDS-FILE
00272                  AT END MOVE 'NO ' TO CARDS-LEFT.
00273              PERFORM B1-GET-A-PAIR-OF-CARDS-INTO-WS.
00274      * FIRST PAIR OF CARDS IN WS: FIRST CARD OF SECOND PAIR IN BUFFER
00275              READ CREDIT-MASTER-OLD-FILE
00276                  AT END MOVE 'NO ' TO OLD-MASTER-RECORDS-LEFT.
00277      * FIRST OLD MASTER RECORD IS IN BUFFER
00278              WRITE PRINT-LINE-OUT FROM LOG-HEADER-WSA1
00279                                   AFTER ADVANCING 3 LINES.
00280
```

Figure 7.5 continued.  MAINTMFS, full compilation, page 6 of 11

```
00281          A2-UPDATE-MASTER.
00282     * BEFORE COMPARING THE UPDATE WITH THE MASTER, WE MUST CHECK
00283     * THAT WE HAVE A VALID PAIR OF CARDS - IF YOUR PROGRAM DOES
00284     * NOT MAKE THIS TEST, IT WILL ONLY WORK WITH VALID PAIRS OF
00285     * CARDS
00286          IF  PAIR-VALIDITY = 'BAD '
00287              PERFORM B1-GET-A-PAIR-OF-CARDS-INTO-WS
00288          ELSE IF  ACCT-NUM-WS IS GREATER THAN ACCT-NUM-MAS-OLD
00289     *                              ACCT-NUM-WS IS CARD ACCOUNT NUM
00290              MOVE CREDIT-MASTER-OLD-RECORD TO
00291                  CREDIT-MASTER-NEW-RECORD
00292              WRITE CREDIT-MASTER-NEW-RECORD
00293              READ CREDIT-MASTER-OLD-FILE
00294                  AT END MOVE 'NO ' TO OLD-MASTER-RECORDS-LEFT
00295          ELSE IF ACCT-NUM-WS = ACCT-NUM-MAS-OLD
00296              PERFORM B2-CHANGE-OR-DELETE-MASTER
00297              PERFORM B1-GET-A-PAIR-OF-CARDS-INTO-WS
00298              READ CREDIT-MASTER-OLD-FILE
00299                  AT END MOVE 'NO ' TO OLD-MASTER-RECORDS-LEFT
00300          ELSE
00301     *                              ACCT-NUM-WS IS LESS THAN
00302     *                              ACCT-NUM-MAS-OLD
00303              PERFORM B3-ADD-NEW-MASTER
00304              PERFORM B1-GET-A-PAIR-OF-CARDS-INTO-WS.
00305
00306       A3-COPY-REMAINING-OLD-MASTER.
00307          MOVE CREDIT-MASTER-OLD-RECORD TO
00308              CREDIT-MASTER-NEW-RECORD
00309          WRITE CREDIT-MASTER-NEW-RECORD,
00310          READ CREDIT-MASTER-OLD-FILE
00311              AT END MOVE 'NO ' TO OLD-MASTER-RECORDS-LEFT
00312
00313       A4-ADD-REMAINING-CARDS.
00314          PERFORM B3-ADD-NEW-MASTER,
00315          PERFORM B1-GET-A-PAIR-OF-CARDS-INTO-WS,
00316
00317       A5-REINITIALIZE-FOR-TAPE-WRITE.
00318          CLOSE APPLICATION-CARDS-FILE
00319                CREDIT-MASTER-OLD-FILE
00320                CREDIT-MASTER-NEW-FILE.
00321          OPEN INPUT CREDIT-MASTER-NEW-FILE.
00322          WRITE PRINT-LINE-OUT FROM HEADER-WSA5
00323                              AFTER ADVANCING 10 LINES,
00324          MOVE 'YES' TO NEW-MASTER-RECORDS-LEFT,
00325          READ CREDIT-MASTER-NEW-FILE
00326              AT END MOVE 'NO ' TO NEW-MASTER-RECORDS-LEFT,
00327
00328       A6-LIST-CONTENTS-OF-MASTER.
00329          MOVE SPACES TO CREDIT-MASTER-PRINT-LINE,
00330          MOVE CREDIT-MASTER-NEW-RECORD TO CREDIT-MASTER-OUT,
00331          WRITE PRINT-LINE-OUT FROM CREDIT-MASTER-PRINT-LINE
00332                              AFTER ADVANCING 2 LINES.
00333          READ CREDIT-MASTER-NEW-FILE
00334              AT END MOVE 'NO ' TO NEW-MASTER-RECORDS-LEFT,
00335
00336       A7-END-OF-JOB.
00337          CLOSE CREDIT-MASTER-NEW-FILE
00338                UPDATE-LISTING.
```

Figure 7.5 continued.  MAINTMFS, full compilation, page 7 of 11

```
00340                   B1-GET-A-PAIR-OF-CARDS-INTO-WS.
00341                       PERFORM C1-EDIT-FIRST-CARD.
00342                       PERFORM C2-MOVE-FIRST-CARD-TO-WS,
00343                       READ APPLICATION-CARDS-FILE
00344                          AT END MOVE 'NO ' TO CARDS-LEFT,
00345                       PERFORM C3-EDIT-SECOND-CARD,
00346                       IF  (FIRST-CARD = 'GOOD')
00347                           AND (SECOND-CARD = 'GOOD')
00348                           AND (ACCT-NUM-MATCH = 'GOOD')
00349                                MOVE 'GOOD' TO PAIR-VALIDITY
00350                                MOVE CREDIT-INFO-IN TO CREDIT-INFO-WS
00351                       ELSE
00352                           MOVE 'BAD ' TO PAIR-VALIDITY
00353                       PERFORM C4-FLUSH-CARDS-TO-ERROR-LINES.
00354                       READ APPLICATION-CARDS-FILE
00355                          AT END MOVE 'NO ' TO CARDS-LEFT,
00356
00357                   B2-CHANGE-OR-DELETE-MASTER.
00358                       IF  CHANGE-CODE-WS = 'CH'
00359                           PERFORM C5-MERGE-UPDATE-WITH-OLD-MAST
00360                           MOVE 'RECORD CHANGED' TO UPDATE-MESSAGE-AREA
00361                           PERFORM C6-LOG-ACTION
00362                           WRITE CREDIT-MASTER-NEW-RECORD
00363                       ELSE IF  CHANGE-CODE-WS = 'DE'
00364                   *                                   CHECK IF DELETE VALID
00365                               IF  CREDIT-INFO-WS IS EQUAL TO SPACES
00366                                   MOVE 'RECORD DELETED' TO UPDATE-MESSAGE-AREA
00367                                   PERFORM C6-LOG-ACTION
00368                               ELSE
00369                                   MOVE 'REC NOT DELETED' TO UPDATE-MESSAGE-AREA
00370                                   MOVE CREDIT-MASTER-OLD-RECORD TO
00371                                       CREDIT-MASTER-NEW-RECORD
00372                                   PERFORM C6-LOG-ACTION
00373                                   WRITE CREDIT-MASTER-NEW-RECORD
00374                       ELSE
00375                           PERFORM C7-INVALID-CHANGE-CODE.
00376
00377
00378                   B3-ADD-NEW-MASTER.
00379                       PERFORM C8-CALC-DISCRETNRY-INCOME,
00380                       PERFORM C9-CALC-CREDIT-LIMIT.
00381                       PERFORM C10-ASSEMBLE-NEW-MASTER-RECORD,
00382                       MOVE 'RECORD ADDED ' TO UPDATE-MESSAGE-AREA,
00383                       PERFORM C6-LOG-ACTION.
00384                       WRITE CREDIT-MASTER-NEW-RECORD,
00385
00386                   C1-EDIT-FIRST-CARD.   COPY EDT1STCD.
00387 C                     MOVE 'GOOD' TO FIRST-CARD.
00388 C                     IF NAME-IN IS EQUAL TO SPACES
00389 C                         MOVE '*** NAME MISSING ***' TO NAME-IN
00390 C                         MOVE 'BAD ' TO FIRST-CARD,
00391 C                     IF ADDRESS-IN IS EQUAL TO SPACES
00392 C                         MOVE '**** ADDRESS MISSING ****' TO ADDRESS-IN
00393 C                         MOVE 'BAD ' TO FIRST-CARD.
00394 C                     IF PHONE-IN IS EQUAL TO SPACES
00395 C                         MOVE 'NO PHONE **' TO PHONE-IN
00396 C                         MOVE 'BAD ' TO FIRST-CARD.
00397
```

Figure 7.5 continued.   MAINTMFS, full compilation, page 8 of 11

```
00398              C2-MOVE-FIRST-CARD-TO-WS.
00399                  MOVE NAME-IN TO NAME-WS.
00400                  MOVE ADDRESS-IN TO ADDRESS-WS.
00401                  MOVE PHONE-IN TO PHONE-WS.
00402                  MOVE CHANGE-CODE-IN TO CHANGE-CODE-WS,
00403                  MOVE ACCT-NUM-IN1 TO ACCT-NUM-WS,
00404
00405              C3-EDIT-SECOND-CARD.  COPY EDT2NDCD,
00406  C              MOVE 'GOOD' TO SECOND-CARD.
00407  C              MOVE 'GOOD' TO ACCT-NUM-MATCH,
00408  C              IF CARD-TYPE-IN IS NOT EQUAL TO 'C'
00409  C                  MOVE 'BAD ' TO SECOND-CARD.
00410  C              IF ACCT-NUM-IN2 IS NOT EQUAL TO ACCT-NUM-WS
00411  C                  MOVE 'BAD' TO ACCT-NUM-MATCH,
00412
00413              C4-FLUSH-CARDS-TO-ERROR-LINES.  COPY FLUSHCDS.
00414  C              MOVE FIRST-CARD TO FIRST-CARD-ERR1,
00415  C              MOVE NAME-WS TO NAME-ERR1,
00416  C              MOVE ADDRESS-WS TO ADDRESS-ERR1,
00417  C              MOVE PHONE-WS TO PHONE-ERR1,
00418  C              MOVE ACCT-NUM-WS TO ACCT-NUM-ERR1,
00419  C              MOVE SECOND-CARD TO SECOND-CARD-ERR2,
00420  C              MOVE CREDIT-INFO-WS TO CREDIT-INFO-ERR2,
00421  C              IF ACCT-NUM-MATCH = 'BAD '
00422  C                  MOVE 'ACCOUNT NUMBERS DO NOT MATCH'
00423  C                                      TO MESSAGE-ERR-LINE-2
00424  C              ELSE
00425  C                  MOVE SPACES TO MESSAGE-ERR-LINE-2,
00426                  MOVE SPACES TO PRINT-LINE-OUT.
00427                  WRITE PRINT-LINE-OUT FROM CARD-ERROR-LINE1-WS
00428                          AFTER ADVANCING 1 LINES,
00429                  MOVE SPACES TO PRINT-LINE-OUT.
00430                  WRITE PRINT-LINE-OUT FROM CARD-ERROR-LINE2-WS
00431                          AFTER ADVANCING 1 LINES.
00432
00433              C5-MERGE-UPDATE-WITH-OLD-MAST.
00434                  MOVE ACCT-NUM-MAS-OLD TO ACCT-NUM-MAS-NEW,
00435                  MOVE NAME-AND-ADDRESS-WS TO NAME-AND-ADDRESS-MAS-NEW,
00436                  MOVE AREA-CODE-WS TO AREA-CODE-MAS-NEW.
00437                  PERFORM D1-REMOVE-HYPHEN-FROM-TEL-NUM.
00438          * THE SECOND INPUT CARD HAS CREDIT DATA, IF THIS HAS TO BE
00439          * UPDATED THEN THE DISCRETIONARY INCOME CALC HAS TO BE RUN
00440                  IF CREDIT-INFO-WS EQUAL TO SPACES
00441                      MOVE CREDIT-INFO-MAS-OLD TO CREDIT-INFO-MAS-NEW
00442                      MOVE ACCOUNT-INFO-MAS-OLD TO ACCOUNT-INFO-MAS-NEW
00443                  ELSE
00444                      PERFORM C8-CALC-DISCRETNRY-INCOME
00445                      PERFORM C9-CALC-CREDIT-LIMIT
00446                      MOVE SEX-WS                 TO SEX-MAS-NEW.
00447                      MOVE MARITAL-STATUS-WS       TO MARITAL-STATUS-MAS-NEW
00448                      MOVE NUMBER-DEPENS-WS        TO NUMBER-DEPENS-MAS-NEW
00449                      MOVE INCOME-HUNDREDS-WS      TO INCOME-HUNDREDS-MAS-NEW
00450                      MOVE YEARS-EMPLOYED-WS       TO YEARS-EMPLOYED-MAS-NEW
00451                      MOVE OWN-OR-RENT-WS          TO OWN-OR-RENT-MAS-NEW
00452                      MOVE MORTGAGE-OR-RENTAL-WS TO MORTGAGE-OR-RENTAL-MAS-NEW
00453                      MOVE OTHER-PAYMENTS-WS       TO OTHER-PAYMENTS-MAS-NEW
00454                      MOVE DISCR-INCOME-WS TO DISCR-INCOME-MAS-NEW
00455                      MOVE CREDIT-LIMIT-WS TO CREDIT-LIMIT-MAS-NEW,
00456                  MOVE CURRENT-BALANCE-OWING-OLD TO CURRENT-BALANCE-OWING-NEW,
00457                  MOVE SPARE-CHARACTERS-OLD TO SPARE-CHARACTERS-NEW,
```

Figure 7.5 continued.  MAINTMFS, full compilation, page 9 of 11

```
00458
00459          C6-LOG-ACTION.
00460              IF CHANGE-CODE-WS = 'CH'
00461          *                                  WRITE OLD TAPE RECORD
00462          *                                  WRITE CARD CONTENTS & MESSAGE
00463          *                                  WRITE NEW TAPE RECORD
00464              ,    MOVE SPACES TO CREDIT-MASTER-PRINT-LINE
00465                   MOVE CREDIT-MASTER-OLD-RECORD TO CREDIT-MASTER-OUT
00466                   WRITE PRINT-LINE-OUT FROM CREDIT-MASTER-PRINT-LINE
00467                                  AFTER ADVANCING 3 LINES
00468                   MOVE SPACES TO UPDATE-RECORD-PRINT-LINE
00469                   MOVE APPLICATION-DATA-WSB2 TO APPLICATION-DATA-OUT
00470                   MOVE UPDATE-MESSAGE-AREA TO MESSAGE-AREA-OUT
00471                   WRITE PRINT-LINE-OUT FROM UPDATE-RECORD-PRINT-LINE
00472                                  AFTER ADVANCING 1 LINES
00473                   MOVE SPACES TO CREDIT-MASTER-PRINT-LINE
00474                   MOVE CREDIT-MASTER-NEW-RECORD TO CREDIT-MASTER-OUT
00475                   WRITE PRINT-LINE-OUT FROM CREDIT-MASTER-PRINT-LINE
00476                                  AFTER ADVANCING 1 LINES
00477              ELSE IF CHANGE-CODE-WS = 'DE'
00478          *                                  WRITE OLD TAPE RECORD
00479          *                                  WRITE CARD CONTENTS & MESSAGE
00480                   MOVE SPACES TO CREDIT-MASTER-PRINT-LINE
00481                   MOVE CREDIT-MASTER-OLD-RECORD TO CREDIT-MASTER-OUT
00482                   WRITE PRINT-LINE-OUT FROM CREDIT-MASTER-PRINT-LINE
00483                                  AFTER ADVANCING 3 LINES
00484                   MOVE SPACES TO UPDATE-RECORD-PRINT-LINE
00485                   MOVE APPLICATION-DATA-WSB2 TO APPLICATION-DATA-OUT
00486                   MOVE UPDATE-MESSAGE-AREA TO MESSAGE-AREA-OUT
00487                   WRITE PRINT-LINE-OUT FROM UPDATE-RECORD-PRINT-LINE
00488                                  AFTER ADVANCING 1 LINES
00489              ELSE IF CHANGE-CODE-WS = ' '
00490          *                                  WRITE CARDS FOR ADDITION
00491          *                                  WRITE NEW TAPE RECORD
00492                   MOVE SPACES TO UPDATE-RECORD-PRINT-LINE
00493                   MOVE APPLICATION-DATA-WSB2 TO APPLICATION-DATA-OUT
00494                   MOVE UPDATE-MESSAGE-AREA TO MESSAGE-AREA-OUT
00495                   WRITE PRINT-LINE-OUT FROM UPDATE-RECORD-PRINT-LINE
00496                                  AFTER ADVANCING 3 LINES
00497                   MOVE SPACES TO CREDIT-MASTER-PRINT-LINE
00498                   MOVE CREDIT-MASTER-NEW-RECORD TO CREDIT-MASTER-OUT
00499                   WRITE PRINT-LINE-OUT FROM CREDIT-MASTER-PRINT-LINE
00500                                  AFTER ADVANCING 1 LINES
00501              ELSE PERFORM C7-INVALID-CHANGE-CODE.
00502
00503          C7-INVALID-CHANGE-CODE.
00504          * THIS ROUTINE WILL HANDLE CARDS WITH NEITHER CH OR DE IN CC73/7
00505
00506          C8-CALC-DISCRETNRY-INCOME.   COPY DISCINCM.
00507 C            COMPUTE ANNUAL-INCOME-WS = INCOME-HUNDREDS-WS * 100.
00508 C            COMPUTE ANNUAL-TAX-WS    = ANNUAL-INCOME-WS * TAX-RATE-WS.
00509 C            COMPUTE MONTHLY-NET-INCOME-WS ROUNDED
00510 C               = (ANNUAL-INCOME-WS - ANNUAL-TAX-WS) / MONTHS-IN-YEAR.
00511 C            COMPUTE MONTHLY-PAYMENTS-WS = MORTGAGE-OR-RENTAL-WS
00512 C                                  + OTHER-PAYMENTS-WS.
00513 C            COMPUTE DISCR-INCOME-WS = MONTHLY-NET-INCOME-WS
00514 C                              - MONTHLY-PAYMENTS-WS
00515 C               ON SIZE ERROR MOVE 999 TO DISCR-INCOME-WS.
00516 C        *    DISCRETIONARY INCOMES OVER $999 PER MONTH ARE SET AT $999
00517
```

Figure 7.5 continued.   MAINTMFS, full compilation, page 10 of 11

```
00518          C9-CALC-CREDIT-LIMIT.  COPY CALCREDT.
00519  C     *    MARRIED?              Y Y Y Y N N N N      THIS DECISION TABLE    *
00520  C     *    OWNED?                Y Y N N Y Y N N      SETS OUT COMPANY POLICY *
00521  C     *    2 OR MORE YEARS? Y N Y N Y N Y N           FOR DETERMINING CREDIT  *
00522  C     *    ------------------------------------       LIMIT FROM DISCRETIONARY*
00523  C     *    CREDIT     FACTOR1              X X        INCOME, FACTOR1 ETC ARE *
00524  C     *    LIMIT IS        2         X   X            SET UP IN WS33.         *
00525  C     *    MULTIPLE        3           X                                      *
00526  C     *    OF DISCR        4     X X                                          *
00527  C     *    INCOME.         5 X                                               *
00528  C          IF MARRIED
00529  C              IF OWNED
00530  C                  IF YEARS-EMPLOYED-WS NOT LESS THAN 02
00531  C                      MOVE FACTOR5 TO CREDIT-FACTOR
00532  C                  ELSE
00533  C                      MOVE FACTOR4 TO CREDIT-FACTOR
00534  C                ELSE
00535  C                  IF YEARS-EMPLOYED-WS NOT LESS THAN 02
00536  C                      MOVE FACTOR4 TO CREDIT-FACTOR
00537  C                  ELSE
00538  C                      MOVE FACTOR2 TO CREDIT-FACTOR
00539  C            ELSE
00540  C              IF OWNED
00541  C                  IF YEARS-EMPLOYED-WS NOT LESS THAN 02
00542  C                      MOVE FACTOR3 TO CREDIT-FACTOR
00543  C                  ELSE
00544  C                      MOVE FACTOR2 TO CREDIT-FACTOR
00545  C                ELSE
00546  C                  MOVE FACTOR1 TO CREDIT-FACTOR.
00547  C          COMPUTE CREDIT-LIMIT-WS = DISCR-INCOME-WS * CREDIT-FACTOR.
00548  C          IF CREDIT-LIMIT-WS IS GREATER THAN UPPER-LIMIT-WS
00549  C              MOVE UPPER-LIMIT-WS TO CREDIT-LIMIT-WS.
00550  C          ADD CREDIT-LIMIT-WS TO TOTAL-CREDIT-GIVEN-WS.
00551
00552          C10-ASSEMBLE-NEW-MASTER-RECORD.
00553              MOVE ACCT-NUM-WS TO ACCT-NUM-MAS-NEW.
00554              MOVE NAME-AND-ADDRESS-WS TO NAME-AND-ADDRESS-MAS-NEW.
00555              MOVE AREA-CODE-WS TO AREA-CODE-MAS-NEW.
00556              PERFORM D1-REMOVE-HYPHEN-FROM-TEL-NUM.
00557              MOVE SEX-WS                TO SEX-MAS-NEW
00558              MOVE MARITAL-STATUS-WS      TO MARITAL-STATUS-MAS-NEW
00559              MOVE NUMBER-DEPENS-WS      TO NUMBER-DEPENS-MAS-NEW
00560              MOVE INCOME-HUNDREDS-WS     TO INCOME-HUNDREDS-MAS-NEW
00561              MOVE YEARS-EMPLOYED-WS      TO YEARS-EMPLOYED-MAS-NEW
00562              MOVE OWN-OR-RENT-WS         TO OWN-OR-RENT-MAS-NEW
00563              MOVE MORTGAGE-OR-RENTAL-WS TO MORTGAGE-OR-RENTAL-MAS-NEW
00564              MOVE OTHER-PAYMENTS-WS      TO OTHER-PAYMENTS-MAS-NEW.
00565              MOVE DISCR-INCOME-WS TO DISCR-INCOME-MAS-NEW.
00566              MOVE CREDIT-LIMIT-WS TO CREDIT-LIMIT-MAS-NEW.
00567              MOVE ZEROS TO CURRENT-BALANCE-OWING-NEW.
00568              MOVE SPACES TO SPARE-CHARACTERS-NEW.
00569
00570          D1-REMOVE-HYPHEN-FROM-TEL-NUM.
00571              MOVE NUMBR-WS TO TEL-NUMBR-WITH-HYPHEN
00572              MOVE EXCHANGE-IN TO EXCHANGE
00573              MOVE FOUR-DIGIT-NUMBR-IN TO FOUR-DIGIT-NUMBR
00574              MOVE TEL-NUMBR-WITHOUT-HYPHEN TO NUMBR-MAS-NEW.
```

Figure 7.5 continued.  MAINTMFS, full compilation, page 11 of 11  – 193

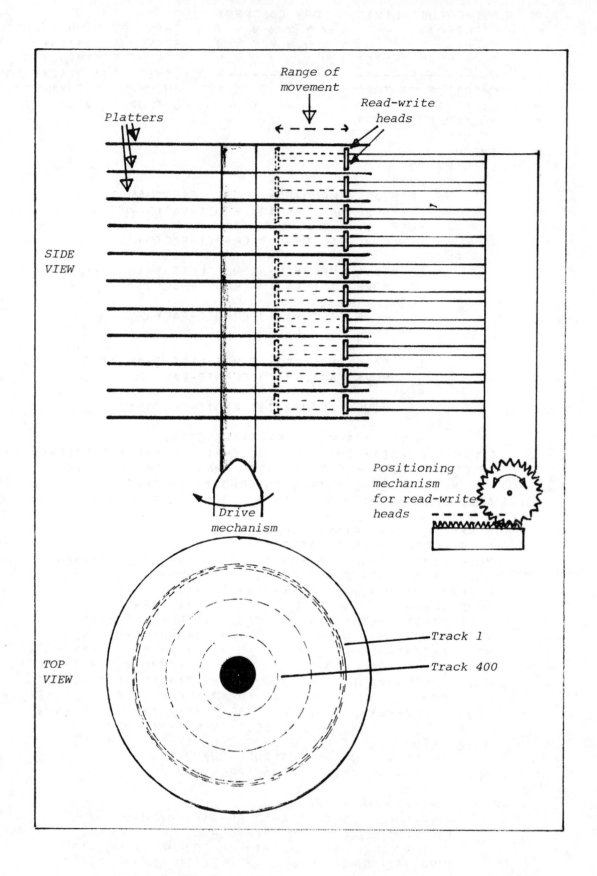

Figure 7.6    Schematic representation of magnetic disk drive

- 194 -

Suppose you had a master file on tape, as maintained by
MAINTMFS, with 30,000 records on it, and you wanted to know
the credit limit of Morris Median, who is the 21,475th record
on the file.  You would need to use a program which read through
the master file, checking each record to see if it was Median's,
until his record was found.  This could take several minutes,
even at computer speeds.  If, five minutes later, you wanted
the credit limit for Marcia Mean, who had the 20,799th record,
you would have to go through the whole process over again.  In
practice, it is usually not economic to search sequentially
through a whole tape file for one name at a time, so inquiries
about data in a sequentially organized file are batched until
there are enough to make a run through the file worthwhile.
Of course, this means that it can take some time to get the
answer to a question about data in a sequential file; if the
program is run once a day, it can take 24 hours or more to
find out someone's credit limit.

Very frequently, we want to access records in random order
and to do it rapidly.  For example, if a customer of a bank wants
to know the balance of his account, he doesn't want to wait.  If
a potential customer calls a supplier to know whether he can de-
liver a certain spare part, he doesn't want to wait.  In each
case we are making an inquiry on the files, and there is no way
of predicting which order the inquiries will come in, or when
they will come.  If the file that holds the relevant data is on
tape, you may need to search through the whole of a reel of tape
to find the information, which, as we have seen, can take too long;
having answered one inquiry, you must rewind the tape and search
all the way through again for the next inquiry.

For this reason, random access storage devices (sometimes
called direct access storage devices, or DASD) were developed,
which can locate any desired record in a fraction of a second.
The most successful DASD to date is the rotating magnetic disk,
shown diagrammatically opposite.

Each surface of the disk can have data recorded on it as
a stream of pulses on a series of tracks.  The read-write heads
can be moved by a precision mechanism, to sit over any one of the
tracks as the disk revolves.  In any one position of the head
movement mechanism, of course, you can read a number of tracks,
one for each read-write head.  To take an example, the IBM 3330
disk drive, which is typical of the disks used on a variety of
computers, has 11 platters, which can be recorded on both surfaces, except for the very top and bottom surfaces (which might
be damaged) and the top surface of the bottom platter (which is
used to position the heads).

Q. How many tracks can be read with a single position of the read-write mechanism?

A. 19 (count them): 11 platters makes 22 sides, less 3 which cannot be written on.

The 19 tracks which can be read at one position of the heads are called a cylinder. Every position of the heads (and the IBM 3330 has 400 possible positions across the face of the platter) reads a different cylinder.

Q. Suppose the data for Victor Grasper is written on track 79 on the side of the platter read by head 11, and that the heads are at present stationed over track 100. What has to happen before we can retrieve Victor Grasper's credit limit?

A. 1. The read-write heads have to be moved from track 100 to track 79.
2. The disk control program has to select head 11 to read.
3. The system has to read track 79 under head 11, as the disk rotates, until it finds Victor Grasper's account number, then transfer the data to the input buffer.

The process of moving the heads to the correct position is called a seek; the process of reading the track as the disk rotates under the head is called a search.

Now for the mind-boggling calculations. The 3330 holds 13,000 characters on each track; there are 19 tracks in each cylinder, and 400 cylinders on each disk pack. So each 3330 drive can hold

13,000 X 19 X 400  or about 100 million characters.

That's roughly 1,250,000 fully punched cards, or a tray of punched cards half a mile long! And the 3330 can locate any item in about 1/30th of a second! That's what we mean by random access.

7.3.1  *Organization of Randomly Accessed Files*

You can put sequentially organized files onto disk, just as you put them onto tape, but to randomly access a file, you have to supply enough information to enable the disk control system to work out which track the record you want is on. This is done in two ways, with indexed organization or relative organization. We shall deal with each in turn in the next two sections.

An indexed file is like a sequential file, except that
at the beginning it has another small file, called the index,
specifying in which cylinder and track each group of records
is to be found.  When you issue a READ calling for a particular
record, the operating system directs the read-write head to the
index file, looks up the cylinder and track; it then goes
directly to the track to find the record.


Suppose we had 38,000 customers on our master file, each
with a record 128 characters long.  Since an IBM 3330 can hold
13,000 characters per track, we would get about 100 customer
records on each track.  Since there are 19 tracks per cylinder we
would need about 20 cylinders to hold the file [ 38,000 /(19 X 100) ].


Suppose further that the 38,000 account numbers range from
100000 to 999999 (with gaps), and that we want customer number
876543, whose record is actually on track 11 of cylinder 16
of the disk drive.  If this were a sequential file, we would have
to read through every track on every cylinder record by record,
saying "Is this account number 876543?  If not, read next record."


In an indexed file, the first cylinder has an index to all
the other cylinders, which in this case would be like this:

| Record Key Range | Cylinder |
|---|---|
| 100000 - 145000 | 1 |
| 145001 - 190500 | 2 |
| 190501 - 230499 | 3 |
| . | . |
| . | . |
| . | . |
| 850001 - 895000 | 16 |
| . | . |
| . | . |

With just one positioning of the read-write head, the disk
control program reads this index comparing the range of keys
for each cylinder with the so-called nominal key of the record
we are looking for, i.e., 876543.  When it gets the match, the
control program sends the read-write head to sit over cylinder 16.
Now the head is in the correct position but which of the 19
read-write heads is the correct one to read from for the track?


You guessed it:  On the first track of each cylinder is a
track index, giving the range of record keys to be found on
each track, like this:

```
          Cylinder 16            Track
       Record Key Range

       850001 - 852500            2
       852501 - 854500            3
                .                 .
                .                 .
       875001 - 880000           11
                .                 .
                .                 .
```

The control program then switches on to read-write head 11 and
searches the track (serially) until it finds the record for 876543.


So with only two seeks of the read-write head (one to the
index and one to the cylinder) we have located the record we
want out of 38,000 others.


As you can appreciate, the programming necessary to do all
of this is somewhat complex; fortunately, the computer manufacturer supplies you with a Disk Control Program which takes
the commands you write in COBOL and works out exactly what to do.
You can write commands in your COBOL program to create indexed
files, access a record randomly as described above, read the
file sequentially, change (update) records on the file, add new
records, and delete records.  Let's look at each of these actions
in turn.


7.4.1      *Creating an Indexed File*


In the FILE-CONTROL paragraph, you need to specify the
information which tells the compiler to create an index; the
file itself is created as a sequential file of records and then
the control program builds the index.

```
     FILE-CONTROL.
          SELECT filename-in-FD ASSIGN TO   (DA-I-CUSTMAST)
               ORGANIZATION IS INDEXED
               ACCESS IS SEQUENTIAL
               RECORD KEY IS data-name.          a typical system-name
```

The RECORD KEY is whatever field you will use to search the file;
in our case, it would be ACCT-NUM.


The system-name, for example DA-I-CUSTMAST above, may
be different depending on the operating system used by your
installation.  This example uses an IBM Operating System name;
earlier we used IBM Disk Operating System (DOS) names -- the
equivalent DOS name might be SYSnnn-DA-2314-I.

In the Data Division, you write an FD for the new indexed
file, normally specifying LABEL RECORDS ARE STANDARD and with a
BLOCK CONTAINS clause.  The input file must be a sequential file,
usually card or tape, with the keys arranged in ascending order.


In the Procedure Division, OPEN the new file as OUTPUT.
READ from the input file and WRITE to the new indexed file.
If for any reason the records are out of order or there are two
records with the same key (a "duplicate key condition"), the
disk system control program will not know what to do.  For this
reason the INVALID KEY clause is provided; the format of the
WRITE statement becomes:

WRITE indexed-record  FROM data-name INVALID KEY imperative.

e.g., WRITE CREATE-INDEX-REC
      INVALID KEY PERFORM DUPLICATE-OR-SEQUENCE-ERROR.

With this information you are now required to write a
program which creates an indexed file out of the customer master
file now held in sequential form on tape.  This will be the first
step in a project to give the Marketing Manager immediate access
to a customer's unpaid balances and other information.  Use
ACCT-NUM as the record key, with a block-size of ten records.
If you find an invalid key, print out the entire tape record with
an appropriate message, and go on to the next record.  Call this
program CREATEMFI.


A model solution is given on the next page; you will see
that unlike the previous programs in the book, it has not been
compiled.  This is because at the time of writing, this particular
form of indexed file, though specified by the 1974 American
National Standard (ANS) for COBOL, had not been implemented by
any manufacturer.  You should check whether your installation
has ANS-74 COBOL, or a compiler which conforms to the earlier
standard, ANS-68.  ANS-68 compilers will have some minor
differences in handling indexed and relative files, and you
should seek advice on what these are.  Hopefully, by the time
you read this, you will have an ANS-74 compiler with which to
work.

```
IDENTIFICATION DIVISION.
PROGRAM-ID.   CREATEMFI.

ENVIRONMENT DIVISION.
INPUT-OUTPUT SECTION.
FILE-CONTROL.
      SELECT TAPE-MASTER   ASSIGN TO UT-S-TAPEINPT.
      SELECT DISK-MASTER   ASSIGN TO DA-I-CUSTMAST
                           ORGANIZATION IS INDEXED
                           ACCESS IS SEQUENTIAL
                           RECORD KEY IS ACCT-NUM-MAS.
      SELECT ERROR-LIST    ASSIGN TO UR-S-SYSPRINT.

DATA DIVISION.
FILE-SECTION.

FD  TAPE-MASTER
    LABEL RECORDS ARE STANDARD
    BLOCK CONTAINS 10 RECORDS.
01  TAPE-MASTER-RECORD.
    05  ACCT-NUM-IN            PIC 9(6).
    05  ACCT-INFO-IN           PIC X(102).
    05  FILLER                 PIC X(20).

FD  DISK-MASTER
    LABEL RECORDS ARE STANDARD
    BLOCK CONTAINS 10 RECORDS.
01  INDEXED-MASTER-RECORD.
    05  ACCT-NUM-MAS           PIC 9(6).
    05  ACCT-INFO-OUT          PIC X(102).
    05  FILLER                 PIC X(20).

FD  ERROR-LIST
    LABEL RECORDS ARE OMITTED.
01  PRINT-LINE-OUT             PIC X(132).

WORKING-STORAGE SECTION.

01  COMMON-WS.
    05  TAPE-RECORDS-LEFT      PIC X(3).

01  ERROR-RECORD-WS.
    05  FILLER                 PIC X(40)
            VALUE 'DUPLICATE OR SEQUENCE ERROR ON ACCT NO  '.
    05  ACCT-NUM-ERR           PIC 9(6).
    05  FILLER                 PIC X(50)
            VALUE 'THIS RECORD IGNORED: CHECK INPUT AND FILE CONTENTS'.
```

Figure 7.7    Model program to create an indexed file

```
PROCEDURE DIVISION.

    PERFORM A1-INITIALIZATION.
    PERFORM A2-LOAD-DISK-FILE
      UNTIL TAPE-RECORDS-LEFT = 'NO '.
    PERFORM A3-END-OF-JOB.
    STOP RUN.

 A1-INITIALIZATION.
    OPEN INPUT  TAPE-MASTER
         OUTPUT DISK-MASTER
                ERROR-LIST.
    MOVE 'YES' TO TAPE-RECORDS-LEFT.
    READ TAPE-MASTER
      AT END MOVE 'NO ' TO TAPE-RECORDS-LEFT.
* FIRST TAPE RECORD IN BUFFER

 A2-LOAD-DISK-FILE.
    MOVE SPACES TO INDEXED-MASTER-RECORD.
    MOVE ACCT-NUM-IN TO ACCT-NUM-MAS.
    MOVE ACCT-INFO-IN TO ACCT-INFO-OUT.
    WRITE INDEXED-MASTER-RECORD
      INVALID KEY PERFORM B1-DUPLICATE-OR-SEQUENCE-ERROR.
    READ TAPE-MASTER
      AT END MOVE 'NO ' TO TAPE-RECORDS-LEFT.

 A3-END-OF-JOB.
    CLOSE TAPE-MASTER
          DISK-MASTER
          ERROR-LIST.

 B1-DUPLICATE-OR-SEQUENCE-ERROR.
    MOVE ACCT-NUM-MAS TO ACCT-NUM-ERR.
    MOVE SPACES TO PRINT-LINE-OUT.
    WRITE PRINT-LINE-OUT FROM ERROR-RECORD-WS.
```

Figure 7.7 continued.  Model program to create an indexed file

Now that we have an indexed file on disk, we want to be able to get at any record on demand.  For example, we might want to be able to get a customer's credit profile, knowing only his account number.  To make an <u>inquiry</u> on the file like this, we want to feed in an account number, or a series of account numbers in any order we please, and get the response to each inquiry printed out.

To make random inquiries, you have to specify ACCESS IS RANDOM in the SELECT statement for the file, and move the key value of the record you want to retrieve into the field named as RECORD KEY, before READing the indexed file.  If the record you ask for can't be found, an INVALID KEY condition will exist, and you will have to specify what the program should do in this case.

We want to develop such an inquiry program, called INXINQIR, which will read in cards, in any order, each with a six-digit account number punched in cc 2 - 7, and with an I (for inquiry) in cc 1.  The program is to retrieve the corresponding record for each account number from the master file, and simply list the contents of the disk record on the printer.  If the record for that account number can't be found, the account number should be printed out with an appropriate message.

The following program will carry out this very basic inquiry function:

```
IDENTIFICATION DIVISION.
PROGRAM-ID.  INXINQIR.

ENVIRONMENT DIVISION.
INPUT-OUTPUT SECTION.
FILE-CONTROL.
    SELECT CARD-FILE    ASSIGN TO UR-S-SYSIN.
    SELECT DISK-MASTER ASSIGN TO DA-I-CUSTMAST
                       ORGANIZATION IS INDEXED
                       ACCESS IS RANDOM
                       RECORD KEY IS ACCT-NUM-MAS.
    SELECT REPORT-LIST ASSIGN TO UR-S-SYSPRINT.

DATA DIVISION.
FILE-SECTION.

FD  CARD-FILE
    LABEL RECORDS ARE OMITTED.
01  INQUIRY-CARD.
    05  CARD-TYPE           PIC X.
    05  ACCT-NUM-IN         PIC 9{6}.
    05  FILLER              PIC X{73}.
```

```
FD   DISK-MASTER
     LABEL RECORDS ARE STANDARD
     BLOCK CONTAINS 10 RECORDS.
01   INDEXED-MASTER-RECORD.
     05   ACCT-NUM-MAS          PIC 9(6).
     05   ACCT-INFO-MAS         PIC X(102).
     05   FILLER                PIC X(20).

FD   REPORT-LIST
     LABEL RECORDS ARE OMITTED.
01   REPORT-LINE.
     05   PRINT-LINE-OUT        PIC X(132).

WORKING-STORAGE SECTION.

01   COMMON-WS.
     05   CARDS-LEFT            PIC X(3).
     05   MASTER-IS-FOUND       PIC X(3).

01   ERROR-LINE-WS.
     05   FILLER               PIC X(15)
             VALUE 'ACCOUNT NUMBER '.
     05   ACCT-NUM-ERR          PIC 9(6).
     05   FILLER                PIC X(25)
             VALUE 'NOT FOUND IN MASTER FILE '.
     05   FILLER                PIC X(86).

PROCEDURE DIVISION.

     PERFORM A1-INITIALIZATION.
     PERFORM A2-PROCESS-INQUIRIES
       UNTIL CARDS-LEFT = 'NO ' .
     PERFORM A3-END-OF-JOB.
     STOP RUN.

A1-INITIALIZATION.
     OPEN   INPUT  CARD-FILE
                   DISK-MASTER
            OUTPUT REPORT-LIST.
     MOVE 'YES' TO CARDS-LEFT.
     READ CARD-FILE
        AT END MOVE 'NO ' TO CARDS-LEFT.

A2-PROCESS-INQUIRIES.
     MOVE ACCT-NUM-IN TO ACCT-NUM-MAS.
     MOVE 'YES' TO MASTER-IS-FOUND.
     READ DISK-MASTER-RECORD
        INVALID KEY MOVE 'NO ' TO MASTER-IS-FOUND.
     IF MASTER-IS-FOUND = 'YES'
          WRITE PRINT-LINE-OUT FROM INDEXED-MASTER-RECORD
     ELSE
          MOVE ACCT-NUM-MAS TO ACCT-NUM-ERR
          WRITE PRINT-LINE-OUT FROM ERROR-LINE-WS.
     READ CARD-FILE
        AT END MOVE 'NO ' TO CARDS-LEFT.

A3-END-OF-JOB.
     CLOSE  CARD-FILE DISK-MASTER REPORT-LIST.
```

When you have compiled a crude skeleton program like INXINQIR and tested it with some account numbers which you know are on the file, as well as with some which you know are not, you have shown that you can successfully retrieve some records from the master file.

A fuller version of this program might check the first column of the card, and reject the card if it did not have an I in cc 1, printing an appropriate message. How would you modify the logic of INXINQIR to do this?

A still fuller version would present the information retrieved for each account as a profile, as we did in CREDCALC. How would you enhance the program to do this? To what extent could you use the Source Statement Library?

Suppose a customer changes his address or his phone number, or his credit circumstances change.  We will want to alter the fields in his record, just as we did when the master file was held on tape.  Similarly, we want to be able to create new records for new customers, and delete records when customers close their accounts.

Changing fields is done with a REWRITE command, adding records is done with a WRITE (there shouldn't be a duplicate key because this is a new key), and deleting records is done with a DELETE command.  In all cases, the file is specified with ACCESS IS RANDOM.

There is, of course, no need to create a fresh copy of an indexed file, as we did with the tape.  When you modify the file, the disk control program reorganizes the index to keep track of all the records, and since the index shows where each record is located, we can add records in any order.  This is especially useful when, as in most cases, there are many fewer changes to the file than there are original records.  For example, if we update only 150 records on a tape containing 38,000 records, we have to rewrite all 38,000 records again on to a new tape.  If we use indexed files, we need only change and rewrite the 150 records.

Let us summarize the program considerations in each case:

## Updates

OPEN the indexed file as I-O (input and output).
The RECORD KEY field should contain the value of the
    record to be updated.
READ the indexed file INVALID KEY PERFORM RECORD-NOT-FOUND.
MOVE the new values to the appropriate fields in the record.
    (Don't change the key field!  If you do, you will update
    the wrong record, or get an invalid key.)
REWRITE the indexed file INVALID KEY PERFORM SERIOUS-ERROR.
    If the invalid key condition exists, it can only be
    because the key has been changed between READ and
    REWRITE, or perhaps because the READ was not done in
    the first place; this would indicate a bug in your
    program.

## Additions

OPEN the indexed file as I-O.
Make sure the RECORD KEY field contains the new value.
WRITE the new record INVALID KEY PERFORM RECORD-ALREADY-IN-FILE.

## Deletions

```
OPEN the indexed file as I-O.
MOVE the key of the record to the key field.
DELETE indexed-file-name RECORD
      INVALID KEY PERFORM RECORD-NOT-FOUND.
```

Having created our indexed master file, and being able to make inquiries on it, we also want to develop a file maintenance program, so that we can add new customers, change information on existing customers, and delete customers whose accounts have been closed.


This program, to be called MAINTMFI, will read pairs of cards laid out as in SAMPLE-4, and like MAINTMFS, changes, additions, and deletions will be submitted using the same card conventions. The only difference will be that where a record is to be added, it will carry the code 'AD' in cc 73 - 74.


Use these specifications to draw up the high-level logic of MAINTMFI. Where the details of a module are not clear, or are not vital to the main logic, define the module by name but code a skeleton version or "stub" as a temporary measure. There are many ways of implementing stubs; the simplest way is to code the paragraph name and add a comment to remind yourself that the code has yet to be written. The compiler will reject your program if you do not at least define the paragraph!


Another means of implementing a stub is to print a simple debugging message when you enter the module. With just a defined name, there is no way of checking that your stub was performed in the right place, unless you are using READY TRACE. We will discuss other stubs in Part II of this book.


An early version of MAINTMFI is shown on the following pages for comparison.

```
IDENTIFICATION DIVISION.
PROGRAM-ID.   MAINTMFI.
.
INPUT-OUTPUT SECTION.
FILE-CONTROL.
    SELECT CUST-MAST-FILE      ASSIGN TO DA-I-CUSTMAST-R
                               ORGANIZATION IS INDEXED
                               ACCESS IS RANDOM
                               RECORD KEY IS ACCT-NUM-MAS.
.
.
PROCEDURE DIVISION.
    PERFORM A1-INITIALIZATION.
    PERFORM A2-UPDATE-INDEXED-FILE
      UNTIL CARDS-LEFT = 'NO '.
    PERFORM A3-END-OF-JOB.
    STOP RUN.

A1-INITIALIZATION.
    OPEN  INPUT   UPDATE-FILE
          I-O     CUST-MAST-FILE
          OUTPUT  UPDATE-LISTING.
    MOVE 'YES' TO CARDS-LEFT.
    PERFORM B1-GET-A-PAIR-OF-CARDS-INTO-WS.
    MOVE ACCT-NUM-WS TO ACCT-NUM-MAS.

A2-UPDATE-INDEXED-FILE.
    IF CHANGE-CODE-WS = 'AD'
        PERFORM B2-ASSEMBLE-NEW-MAST
        PERFORM B3-WRITE-CUSTOMER-MAST
        IF INVALID-KEY-FLAG = 'YES'
            PERFORM B4-DUPLICATE-REC-ON-FILE
        ELSE
            PERFORM B5-PRINT-CHANGE
    ELSE IF CHANGE-CODE-WS = 'CH'
        PERFORM B6-READ-CUSTOMER-MAST
        IF INVALID-KEY-FLAG = 'YES'
            PERFORM B7-CUSTOMER-NOT-FOUND
        ELSE
            PERFORM B8-MERGE-CHANGES-WITH-MAST
            PERFORM B9-REWRITE-CUSTOMER-MAST
            IF INVALID-KEY-FLAG = 'YES'
                PERFORM B10-DSK-OR-PRGM-ERR
            ELSE
                PERFORM B5-PRINT-CHANGE
    ELSE IF CHANGE-CODE-WS = 'DE'
        PERFORM B11-DOUBLE-CHECK-DELETE
        PERFORM B12-DELETE-CUSTOMER-MAST
        IF INVALID-KEY-FLAG = 'YES'
            PERFORM B10-DSK-OR-PRGM-ERR
        ELSE
            PERFORM B13-PRINT-DELETION-MSG
    ELSE
        PERFORM B14-INVALID-CHANGE-CODE.
    PERFORM B1-GET-A-PAIR-OF-CARDS-INTO-WS.
```

Figure 7.8    MAINTMFI, file maintenance program

```
A3-END-OF-JOB.
    CLOSE UPDATE-FILE
          CUST-MAST-FILE
          UPDATE-LISTING.

B1-GET-A-PAIR-OF-CARDS-INTO-WS.   COPY GETPRCDS.

B2-ASSEMBLE-NEW-MAST.
*  THIS ROUTINE WILL BE COPIED FROM THE MAINTMFS PROGRAM

B3-WRITE-CUSTOMER-MAST.
    MOVE 'NO' TO INVALID-KEY-FLAG.
    WRITE CUSTOMER-MAST-RECORD
        INVALID KEY MOVE 'YES' TO INVALID-KEY-FLAG.

B4-DUPLICATE-REC-ON-FILE.
*  THIS ROUTINE WILL BE LEFT AS A STUB FOR EARLY TESTS

B5-PRINT-CHANGE.
*  THIS ROUTINE WILL BE ADAPTED FROM THE MAINTMFS PROGRAM

B6-READ-CUSTOMER-MAST.
    MOVE 'NO' TO INVALID-KEY-FLAG.
    READ CUST-MAST-FILE
        INVALID KEY MOVE 'YES' TO INVALID-KEY-FLAG.

B7-CUSTOMER-NOT-FOUND.
*  THIS ROUTINE WILL BE LEFT AS A STUB FOR EARLY TESTS

B8-MERGE-CHANGES-WITH-MAST.
*  THIS ROUTINE WILL BE COPIED FROM THE MAINTMFS PROGRAM

B9-REWRITE-CUSTOMER-MAST.
    MOVE 'NO' TO INVALID-KEY-FLAG.
    REWRITE CUST-MAST-RECORD
        INVALID KEY MOVE 'YES' TO INVALID-KEY-FLAG.

B10-DSK-OR-PRGM-ERR.
*  THIS ROUTINE WILL BE LEFT AS A STUB FOR EARLY TESTS

B11-DOUBLE-CHECK-DELETE.
*  THIS ROUTINE WILL BE LEFT AS A STUB FOR EARLY TESTS

B12-DELETE-CUSTOMER-MAST.
    MOVE 'NO' TO INVALID-KEY-FLAG.
    DELETE CUST-MAST-FILE RECORD
        INVALID KEY MOVE 'YES' TO INVALID-KEY-FLAG.

B13-PRINT-DELETION-MSG.
*  THIS ROUTINE WILL BE LEFT AS A STUB FOR EARLY TESTS

B14-INVALID-CHANGE-CODE.
*  THIS ROUTINE WILL BE LEFT AS A STUB FOR EARLY TESTS
```

Figure 7.8 continued.   MAINTMFI, file maintenance program

### 7.4.4  Other Facilities with Indexed Files

Should you want to print out a complete listing of a file, you can read an indexed file sequentially by specifying ACCESS IS SEQUENTIAL and writing the READ statement as you would do for a tape file.

Suppose you want to look at a group of records with keys close together, say the ten records following account 876543. You don't want to read through the whole file sequentially to get there, and you want to make other random accesses in the same program.  With ANS-74 COBOL compilers, you can do this by specifying ACCESS IS DYNAMIC, and READing the first record you want to look at, then writing:

           READ filename NEXT RECORD.

This enables you to mix random access and sequential processing, if your problem demands it.  The details of these techniques are given in Part II, Chapter 11.

### 7.4.5  Disadvantages of Indexed Files

We said that you can access any record with only two move-ments of the read-write heads, one to the cylinder index and one to the cylinder.  This is true when an indexed file is newly created.  However, once you start to add records to a file, the disk control system inserts them in their sequential position in the file, moving other records up to make room.  Once a track is full, records may go into a special overflow area, which may be on another cylinder or cylinders.  When a lot of records have been added to the file, the overflow situation may be such that to find any given record can mean four seeks of the read-write head.  This can slow processing significantly.

The other type of random access file organization, relative organization, attempts to speed up random access by going directly to the record.  This is dealt with in the next section.

Of course, if you never require random access, you can create a sequential file on disk which has the same features as a sequen-tial file on tape.  The statements used are very similar to those for a sequential tape file, and you should consult the manufacturer's COBOL reference manual for your installation if you need to use a disk sequential file.  Bear in mind that holding sequential files on tape is much cheaper than disk.

The idea behind relative file organization is to look up each record by specifying to the disk control system its relative position in the file. With relative organization, the disk control system knows the number of records on each track, and the track at which the file begins. So, if we specify that the record we want is the 379th in the file, the disk control system can work out which track this record is on, and position the read-write heads to read or write the record. The relative record number (RRN), 379 in this case, is a unique number specifying the relative position of the record in the file.

Notice that, once we specify the RRN, the read-write heads can reach the record in only one seek movement, compared with a minimum of two seeks for an indexed file. This makes relative organization inherently faster than indexed organization.

The drawback is that it can be quite difficult to arrange the record keys so that the programmer can specify the RRN. In some cases, the nature of the problem makes this comparatively simple. For instance, suppose we wanted to keep a day-to-day record of the volume of business conducted by our company. We also want to retrieve this information, by specifying the Julian date of the day whose volume of business record we wish to see. The Julian date is the number of the day in the year: January 31st (a Gregorian date) corresponds to a Julian date of 031. February 27th has a Julian date of 058. We could use the Julian date as the RRN for the file, and write a program which would convert each date, supplied as MMDDYY, to the Julian date before reading the relatively organized disk file.

Q.    Apart from the inconvenience in programming, what are the disadvantages of this approach, assuming no business is done on Saturdays, Sundays, and holidays?

A.    A considerable amount of disk space will be wasted, because the disk control system will leave a space for each Julian date, no matter whether there is a record or not.

Problem situations in which the relative record number can be obtained directly, are rare. Consider the case of our mail-order master file. Suppose we have 500 records, with account numbers from 000001 through 999999. How can we transform the account number into a RRN?

One way of dealing with this is to use a <u>randomizing</u> routine: Divide the account number by the prime number which is just less than the total number of records in the file. Use the remainder as the RRN. For example, if you were to divide Victor Grasper's account number, 010101, by 499 (which happens to be a prime number), the integer result is 20 and the remainder is 121, Victor Grasper will thus become the 121st record in the file. If there were a customer allocated the account number 010480, the result would be 21 and the remainder would be 1. This account would therefore be the first record. Since the remainder will always be between 0 and 498, if you add 1 to these remainders, they can be used as RRNs.

    Q.  What is the drawback of this method?

    A.  You may have two account numbers which randomize to the same remainder. For example, 998121 randomizes to the same RRN as does Victor Grasper's account number. These two account numbers -- 010101 and 998121 -- are said to be <u>synonyms</u>. With only 500 accounts spread across 1 million possible account numbers, the probability of synonyms is rather low. But what if there were 100,000 accounts?

If relative organization is used, the programmer has to specify what action should be taken in the case of synonyms. For this reason, indexed file organization is much more common than relative organization; relative files are mainly used

- where speed of response to inquiries or speed of updating is very important

or

- where the keys can easily be transformed to relative record numbers.

The COBOL that you write for relative files is very similar to that for indexed files, the main difference being in the SELECT statement; as an example:

```
SELECT DISK-MASTER ASSIGN TO DA-R-RELMAST
       ORGANIZATION IS RELATIVE
       ACCESS IS RANDOM
       RELATIVE KEY IS ACCT-NUM-REMAINDER.
```

Relative organization is dealt with in greater detail in Chapter 11, Part II.

Up till now we have controlled spacing on printed output by adding AFTER ADVANCING n LINES to each WRITE statement. As you will have noticed, the continuous forms used for printer output usually have perforations every 11 inches (or, at 6 lines per inch, 66 lines).  We have simply written over these perforations.

For professionally produced reports, we may want to print headings at the top of each page, or jump to the top of a new page when we get near the bottom of the page we are printing. This can be done by specifying the page layout you want in an optional LINAGE clause in the FD for the printer file.  The variables you can specify are shown in the diagram:

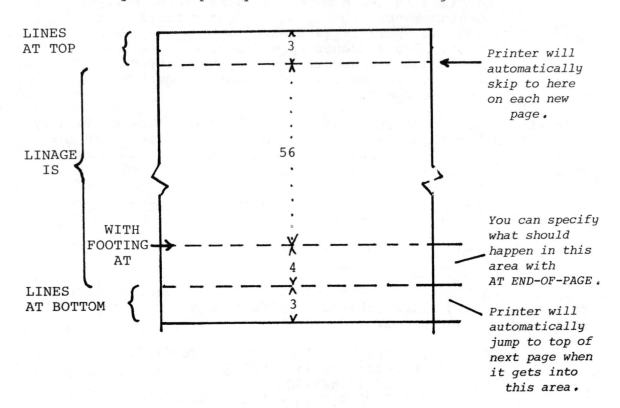

Thus, if you were to write the following in SAMPLE-3:

```
FD  PROFILE-LISTING
    LABEL RECORDS ARE OMITTED
    LINAGE IS 60 LINES
        WITH FOOTING AT 56
        LINES AT TOP 3
        LINES AT BOTTOM 3.
```

each page would start three lines from the top, and the compiler would automatically set up a field called LINAGE-COUNTER, which is set to a value of 1 at the top of each page, and is incremented appropriately by every WRITE statement. Before each WRITE, the program will test to see whether the LINAGE-COUNTER has reached or exceeded the LINAGE value specified in the FD. If it has, the printer will jump to the top of the next page, leaving three lines at the bottom of the previous page.

This automatic page overflow can be inconvenient when, as in SAMPLE-3, you are printing lines in groups of three, because it might cause a group to be split between pages. For this reason, you have an optional AT END-OF-PAGE clause in the WRITE statement. The END-OF-PAGE condition exists when the LINAGE-COUNTER is equal to or greater than the FOOTING value. So if you were to modify the WRITE-PROFILE paragraph in SAMPLE-3 like this:

```
WRITE-PROFILE.
    MOVE SPACES TO PRINT-LINE-OUT.
    WRITE PRINT-LINE-OUT FROM LINE-1-WS
        AFTER ADVANCING 4 LINES.
    MOVE SPACES TO PRINT-LINE-OUT.
    WRITE PRINT-LINE-OUT FROM LINE-2-WS
        AFTER ADVANCING 1 LINE.
    MOVE SPACES TO PRINT-LINE-OUT.
    WRITE PRINT-LINE-OUT FROM LINE-3-WS
        AFTER ADVANCING 1 LINE
        AT END-OF-PAGE
            WRITE PRINT-LINE-OUT FROM HEADER-WS
                AFTER ADVANCING PAGE.
```

when the group of three lines ends at or below the line specified in WITH FOOTING AT, the AFTER ADVANCING PAGE will cause the printer to skip to the top of the next page (as specified in LINES AT TOP) and write a heading. Always check your printing layout to be sure that the footing area is large enough for all the lines you might possibly want printed in it, so that automatic overflow does not spoil your report.

We should point out that these very useful facilities only apply to ANS-74 COBOL compilers. Some ANS-68 compilers have the END-OF-PAGE facility; often it is the programmer's responsibility to keep track of where he is on the page. Once again, you must check the provisions of the COBOL compiler you are using.

### 7.7.1      Functional Specifications

Now that we have our customer master file created and maintainable as an indexed file, we are in a position to start doing business.

When we get an order for goods from customers, we send them the goods in the mail with an invoice, stating the date of shipment, a serial number, a description of what goods were sent, and the amount payable.

When the customers get the goods, they will send us back a check, money order, or cash in payment.

At the end of each month, we want to send each customer a statement with details of all the invoices sent out, the payments received, and the net amount owing, if any.

Naturally, we don't want to send out goods to someone if that would mean the amount they owed exceeded their credit limit.  Nor do we want to send out goods to someone who is not on our master file.

So the system you have to design and write will have three main functions:

- to accept orders and payments, and keep a record of the transactions and balances for each account

- to check the credit information on the master file for each person ordering and to reject orders from people who do not have accounts, or who would be exceeding their credit limit, and to make out invoices for good orders

- to produce at intervals a statement for each account that ·has had a transaction since the last statement.

The information we need to store about an order is:

- Customer's account number
- Date we processed the order
- An invoice serial number consisting of
  3 letters for the initials of the account
  representative plus a 3-digit serial
  number, e.g., CPA903
- 10 letters of description of the item,
  e.g., SNOWMOBILE
- The amount of the invoice in dollars and
  cents up to $9999.99.  Ignore tax

The information we need to store about a payment is:

- Customer's account number
- Date we received the payment
- Serial number of the check or money order
- Whether the payment was by check, money
  order or cash
- The amount of the payment in dollars and
  cents.

Clearly, these two transaction types have a lot in common;
maybe we can use the same card layout.

Each invoice should have the following information and layout:

```
+-----------------------------------------------------------+
|            YOURDON MAIL-ORDER CORPORATION                 |
| 1133 AVENUE OF THE AMERICAS    NEW YORK, NY 10036 212 730-2670 |
|                                                           |
|                                                           |
|         TO:     VICTOR S GRASPER                          |
|                 990 GAUNTLET AVE                          |
|                 BURLINGAME CA                             |
|                         94010                             |
|                                                           |
|    DATE          INVOICE   DESCRIPTION   AMOUNT           |
|                  SERIAL                  $                |
|                    NO                                     |
|                                                           |
| MAY 8th 1977  CPA421    SNOWMOBILE     1191.12            |
|                                                           |
| PAYMENT IS DUE ON RECEIPT OF GOODS                        |
| PLEASE QUOTE YOUR ACCOUNT NUMBER 010101 ON ALL            |
| PAYMENTS AND CORRESPONDENCE                               |
+-----------------------------------------------------------+
```

Each statement should look like this:

```
┌─────────────────────────────────────────────────────────────────┐
│                                                                   │
│                  YOURDON MAIL-ORDER CORPORATION                   │
│       1133 AVENUE OF THE AMERICAS  NEW YORK, NY 10036  212 730-2670│
│                                                                   │
│                                                                   │
│            TO:    VICTOR S. GRASPER                                │
│                   990 GAUNTLET AVE                                 │
│                   BURLINGAME  CA                                   │
│                            94010                                  │
│                                                                   │
│                                                                   │
│             STATEMENT OF ACCOUNT AT MAY 31st 1977                 │
│                                                                   │
│                                                                   │
│          BALANCE OWING AT APRIL 30th 1977              293.24     │
│                                                                   │
│       DATE                DESCRIPTION         AMOUNT   BALANCE     │
│                                                 $        $         │
│     MAY  8th    INVOICE   CPG421   SNOWMOBILE  1191.12  1484.36    │
│     MAY 17th    CHECK     423      RECEIVED-THANK YOU 293.24 1191.12│
│     MAY 29th    INVOICE   CPG903   BOOKS         8.88  1200.00     │
│                                                                   │
│                                                                   │
│                                                                   │
│     BALANCE OWING AT MAY 31st 1977                  $1200.00      │
├─────────────────────────────────────────────────────────────────┤
│                                                                   │
│     YOU ARE REMINDED THAT PAYMENT IS DUE ON RECEIPT OF GOODS.     │
│     PLEASE QUOTE YOUR ACCOUNT NUMBER 010101 ON ALL PAYMENTS       │
│     AND CORRESPONDENCE.                                           │
│                                                                   │
└─────────────────────────────────────────────────────────────────┘
```

The systems analyst tells you that you should allow for up to
20 invoices in one month, but you can assume there will never
be more than one item per invoice, or more than one invoice
per day.  There may be up to 5, but usually only 1, payments
per month.

Give some thought to a system that would meet these functional specifications, knowing that you already have the indexed master file and MAINTMFI. This will be very useful if a customer calls up and asks how much he owes, or if management wants to know.

### 7.7.2    *System Design*

Let us assume that the transactions will be punched onto cards, with a card format that we will specify later. We need to edit these cards, first to make sure as far as possible that the punching has been done correctly, then to check that the customer account number exists on our master file. Next, orders must be validated to ensure that they will not exceed the credit limit. Then invoices can be printed.

For reference and auditing purposes, we want to print a journal, or log, of every transaction in the order it was received, giving full details of the transaction and the reason for rejection, if any. You are free to design the layout of this transaction journal.

Many commercial systems separate out orders and payments into separate batches, and edit them with separate programs. We do not want to do this, as it puts an extra clerical load on the people opening the mail; you should design a card input format that can be used for invoices or payments (though of course you will need a transaction type code so the system can tell which is which).

The data flow diagram for daily processing will thus look like:

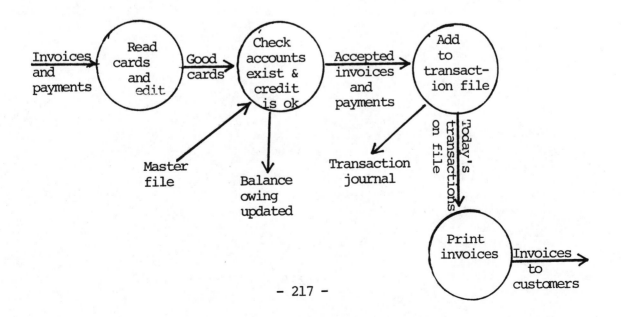

There is no theoretical reason why you can't print the invoice at the same time as the transaction journal, except that many computers only have one printer, and it would be very tedious for the operator to have to go through the print-out and separate the invoices. Anyway we need to save the transactions for printing statements at the end of the month.

The structure chart will look like

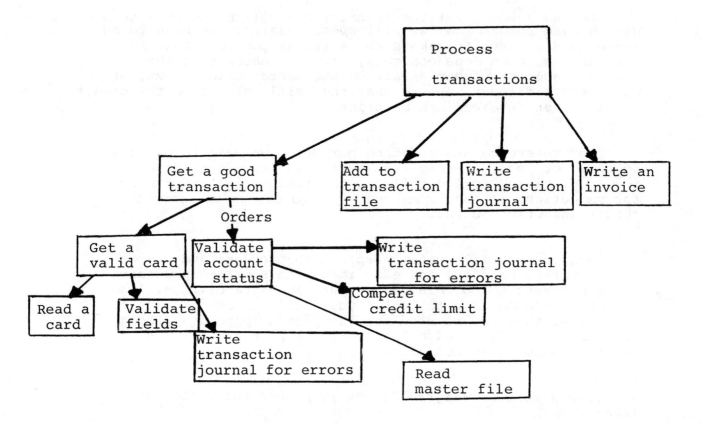

You could implement this structure with two programs, the first of which would build the transaction file and the second of which would read the transaction file to write the invoices; or you could do it all with one program which, like CREATEMF, closes the transaction file and reopens it to write the invoices. This packaging choice is largely one of the size of program that you can run on your computer, and the convenience of the operator if the invoices are to be written on special paper.

The statement writing program will have to be separate, since it will usually be run only once a month.

## 7.7.3 File Design

The transactions, of course, will come in random order, depending on what arrives in the mail each day. When we produce the statements, we want to do so one account at a time -- with the transactions for that statement all together in date order. This involves sorting the transactions in some way to get them into order, a facility which we have not yet covered, or loading the transactions to an indexed file in such a way as to be able to retrieve them in the desired way by reading the file sequentially.

This is achieved by making the record key of the transaction file a field which is a combination of account number, transaction date in the form MMDD, and transaction type. Thus, the data for the invoice shown previously could be stored in a record with the key 0101015081 where I is the code for invoice. An invoice the following day would have the key 0101010509I and be retrieved next in a sequential read.

## 7.8    BUILDING THE SYSTEM WITH A SKELETON AND SUCCESSIVE VERSIONS

With these main design considerations, you should do a detailed design of the file and the programs, writing the logic in pseudocode. For instance, the main logic of "Get a good transaction" might be:

```
IF the transaction is for an invoice
    Add the invoice amount to the current balance owing
    IF the new current balance would be greater than the
                                        credit limit
        Write a message to the transaction journal & reject
    ELSE
        Write the new value of the current balance on the
                                        master file
    Write the transaction to the transaction file
```

ELSE (transaction is a payment)
    Subtract the amount from the current balance on the
                                       master file
    Write the transaction to the transaction file

If you can work with some colleagues, divide the work up
among you, with perhaps one person being responsible for the
editing of cards, one for the invoice production, and one for
statement production.


Where several people and their programs must interface,
it is best to code the high levels of each program first,
leaving as much as possible as stubs in the way we did with
MAINTMFI, and get a "skeleton" or "Version Ø" of the whole
system going as soon as possible.

Version Ø for your system might be a version which:

- reads in a correctly punched order card and a
  correctly punched payment card
- does no editing of fields for numeric, alphabetic, etc.
- verifies that the account exists but assumes the
  credit check is OK
- writes the transactions to the transaction file
- writes an unformatted invoice for the order from the
  transaction file with, for example, no conversion of
  dates to the form specified

That is, Version Ø would contain almost no editing, no transaction journal, and no statement. It would however prove that
your team could load and read the transaction file, and read
the master file.


Version 1 might write a crude statement, simple transaction journal, and a formatted invoice.


Version 2 might reject orders for credit, and edit some
fields in the cards, rejecting them if they are not numeric or
alphabetic when they should be. It could require a fully formatted invoice and statement.


This so-called top-down implementation of a system has the
advantage that communication between several people on a project is simplified by having a skeleton version of the system
on the machine for everyone to work with. It also enables you
to see visible progress much earlier in the project than you
would if you were to code each program completely before
putting the system together.

<u>CONCLUSION TO PART I</u>

If you have understood everything you have read so far, and you have worked the program exercises, producing working programs, you are competent to be a junior member of a programming team. You have learned the basics of COBOL, and can use them to solve a wide variety of commercial problems. There are a number of features and facilities in COBOL which you have yet to learn; they will be covered in Part II of this book.

If you find you have to maintain or enhance programs written by other people, you may see use of the GO TO statement, which transfers control to some other part of the program. Unlike the PERFORM statement, the GO TO does not bring control back to the original point, and unless used with great care, the GO TO can make the program difficult to follow. The GO TO statement is dealt with in detail in Part II, Chapter 8; if you have trouble working with programs which use it, express the programs as structured flowcharts, and rewrite the code using the structures with which you are familiar.

PART II of <u>Learning to Program in Structured COBOL</u> will be published by YOURDON inc. in late-1976.  The Table of Contents follows:

# APPENDIX A:    ACKNOWLEDGEMENTS

The following paragraphs are reprinted from "American National Standard, Programming Language, COBOL" published in 1974 by the American National Standards Institute.

Any organization interested in reproducing the COBOL standard and specifications in whole or in part, using ideas from this document as the basis for an instruction manual or for any other purpose, is free to do so.  However, all such organizations are requested to reproduce the following acknowledgement paragraphs in their entirety as part of the preface to any such publication (any organization using a short passage from this document, such as in a book review, is requested to mention "COBOL" in acknowledgement of the source, but need not quote the acknowledgement):

COBOL is an industry language and is not the property of any company or group of companies, or of any organization or group of organizations.

No warranty, expressed or implied, is made by any contributor or by the CODASYL Programming Language Committee as to the accuracy and functioning of the programming system and language.  Moreover, no responsibility is assumed by any contributor, or by the committee, in connection therewith.

The authors and copyright holders of the copyrighted material used herein

FLOW-MATIC (trademark of Sperry Rand Corporation), Programming for the UNIVAC® I and II, Data Automation Systems copyrighted 1958, 1959, by Sperry Rand Corporation; IBM Commercial Translator Form No. F 28-8013, copyrighted 1959 by IBM; FACT, DSI 27A5260-2760, copyrighted 1960 by Minneapolis-Honeywell

have specifically authorized the use of this material in whole or in part, in the COBOL specifications.  Such authorization extends to the reproduction and use of COBOL specifications in programming manuals or similar publications.

# APPENDIX B:    RESERVED WORDS

This list of reserved words includes all those specified by the 1974 American National Standard, plus others (marked with an *) which may be found in other compilers, but which are not part of the standard.   You should avoid using any of the words on this list as programmer-defined names, even if they are not reserved words for the compiler you happen to be using.   Be sure to check out each compiler you use to see that it has no other reserved words.

|   | | |   | | |
|---|---|---|---|---|---|
| | ACCEPT | | * | CHANGED | |
| | ACCESS | | * | CHANNEL | |
| * | ACTUAL | | | CHARACTER | |
| | ADD | | | CHARACTERS | |
| * | ADDRESS | | | CLOCK-UNITS | |
| | ADVANCING | | | CLOSE | |
| | AFTER | | | COBOL | |
| | ALL | | | CODE | |
| | ALPHABETIC | | | CODE-SET | |
| | ALSO | | | COLLATING | |
| | ALTER | | | COLUMN | |
| | ALTERNATE | | * | COM-REG | |
| | AND | | | COMMA | |
| * | APPLY | | | COMMUNICATION | |
| | ARE | | | COMP | |
| | AREA | | * | COMP-1 | |
| | AREAS | | * | COMP-2 | |
| | ASCENDING | | * | COMP-3 | |
| * | ASCII | | * | COMP-4 | |
| | ASSIGN | | | COMPUTATIONAL | |
| | AT | | * | COMPUTATIONAL-1 | |
| | AUTHOR | | * | COMPUTATIONAL-2 | |
| | | | * | COMPUTATIONAL-3 | |
| | | | * | COMPUTATIONAL-4 | |
| * | BASIS | | | COMPUTE | |
| | BEFORE | | | CONFIGURATION | |
| * | BEGINNING | | * | CONSOLE | |
| * | BINARY | | | CONTAINS | |
| | BLANK | | | CONTROL | |
| | BLOCK | | | CONTROLS | |
| | BOTTOM | | | COPY | |
| | BY | | * | CORE-INDEX | |
| | | | | CORR | |
| | | | | CORRESPONDING | |
| | CALL | | | COUNT | |
| | CANCEL | | * | CSP | |
| * | CARD-PUNCH | | | CURRENCY | |
| * | CARD-READER | | * | CURRENT-DATE | |
| * | CBL | | * | CYL-INDEX | |
| | CD | | * | CYL-OVERFLOW | |
| | CF | | * | CO1 | |
| | CH | | * | CO2 | |

| | | |
|---|---|---|
| * | CO3 | |
| * | CO4 | |
| * | CO5 | |
| * | CO6 | |
| * | CO7 | |
| * | CO8 | |
| * | CO9 | |
| * | C10 | |
| * | C11 | |
| * | C12 | |
| | | |
| | DATA | |
| | DATE | |
| | DATE-COMPILED | |
| | DATE-WRITTEN | |
| | DAY | |
| | DE | |
| * | DEBUG | |
| | DEBUG-CONTENTS | |
| | DEBUG-ITEM | |
| | DEBUG-LINE | |
| | DEBUG-NAME | |
| | DEBUG-SUB-1 | |
| | DEBUG-SUB-2 | |
| | DEBUG-SUB-3 | |
| | DEBUGGING | |
| | DECIMAL-POINT | |
| | DECLARATIVES | |
| * | DEFERRED | |
| | DELETE | |
| | DELIMITED | |
| | DELIMITER | |
| * | DENSITY | |
| | DEPENDING | |
| * | DEPTH | |
| | DESCENDING | |
| | DESTINATION | |
| | DETAIL | |
| | DISABLE | |
| * | DISP | |
| | DISPLAY | |
| * | DISPLAY-ST | |

| | | |
|---|---|---|
| * DISPLAY-6 | GO | * LINE-PRINTER |
| * DISPLAY-7 | * GOBACK | LINES |
| DIVIDE | GREATER | LINKAGE |
| DIVISION | GROUP | LOCK |
| DOWN | | LOW-VALUE |
| DUPLICATES | | LOW-VALUES |
| DYNAMIC | HEADING | |
| | HIGH-VALUE | |
| | HIGH-VALUES | |
| * EBCDIC | | * MACRO |
| EGI | | * MAP4 |
| * EJECT | I-O | * MAP5 |
| ELSE | I-O CONTROL | * MAP6 |
| EMI | * ID | * MAP7 |
| ENABLE | IDENTIFICATION | * MAP8 |
| END | IF | * MASTER-INDEX |
| END-OF-PAGE | IN | MEMORY |
| * ENDING | INDEX | MERGE |
| ENTER | INDEXED | MESSAGE |
| * ENTRY | INDICATE | MODE |
| ENVIRONMENT | INITIAL | MODULES |
| EOP | INITIATE | * MORE-LABELS |
| EQUAL | INPUT | MOVE |
| * EQUALS | INPUT-OUTPUT | MULTIPLE |
| ERROR | * INSERT | MULTIPLY |
| ESI | INSPECT | |
| * EVEN | INSTALLATION | |
| EVERY | INTO | * NAMED |
| * EXAMINE | INVALID | NATIVE |
| EXCEPTION | IS | NEGATIVE |
| * EXHIBIT | | NEXT |
| EXIT | | NO |
| EXTEND | JUST | * NOMINAL |
| * EXTENDED-SEARCH | JUSTIFIED | NOT |
| | | * NOTE |
| | | * NSTD-REELS |
| FD | KEY | NUMBER |
| FILE | * KEYS | NUMERIC |
| FILE-CONTROL | | |
| * FILE-LIMIT | | |
| * FILE-LIMITS | LABEL | OBJECT-COMPUTER |
| FILLER | * LABEL-RETURN | OCCURS |
| FINAL | LAST | * ODD |
| FIRST | LEADING | OF |
| FOOTING | * LEAVE | OFF |
| FOR | LEFT | OMITTED |
| * FORTRAN | LENGTH | ON |
| * FORTRAN-IV | LESS | OPEN |
| FROM | LIMIT | OPTIONAL |
| | LIMITS | OR |
| | LINAGE | ORGANIZATION |
| GENERATE | LINAGE-COUNTER | * OTHERWISE |
| GIVING | LINE | OUTPUT |
| | LINE-COUNTER | OVERFLOW |

PAGE
PAGE-COUNTER
* PAPER-TAPE-PUNCH
* PAPER-TAPE-READER
* PARITY
PERFORM
PF
PH
PIC
PICTURE
PLUS
POINTER
POSITION
* POSITIONING
POSITIVE
* PRINT-CONTROL
* PRINT-SWITCH
PRINTING
PROCEDURE
PROCEDURES
PROCEED
* PROCESSING
PROGRAM
PROGRAM-ID

QUEUE
QUOTE
QUOTES

RANDOM
RD
READ
* READ-AHEAD
* READY
RECEIVE
RECORD
* RECORD-OVERFLOW
* RECORDING
RECORDS
REDEFINES
REEL
REFERENCES
RELATIVE
RELEASE
* RELOAD
REMAINDER
* REMARKS
REMOVAL
RENAMES

* REORG-CRITERIA
REPLACING
REPORT
REPORTING
REPORTS
* REREAD
RERUN
RESERVE
RESET
RETURN
* RETURN-CODE
REVERSED
REWIND
REWRITE
RF
RH
RIGHT
ROUNDED
RUN

SAME
SD
SEARCH
SECTION
SECURITY
* SEEK
SEGMENT
SEGMENT-LIMIT
SELECT
SEND
SENTENCE
SEPARATE
SEQUENCE
SEQUENTIAL
* SERVICE
SET
SIGN
SIZE
* SKIP1
* SKIP2
* SKIP3
SORT
* SORT-CORE-SIZE
* SORT-FILE-SIZE
SORT-MERGE
* SORT-MESSAGE
* SORT-MODE-SIZE
* SORT-RETURN
SOURCE
SOURCE-COMPUTER

SPACE
SPACES
SPECIAL-NAMES
STANDARD
STANDARD-1
START
STATUS
STOP
STRING
SUB-QUEUE-1
SUB-QUEUE-2
SUB-QUEUE-3
SUBTRACT
SUM
SUPPRESS
* SWITCH
SYMBOLIC
SYNC
SYNCHRONIZED
* SYSIN
* SYSIPT
* SYSLST
* SYSOUT
* SYSPCH
* SYSPUNCH
* SO1
* SO2

TABLE
* TALLY
TALLYING
TAPE
TERMINAL
TERMINATE
TEXT
THAN
* THEN
THROUGH
THRU
TIME
* TIME-OF-DAY
TIMES
TO
* TODAY
TOP
* TOTALED
* TOTALING
* TRACE
* TRACK
* TRACK-AREA

- 229 -

```
*   TRACK-LIMIT              +
*   TRACKS                   -
    TRAILING                 *
*   TRANSFORM                /
    TYPE                     **
                             >
                             <

    UNIT                     =
    UNSTRING
    UNTIL
    UP
    UPON
*   UPSI-O
*   UPSI-1
*   UPSI-2
*   UPSI-3
*   UPSI-4
*   UPSI-5
*   UPSI-6
*   UPSI-7
    USAGE
    USE
*   USER-NUMBER
    USING


    VALUE
    VALUES
    VARYING


    WHEN
    WITH
    WORDS
    WORKING-STORAGE
    WRITE
*   WRITE-BEHIND
*   WRITE-ONLY
*   WRITE-VERIFY


    ZERO
    ZEROES
    ZEROS
```

APPENDIX C:   LESSON PLANS AND LECTURE NOTES

The following pages set out suggested lesson
plans and lecture notes for a course with 30
three-hour sessions, suitable for a three-week
full-time course for industry entrants or a
two-semester college course.

The references are to pages in Part I of this
book, which serves as the text for such a
course.

## Session 1

*Preparation:*

A card for each student with Hollerith code (p. 6).

*Lecture:*

Administration, hours, etc.  Go around the class to assess each student's background in DP, if any.

Introduce function of computers in light of class background, stressing that machine only obeys programmer.

Explain in simple terms COBOL, compiler, machine language.

Explain the coupon listing problem (p. 2).

Get students to compare list of raw names, addresses, and phone numbers with printed output (pp. 3-4).

Get students to count number of columns required for each field.  Show a typical card.

Give each student a coded card and explain Hollerith code, row, column, 12-row, 11-row, 9-edge, corner cut, interpreted, digit, letter, special character, ampersand, hyphen, not-sign, apostrophe, quote, hash-mark.

Explain how card data gets into the computer, function of card-reader, hopper, stacker.

Explain in simple terms the function of the CPU and the printer (p. 7).

How do the holes get in the card?  Explain functions of key-punch, including duplication (but not control card).

*Exercise:*

Demonstrate key-punch if one is available, and assign each student to punch a transaction card from the list on page 3.

(If the class is too large for the number of key-punches available, demonstrate by punching one card, and have the others already punched.)

*Lecture:*

Explain the printer spacing chart (p. 8).  Get students to compare field lengths on card with printer spacing chart.  Refer to spaces as "fillers."

<u>Session 2</u>

*Preparation:*

One source deck of SAMPLE-1  ⎫
One compilation listing            ⎬   for
One execution listing               ⎭   each
                                                    student

*Lecture:*

Review Session 1

What does the programmer have to do?

Explain SAMPLE-1 line by line. Stress that the
detailed meaning will be made clear later in the
course, but that the important thing is to see how
everything fits together.

Hand out decks to each student. Get students to
compare the deck with the visual.

*Exercise:*

Visit the machine room. Identify pieces of hardware.
Compile a deck, then execute with the data cards
punched during the morning.

Allow each student to do this if time and cost permit.

*Lecture:*

Hand out compilation listings and execution listings.

Review the process of compilation and execution.
Explain that the result of compilation may be stored
internally or punched out in an object deck.

*Preparation:*

Execution of SAMPLE-1 with statement 48 (MOVE SPACES
TO PRINT-RECORD.) taken out.

*Lecture:*

Review SAMPLE-1 again comparing compilation deck with
compilation listing and with COBOL coding sheets.
Answer any questions as simply as possible.  Review
structure of the course now the students have seen a
program and had an overview.

Explain MOVE using non-numeric example, and just
treating main storage as a number of storage positions.
Get students to work out how to swap two fields
with-MOVE's (p. 15).

Explain the need for initializing to blanks.  Use of
MOVE SPACES.  Hand out execution listing of SAMPLE-1
without print-lines initialized and show the garbage
in the print-lines.  Get students to explain why garbage
stays the same after the first line.

Explain qualified data-names (p. 16).

Explain literals (p. 17).

Explain numeric MOVE's and contrast with non-numeric
(pp. 18-20).

Get students to do exercise on numeric moves.

Explain ZEROS by comparison with SPACES.

Explain difference between numbers represented by
PIC X and by PIC 9.

Review IF statement in SAMPLE-1.

Explain process of execution is normally sequential,
but the IF allows the computer to choose, and so
appear to "think" (pp. 22-23).

Explain structured flowchart and get students to
answer questions.

*Exercise:*

Get students to transform structured flowcharts to
code (p. 23).

<u>Session 4</u>

*Preparation:*

COBOL coding pads. Decks of additional cards for insertion in SAMPLE-1 to make SAMPLE-2. Decks of additional data cards for SAMPLE-2.

*Lecture:*

Review the PERFORM statement in SAMPLE-1.

Define a procedure.

Explain a flow of control in a PERFORM executed only once.

Explain meaning of PERFORM ... UNTIL ...

Show structured flowchart representation (p. 25).

Get students to answer questions about PERFORM.

Explain specification for SAMPLE-2 (p. 27).

*Exercise:*

Get students to draw a structured flowchart, then explain solution.

*Lecture:*

Hand out COBOL coding pads and review Margin A, B, and Numbering of statements.

*Exercise:*

Get students to code SAMPLE-2 with closed books (about 1 hour).

Get students to compare their solution to listing on page 30 and with SAMPLE-1.

Hand out decks of additional cards (or have students punch up cards needed) and have each student submit his job of SAMPLE-2.

## Session 5

Review compilations (and executions of successful compiles) of SAMPLE-2.

Define character set, special characters, alphabetic, numeric, alphanumeric (p. 33).

Explain elementary item, group item, level number.

Explain PIC, A, 9, X.

Define division names, section names, procedure-names, data-names.

Explain rules for programmer-defined names.

Get students to work exercise (p. 38).

Explain good practice on data-names.

Explain punctuation rules:  Define statement and sentence.

Explain good practice on layout.

Explain handwriting conventions (p. 42).

Explain rules and good practice for comments and continuation (pp. 43-44).

Explain that FD's set up I/O areas (buffers), for use by READ and WRITE.

Explain need for W-S.

Explain use of flags.

Explain VALUE statement, and diagram of W-S.

Explain level-88 condition names.

Get students to answer Review Quiz (p. 50).

## Session 6

*Preparation:*

Data cards for SAMPLE-3.  Coding supplies.

*Lecture:*

Explain specifications for SAMPLE-3 (pp. 52-53).

Explain specimen report (p. 54).

*Exercise:*

Get students to produce a printer spacing chart and check it against the report.

*Lecture:*

Discuss program design:  Lead students to the conclusion that the input is really a 92-character record which should be set up in W-S for each pair of cards, and that the output is three 132-character lines which should also be set up in W-S.

Explain DATA RECORDS ARE (p. 57).

*Exercise:*

Get students to code Data Division and check with sample (pp. 58-59).

*Lecture:*

Develop the program graph.

Show how the structure chart is derived and explain passing of control up and down structure chart.

Develop pseudocode from the chart.  Get students to draw a structured flowchart and check with sample.

Explain WRITE AFTER ADVANCING.

Get students to code Procedure Division and compare with sample.

Arrange for key-punching and submission of solutions. Provide JCL for compilation.

*Preparation:*

Copies of SAMPLE-3 compilation with some interesting diagnostics.

*Lecture:*

Explain briefly why job control cards are needed; function of operating system. Specify JCL to compile and execute on your installation.

Review SAMPLE-3 solution, answering any questions. Explain diagnostic codes (-W, -C, -E, -D) or relevant severity levels if non-IBM (p. 70).

*Exercise:*

Get students to locate cause of diagnostics in each other's SAMPLE-3 output.

*Lecture:*

Explain two forms of ADD (p. 73).

Explain two forms of SUBTRACT.

Explain two forms of MULTIPLY.

Explain two forms of DIVIDE.

*Exercise:*

Get students to code instructions to determine discretionary income.

*Lecture:*

Explain rounding (p. 76).

Explain COMPUTE, stressing the importance of ON SIZE ERROR.

Explain use of signed variables.

*Exercise:*

Get students to do Review Quiz (p. 80).

## Session 8

*Preparation:*

Catalog SAMPLE-3 data structures and paragraphs on Source Statement Library (p. 92).

*Lecture:*

Explain purpose of SSL and its advantages to the programmer.

Explain COPY
        COPY REPLACING (p. 83).

Review the steps to follow in developing a program (p. 84).

Explain program checks, with an example of a data exception (p. 86).

Explain READY TRACE and EXHIBIT NAMED, with their use, to locate a data exception (pp. 87-88).

Explain the specification for SAMPLE-4.

Lead students through the development of the structure chart.

Walk through the modules available on the SSL.

*Exercise:*

Get students to code SAMPLE-4 using SSL and COPY.

*Exercise:*

    Get students to complete coding of SAMPLE-4, and to
review each other's coding sheets in pairs before
key-punching, compiling, and testing.

## Session 10

*Lecture:*

    Explain five types of logical conditions (pp. 101-108).
      - relational:  advise not to use $>$ $<$
      - class
      - condition name
      - sign
      - complex:  relate to truth-table

    Explain use of nested IF's to structure AND conditions
(p. 109).

    Get students to code a nested IF (p. 112).

    Explain the block structure problem and ways of
solving it (pp. 112-115).

    Explain the null ELSE (p. 116).

    Explain the CASE structure (p. 118) and get students
to code one.

Session 11

*Lecture:*

Review ways of simplifying nested IF's (p. 120).

Explain the conventions for decision tables, conditions, actions, rules, how to derive the number of rules in an exhaustive table.

*Exercise:*

Get the students to draw a decision table from an English statement (p. 122).

*Lecture:*

Explain selective decision tables, the "don't-care" entry, the ELSE rule (p. 125).

*Exercise:*

Get students to produce an exhaustive decision table for credit limit as specified on page 127, and simplify it as far as possible.

Review decision table, and get students to code a nested IF to express the logic (p. 129).

Session 12

*Exercise:*

Explain the full specification for CREDCALC (p. 131).

Get students to design down to pseudocode, and review their designs in pairs.

*Lecture:*

Discuss a model structure for CREDCALC and walk through pseudocode for each module.

## Sessions 13 and 14

*Preparation:*

Test data deck for CREDCALC.

*Exercise:*

Students code, compile, and test CREDCALC, using COPY as far as possible.

## Session 15

*Preparation:*

Additional CREDCALC module cataloged on COPYLIB (p. 159).

*Lecture:*

Explain that cards become inconvenient in high volume.

Define magnetic tape, characters per inch, IRG, blocking, BLOCK CONTAINS, labels, LABEL RECORDS ARE STANDARD (p. 153).

Explain difference between sequential and random access, UR, UT, DA, SELECT statement for tape file on your installation.

Explain function of OPEN and CLOSE, READ and WRITE for single-volume, single-file tapes (p. 154).

Explain specification for CREATEMF: Get students to produce a structure chart and pseudocode (pp. 157-158).

## Session 16

*Exercise:*

Students complete coding of CREATEMF and compare their solution with the model (pp. 160-174).

Visit to installation to see tape units demonstrated and tape file loaded. Demonstration of disks.

*Lecture:*

Discuss the considerations in updating the sequential
master file with a presorted addition, deletion, and
change file:  specification for MAINTMFS (p. 181).

Develop program graph for students.

Get students to draw structure chart and pseudocode.

Walk through solution (pp. 183-193).


Session 18

*Lecture:*

Explain random access, magnetic disk, track, read-write
head, platter, cylinder, seek, search, rotational
delay (p. 195).

*Exercise:*

Get students to calculate the capacity and average
access time of the disk drives used in your
installation from basic data.

*Lecture:*

Explain indexed file organization, track, index,
record key (p. 197).

Explain creation of an indexed file, FILE-CONTROL
paragraph, ORGANIZATION, ACCESS, RECORD KEY.

Explain use of INVALID KEY.

Walk through model for CREATEMFI (pp. 200-201).

Explain differences for accessing the new indexed
file randomly and walk through a model (p. 202).

## Session 19

*Lecture:*

Explain updating, addition, and deletion of records on an indexed file: REWRITE and DELETE (p. 205).

Explain specification for MAINTMFI (p. 206). Get students to develop structure chart and pseudocode, and review.

## Sessions 20 and 21

*Preparation:*

Master file on disk built by CREATMFI. Updates, addition, and deletion cards for master file.

*Exercise:*

Students code, review, compile, and test MAINTMFI.

## Session 22

*Lecture:*

Explain disadvantages of indexed files, overflow leads to long access times (p. 209).

Explain relative file concept, transforming a key to a relative record number and retrieving with a single access.

Give example of division by prime number and using remainder.

Explain synonyms and how they may be handled.

Explain difference in coding between indexed and relative files.

Explain differences between ANS-74 and access methods used in your installation.

## Session 23

*Lecture:*

Explain the printer spacing facilities of ANS-74, the LINAGE clause and its options, the AT END-OF-PAGE option, other options of the WRITE statement (p. 212).

Explain the printer control features of your COBOL compiler if not ANS-74.

*Lecture:*

Explain specification for credit account system:
processing transactions of invoice and payment data
against master file to keep a balance owing available
on-line against credit limit, and printing statements
of account when required (p. 215).

*Exercise:*

Get students to work in pairs on the system design
and then review a structure chart with them.

Plan the successive versions for top-down implementation.

Sessions 25-30

Have students implement the credit account system
top-down to as great a level of detail as time allows.

## 1.   ANSWERS TO 3.9 REVIEW QUIZ

Q1.   Which of the characters shown in the specimen card on page 6
      are <u>not</u> in the COBOL character set?

A1.   11 characters: &, !, *, ¬ , %, _, ?, :, #, @, "

Q2/   What is wrong with this FD?
A2

```
      FD   OUT-PRINT◄────no period
      01   LINE◄───no period          PIC X{132}◄────PIC on 01 level items
           05  FILLER                 PIC X{60}.
           05  FILLER                 PIC X{12}    VALUE REPORT   no quotes
                                               HEADING.◄──
           05  FILLER                 PIC X{60}.
                                              └── 14 chars.
```

Q3/   What is wrong with this FD?
A3

```
      FD   CARD-FILE ◄──no period
      01   CARD◄──────no period
           02  NAME.◄──period     PIC A {20}.
           02  ADDRESS◄──no period
               03  STREET.◄        PIC X {20}.    spaces between
               03  CITY.◄──periods PIC A {20}.    character and
               03  STATE-ZIP.◄     PIC X {20}.    parentheses
```

Q4/   Here are some programmer-defined names.  Decide if they are
A4    OK  a) as data-names, b) as procedure-names, and if not, why
      not:

| Name | Data-Name | Procedure-Name |
|------|-----------|----------------|
| MASTER-FILE-INVENTORY-CODE | OK | OK |
| M9999 | OK* | OK* |
| HEADING- | Ends with hyphen | same |
| -TITLE- | Begins and ends with hyphen | same |
| 111X | OK* | OK* |
| LINE-COUNTER | OK | OK |
| ZIP CODE | Spaces in name | same |
| ZIP.CODE | Special character | same |
| POSITION | OK** | OK* |
| 666 | Data name <u>must</u> contain at least one alpha character | OK* |

   \* Meaningless name
  \*\* Ambiguous name, possibly meaningless

Q5/   What is wrong with this Working Storage section?
A5

```
                                                           PIC X(3)
          01   CARDS-LEFT-FLAG              PIC 999 VALUE 'YES'.
          01   PRINT-LINE-WS        VALUE SPACES. ◄── VALUE on 01 level
             05   FILLER.                  (no PIC)
             05   FILLER          PIC X{24} ◄──── 25 characters
                           VALUE 'MONTHLY PRODUCTION REPORT'.
             05   FILLER.                  (no PIC)
```

Q6.   Write the FD entries to set up meaningful condition-names
      for a one-column card code called JOB-CODE with the following
      meanings:

```
          T   Trainee              P   Programmer
          J   Junior Programmer    A   Systems Analyst
```

A6.

```
          FD   CARD-FILE.
          01   CARD.
             05   JOB-CODE            PIC X.
                88   TRAINEE         VALUE 'T'.
                88   JNR-PROG        VALUE 'J'.
                88   PROGRAMMER      VALUE 'P'.
                88   SYS-ANALYST     VALUE 'A'.
             05   FILLER             PIC X{79}.
```

Q7.   Rewrite the Working Storage section specified in question 5,
      using correct COBOL, and changing the print-line to read
      REPORT OF MONTHLY SALES, PRODUCTION AND PROFITABILITY, cen-
      tered in a 132-position print-line.

A7.

```
          01   CARDS-LEFT-FLAG       PIC X{3}   VALUE 'YES'.
          01   PRINT-LINE-WS.
             05   FILLER             PIC X{39}.
             05   FILLER             PIC X{53}
                   VALUE 'REPORT OF MONTHLY SALES, PRODUCTION
          -        ' AND PROFITABILITY'.
             05   FILLER             PIC X{40}.
```

Q1.  Write the code to increase the value of VERMOUTH
     by the amount stored in GIN and store the new value
     in MARTINI.

A1.

         ADD GIN VERMOUTH GIVING MARTINI.
     or
         COMPUTE MARTINI = GIN + VERMOUTH.

Q2.  Write the code to increase the value of LOOP-COUNT
     by 1.

A2.

         ADD 1 TO LOOP-COUNT.

Q3.  If field TOTAL contains 480 and field NUMBR contains
     24, what is in each field after executing

         DIVIDE NUMBR INTO TOTAL.

A3.

         NUMBR:  24
         TOTAL:  20

Q4.  If RESULT is defined as PIC 9V99, what is in RESULT
     after execution of

         DIVIDE 8 INTO 9 GIVING RESULT ROUNDED.

A4.

         RESULT: 1.13

Q5.  If ABSOLUTE-VALUE is defined as PIC 9(3), what is in
     ABSOLUTE-VALUE after execution of

         SUBTRACT 1000 FROM 2 GIVING ABSOLUTE-VALUE.

A5.

         ABSOLUTE-VALUE:  998    The sign will be missing since
                                 ABSOLUTE-VALUE was not defined
                                 as PIC S9V99.

Q6.  Use the COMPUTE statement to write the code calculating
     the interest due on an amount up to $100,000 at a rate
     of interest which may be set to the nearest 1/4% up to
     20%, over a period to the nearest year, expressing the
     result to the nearest cent.  Include the Data Division
     entries for your data-names.

```
A6.          WORKING-STORAGE SECTION.

             01   INTEREST-CALC-WS.
                  05   PERIOD-IN-YEARS        PIC 9(3).        (two decimal places
                  05   INTEREST-RATE          PIC 99V99.       are needed to hold ¼%)
                  05   AMOUNT                 PIC 9(5)V99.
                  05   INTEREST-DUE           PIC 9(6)V99.

             .                                                (if the period is
             .                                                long enough, the
             .                                                interest may be more
             .                                                than the principal
             PROCEDURE DIVISION.                              amount)
             .
             .
             INTEREST-CALC.
             COMPUTE INTEREST-DUE ROUNDED =
              (AMOUNT * INTEREST-RATE * PERIOD-IN-YEARS) / 100.
```